IMPLEMENTING DATA SCIENCE AND ANALYTICS

A Comprehensive Guide to Success

Rick Spair

Introduction

Welcome to "Implementing Data Science and Analytics: A Comprehensive Guide to Success." In today's data-driven world, organizations across industries are realizing the immense value of harnessing data to drive decision-making, gain insights, and unlock new opportunities. Data science and analytics have emerged as crucial disciplines for organizations to stay competitive, make informed choices, and create innovative solutions.

This comprehensive guide is designed to provide you with a deep understanding of the principles, methodologies, and best practices necessary to implement data science and analytics successfully. Whether you are a seasoned data professional looking to enhance your skills or a beginner embarking on your data journey, this book will serve as your trusted companion.

Part I: Getting Started introduces you to the foundations of data science and analytics. You will gain a clear understanding of the definitions, concepts, and importance of data science and analytics in today's business landscape. We will explore the benefits of data-driven decision-making and its impact on organizational success. Additionally, we will delve into the implementation process, discussing the key considerations, challenges, and strategies for achieving success in data science initiatives.

Part II: Building a Data Science Team focuses on the crucial aspect of assembling a skilled and effective data science team. We will explore the key roles and responsibilities within a data science team and provide guidance on identifying and hiring top talent. Moreover, we will discuss strategies for fostering a collaborative and productive team environment, ensuring the team's success in delivering impactful insights and solutions.

Part III: Defining Objectives and Key Metrics emphasizes the importance of setting clear goals and objectives for data science initiatives. We will delve into the process of defining objectives that align with organizational priorities, and we will explore various frameworks and methodologies for selecting key performance indicators (KPIs). By establishing measurable goals and KPIs, organizations can effectively track progress, evaluate success, and drive continuous improvement.

Part IV: Data Collection and Management dives into the critical aspects of data collection, quality assurance, and governance. You will learn how to select relevant data sources, ensuring that the data collected is accurate, comprehensive, and aligned with the objectives of your project. We will discuss best practices for data cleansing, data integration, and data storage, along with strategies for implementing effective data governance practices.

Part V: Data Exploration and Visualization explores the essential process of exploring and understanding the data. We will discuss techniques for data exploration, including descriptive statistics, data profiling, and visualization. You will learn how to extract insights, identify patterns, and uncover hidden relationships within your data. Moreover, we will explore various visualization techniques to effectively communicate your findings and insights to stakeholders.

Part VI: Statistical Analysis and Machine Learning introduces you to the core concepts of statistical analysis and machine learning. We will cover a range of statistical techniques, such as hypothesis testing, regression analysis, and clustering. Additionally, we will explore machine learning algorithms, including supervised learning, unsupervised learning, and reinforcement learning. You will gain hands-on experience in applying these techniques to real-world datasets.

Part VII: Implementing Predictive Analytics focuses on leveraging the power of predictive analytics to forecast future trends and outcomes. We will explore techniques such as time series analysis, regression modeling, and ensemble methods. You will learn how to build predictive models that enable organizations to make accurate forecasts, optimize resources, and drive strategic decision-making.

Part VIII: Data-Driven Decision-Making delves into the practical aspects of integrating data insights into decision-making processes. We will discuss methodologies for evaluating and prioritizing options, conducting cost-benefit analyses, and assessing risks. Furthermore, we will explore effective strategies for communicating results to stakeholders and fostering a data-driven decision-making culture within organizations.

Part IX: Data Privacy and Security explores the critical considerations for protecting data privacy and ensuring data security. We will delve into the regulatory landscape, discussing the importance of compliance with data protection regulations. You will learn about best practices for safeguarding sensitive information, implementing robust security measures, and managing data breaches effectively.

Part X: Scaling Data Science Projects focuses on the challenges and strategies for scaling data science projects to handle large volumes of data. We will discuss techniques for handling big data, leveraging cloud computing, and managing infrastructure and scalability challenges. Moreover, we will explore emerging technologies and trends that enable organizations to tackle scalability issues effectively.

Part XI: Real-Time Analytics and Stream Processing explores the realm of real-time analytics and stream processing. We will discuss the concepts, frameworks, and tools used to analyze data streams and make instant decisions. You will learn how to implement stream processing frameworks, build real-time dashboards, and set up alerts to monitor critical events and trends.

Part XII: Ethical Considerations in Data Science delves into the ethical and societal implications of data science. We will examine topics such as bias and fairness in algorithms, the ethical use of data, and promoting transparency and accountability. You will gain insights into the importance of responsible data practices and how to navigate ethical challenges in your data science initiatives.

Part XIII: Data Science in Business Domains explores the application of data science in specific industry domains. We will cover various domains, including marketing and sales, operations and supply chain, finance and risk management, healthcare and life sciences, human resources, and the Internet of Things (IoT). You will learn about the specific challenges, opportunities, and best practices in applying data science techniques to these domains.

Part XIV: Evaluating Data Science Projects focuses on evaluating the success of data initiatives and identifying areas for improvement. We will discuss methodologies for measuring the impact and effectiveness of data projects, evaluating model performance, and assessing the return on investment (ROI) of data science initiatives. Additionally, we will explore strategies for creating a culture of experimentation and learning, enabling continuous improvement and innovation.

Part XV: Future Trends in Data Science and Analytics provides an exciting glimpse into the future of data science. We will explore emerging technologies, techniques, and trends shaping the field, such as artificial intelligence (AI), deep learning, natural language processing (NLP), and explainable AI. You will gain insights into the potential impact of these advancements and how they are reshaping data science and analytics.

Finally, the appendix, Chapter 21, serves as a valuable resource, providing an overview of recommended books, articles, online courses, data science platforms, and tools. It aims to equip you with a comprehensive set of resources to further enhance your knowledge, skills, and proficiency in data science and analytics.

By embarking on this comprehensive guide, you have taken a significant step towards becoming a proficient data scientist or analyst. With each chapter, you will deepen your understanding, acquire new skills, and gain the confidence to tackle real-world data challenges. The world of data science and analytics is evolving at a rapid pace, and by mastering the concepts and techniques in this guide, you will be well-prepared to make a meaningful impact in your organization and beyond.

Let us begin this transformative journey into the realm of data science and analytics, where the power of data unlocks endless possibilities for innovation, growth, and success.

CONTENTS

CHAPTER 1: INTRODUCTION TO DATA SCIENCE AND ANALYTICS

In this chapter, we provide an overview of data science and analytics, highlighting their significance and the value they bring to organizations. We explore the fundamental concepts and processes involved in implementing data-driven decision-making strategies.

Defining Data Science and Analytics

We begin by defining data science and analytics, explaining how they involve extracting actionable insights from raw data to drive informed decision-making. We emphasize the interdisciplinary nature of data science, which combines statistics, mathematics, computer science, and domain expertise.

Importance and Benefits of Data-Driven Decision-Making

Next, we delve into the importance of data-driven decision-making in today's business landscape. We discuss how leveraging data insights can lead to improved efficiency, cost reduction, enhanced customer experiences, and a competitive advantage. We provide real-world examples of organizations that have successfully implemented data science and analytics to achieve remarkable outcomes.

Overview of the Implementation Process

In this section, we outline the key steps involved in implementing data science and analytics initiatives. We highlight the importance of a well-defined strategy, clear objectives, and an understanding of the available data sources. We touch upon topics such as data collection, management, exploration, visualization, statistical analysis, machine learning, and predictive analytics.

Challenges and Considerations

Implementing data science and analytics comes with its share of challenges. We discuss common obstacles organizations may face, such as data quality issues, talent acquisition, infrastructure requirements, and ethical considerations. We emphasize the need for proper data governance and privacy measures to ensure compliance with regulations and maintain public trust.

Key Takeaways

We conclude the chapter by summarizing the main points covered and providing key takeaways for readers. We stress the importance of data science and analytics as powerful tools for driving organizational success and highlight the subsequent chapters in the guide, which will explore various aspects of implementing data science and analytics in greater detail.

By the end of this chapter, readers will have a clear understanding of what data science and analytics entail, their significance in decision-making, and the overall implementation process. This foundational knowledge will serve as a solid basis for exploring the subsequent chapters and gaining practical insights and strategies for successful implementation.

Defining Data Science and Analytics

Data science and analytics have emerged as critical disciplines in today's data-driven world. They involve the systematic exploration, analysis, and interpretation of vast amounts of data to uncover valuable insights and drive informed decision-making. In this section, we will delve into the definitions of data science and analytics, highlighting their core components and their roles in organizations.

Data Science:

Data science can be defined as an interdisciplinary field that combines various techniques, tools, and methodologies to extract knowledge and insights from structured and unstructured data. It encompasses a wide range of disciplines, including statistics, mathematics, computer science, and domain expertise. The ultimate goal of data science is to extract actionable insights that can be used to solve complex problems, improve processes, and drive innovation.

Data science involves a systematic approach to data exploration, preprocessing, analysis, modeling, and visualization. It utilizes statistical techniques, machine learning algorithms, and data mining methods to uncover patterns, trends, and relationships within the data. By leveraging data science, organizations can gain a deeper understanding of their operations, customers, and market dynamics.

Analytics:

Analytics is the process of examining data to gain insights and support decision-making. It involves the application of statistical analysis, quantitative methods, and predictive modeling techniques to extract actionable insights from data. Analytics focuses on understanding past and present data patterns and using them to make predictions, optimize processes, and improve performance.

Analytics can be broadly categorized into descriptive, diagnostic, predictive, and prescriptive analytics:

Descriptive Analytics: Descriptive analytics focuses on summarizing and interpreting historical data to understand what has happened. It involves generating reports, dashboards, and visualizations that provide a clear snapshot of the current state of affairs.

Diagnostic Analytics: Diagnostic analytics aims to answer why something has happened by investigating the root causes and relationships within the data. It involves exploring correlations, conducting regression analysis, and performing hypothesis testing to uncover insights into the factors influencing outcomes.

Predictive Analytics: Predictive analytics utilizes historical data to make predictions about future outcomes. By applying statistical models, machine learning algorithms, and forecasting techniques, organizations can anticipate trends, forecast demand, and optimize decision-making based on expected outcomes.

Prescriptive Analytics: Prescriptive analytics takes predictive analysis a step further by providing recommendations on the actions to take in order to optimize outcomes. It combines historical data, predictive models, and optimization algorithms to suggest the best course of action to achieve desired goals.

Data science and analytics share a close relationship, with data science providing the foundation and methodologies for analyzing and extracting insights from data, while analytics focuses on utilizing those insights to inform decision-making.

In organizations, data science and analytics are used across various domains and functions. They play a crucial role in marketing and sales, helping organizations understand customer preferences, optimize campaigns, and forecast sales. In operations and supply chain management, data science and analytics enable process optimization, inventory management, and predictive maintenance. In finance and risk management, they support fraud detection, risk modeling, and portfolio optimization. In healthcare and life sciences, data science and analytics drive advancements in precision medicine, clinical decision support, and drug discovery.

In summary, data science and analytics are powerful disciplines that enable organizations to harness the potential of data. They involve the systematic exploration and analysis of data to generate valuable insights that support decision-making and drive organizational success. By leveraging the techniques and methodologies of data science and analytics, organizations can gain a competitive advantage, optimize processes, and unlock new opportunities for growth and innovation.

Importance and Benefits of Data-Driven Decision-Making

In today's fast-paced and data-rich world, organizations are increasingly realizing the importance of data-driven decision-making. Data-driven decision-making refers to the process of utilizing data and insights to guide strategic choices, operational improvements, and resource allocations. In this section, we will explore the significance and benefits of adopting a data-driven approach in decision-making.

Enhanced Accuracy and Precision:

Data-driven decision-making allows organizations to move away from intuition-based or anecdotal decision-making and rely on empirical evidence and facts. By leveraging data, organizations can gain a more accurate and precise understanding of their business operations, market dynamics, and customer behavior. This enables them to make informed decisions based on real-world data, reducing the risk of biased or subjective judgments.

Improved Efficiency and Cost Reduction:

Data-driven decision-making can lead to improved operational efficiency and cost reduction. By analyzing data, organizations can identify inefficiencies, bottlenecks, and areas for improvement. This helps optimize processes, streamline workflows, and eliminate waste. For example, analyzing production data can identify areas where resources are underutilized, allowing for better resource allocation and cost savings.

Better Customer Understanding and Personalization:

Data-driven decision-making enables organizations to gain a deeper understanding of their customers. By analyzing customer data, such as demographics, preferences, and purchase history, organizations can tailor their products, services, and marketing efforts to meet specific customer needs. This leads to enhanced customer experiences, increased customer satisfaction, and improved customer retention.

Competitive Advantage:

Data-driven decision-making provides organizations with a competitive edge. By leveraging data insights, organizations can identify emerging trends, market opportunities, and customer demands faster than their competitors. This allows them to adapt quickly, develop innovative products or services, and seize market share. Organizations that effectively leverage data-driven decision-making are better positioned to stay ahead in a rapidly evolving business landscape.

Proactive Risk Management:

Data-driven decision-making enables organizations to proactively identify and manage risks. By analyzing historical data and patterns, organizations can detect potential risks and anticipate future challenges. This helps in implementing preventive measures, developing risk mitigation strategies, and reducing the likelihood of adverse events. For example, financial institutions use data-driven models to detect fraudulent transactions and minimize financial risks.

Optimized Resource Allocation:

Data-driven decision-making enables organizations to allocate resources more effectively. By analyzing data on resource utilization, market demand, and customer behavior, organizations can allocate their resources - such as budget, manpower, and inventory - in a manner that maximizes efficiency and delivers the highest return on investment (ROI). This leads to better resource utilization, reduced waste, and improved financial performance.

Continuous Improvement and Agility:

Data-driven decision-making fosters a culture of continuous improvement and agility within organizations. By collecting and analyzing data on performance metrics, organizations can identify areas for improvement, implement changes, and measure the impact of those changes. Data-driven insights enable organizations to adapt and respond quickly to market shifts, customer preferences, and emerging trends, allowing for continuous innovation and growth.

Objective Evaluation and Accountability:

Data-driven decision-making promotes objective evaluation and accountability. Decisions made based on data can be objectively measured and evaluated against predefined metrics. This allows organizations to assess the effectiveness of their decisions, identify areas of success or improvement, and hold individuals or teams accountable for their performance. Data-driven decision-making supports a culture of transparency and evidence-based evaluation.

In conclusion, data-driven decision-making has become essential for organizations seeking to thrive in today's data-centric world. By leveraging data and insights, organizations can make informed decisions that lead to improved accuracy, enhanced efficiency, better customer experiences, and a competitive advantage. With the ability to identify risks, optimize resource allocation, foster continuous improvement, and drive objective evaluation, data-driven decision-making enables organizations to navigate complex business challenges and seize new opportunities for growth and innovation.

Overview of the Implementation Process

Implementing data science and analytics initiatives requires a systematic and well-structured approach. In this section, we will provide an overview of the key steps involved in the implementation process. Understanding these steps will help organizations effectively navigate the complexities of implementing data science and analytics projects and maximize their chances of success.

Define Clear Objectives:

The first step in the implementation process is to define clear objectives for the data science and analytics initiative. This involves identifying the specific business problems or opportunities the organization aims to address using data-driven insights. Clear objectives provide a focused direction and ensure that the implementation efforts align with the overall strategic goals of the organization.

Identify Relevant Data Sources:

Once the objectives are established, the next step is to identify and gather the relevant data sources needed to address the objectives. This includes internal data sources, such as databases, customer records, and transactional data, as well as external data sources, such as third-party data, social media data, and public data repositories. Ensuring data quality and reliability is crucial at this stage to ensure accurate and meaningful analysis.

Data Collection and Preprocessing:

After identifying the data sources, the data needs to be collected and prepared for analysis. This involves data collection from various sources, data cleaning to remove errors and inconsistencies, data integration to combine different datasets, and data transformation to make it suitable for analysis. Data preprocessing also includes handling missing data, outlier detection, and normalization, among other techniques.

Exploratory Data Analysis:

Exploratory Data Analysis (EDA) is a crucial step to gain initial insights into the data. This involves applying statistical techniques, visualizations, and data mining methods to understand the underlying patterns, relationships, and distributions in the data. EDA helps identify variables of interest, potential correlations, and outliers, which can guide subsequent analysis and modeling steps.

Data Visualization:

Data visualization plays a vital role in conveying complex information and insights in a visually appealing and understandable manner. Effective data visualization techniques, such as charts, graphs, and interactive dashboards, help stakeholders interpret the findings and derive actionable insights from the data. Visualizations facilitate better communication of data-driven insights across the organization.

Statistical Analysis and Modeling:

Statistical analysis and modeling techniques are employed to derive meaningful insights from the data. This includes applying statistical tests, hypothesis testing, regression analysis, and other advanced statistical methods. Additionally, machine learning algorithms, such as classification, clustering, and predictive modeling, can be utilized to uncover hidden patterns, make predictions, and generate actionable insights.

Predictive Analytics:

Predictive analytics focuses on forecasting future outcomes and trends based on historical data patterns. By leveraging statistical modeling, machine learning algorithms, and time series analysis, organizations can make predictions about customer behavior, market trends, demand forecasting, and other relevant factors. Predictive analytics enables proactive decision-making and helps organizations stay ahead of the curve.

Data-Driven Decision-Making:

The insights generated from the data analysis and predictive modeling are used to inform decision-making processes. Data-driven decision-making involves integrating data insights into the decision-making frameworks, processes, and workflows of the organization. It requires effective communication of the findings to stakeholders, ensuring that decisions are made based on evidence and data-driven insights.

Implementation and Execution:

Once decisions are made based on data-driven insights, it is important to implement and execute the recommended actions or strategies. This may involve changes to operational processes, resource allocations, marketing campaigns, product development, or other business initiatives. Proper planning, stakeholder involvement, and change management strategies are critical during the implementation phase.

Evaluation and Continuous Improvement:

The implementation process should be accompanied by robust evaluation and continuous improvement efforts. Measuring the outcomes against predefined metrics and objectives allows organizations to assess the effectiveness of their data science and analytics initiatives. Feedback loops and performance tracking help identify areas for improvement, refine models and strategies, and drive continuous learning and optimization.

Throughout the implementation process, it is crucial to have a strong data governance framework in place. This includes data privacy, security, and compliance measures, as well as proper documentation and documentation of data processes. Regular monitoring and maintenance of the implemented solutions are also necessary to ensure ongoing accuracy, relevance, and effectiveness.

In conclusion, the implementation process of data science and analytics initiatives involves a series of steps, starting from defining clear objectives and gathering relevant data to analysis, modeling, and data-driven decision-making. Effective implementation requires a combination of technical expertise, stakeholder engagement, and a robust data governance framework. By following a structured approach and continuously evaluating and improving the implemented solutions, organizations can harness the power of data science and analytics to drive innovation, efficiency, and informed decision-making.

CHAPTER 2: BUILDING A DATA SCIENCE TEAM

Chapter 2 focuses on the crucial aspect of building a data science team within an organization. It covers the key considerations, roles, and strategies involved in creating and nurturing a high-performing data science team.

Importance of a Data Science Team:

This section highlights the growing importance of data science in today's data-driven world and explains why organizations need dedicated teams to leverage the power of data. It emphasizes that a data science team brings the necessary expertise and domain knowledge to extract valuable insights from data and drive data-driven decision-making.

Identifying Key Roles and Responsibilities:

Building an effective data science team requires identifying and defining key roles and responsibilities. This section explores the core roles typically found in a data science team, such as data scientists, data engineers, machine learning engineers, and domain experts. It explains the unique skill sets and responsibilities of each role and how they collaborate to deliver impactful outcomes.

Hiring and Retaining Top Talent:

Recruiting and retaining top talent in the competitive field of data science is crucial for building a successful team. This section provides insights into effective hiring strategies, including defining clear job descriptions, conducting targeted talent searches, and utilizing specialized recruitment platforms. It also highlights the importance of creating an attractive work environment, offering competitive compensation packages, and providing professional growth opportunities to retain top data science talent.

Collaboration and Interdisciplinary Approach:

Effective collaboration is essential for a data science team to succeed. This section explores strategies to foster collaboration within the team and with other departments in the organization. It emphasizes the importance of an interdisciplinary approach, encouraging collaboration between data scientists, business stakeholders, IT teams, and domain experts to ensure a holistic understanding of data challenges and align data initiatives with business objectives.

Building a Collaborative Environment:

Creating a collaborative and inclusive environment is key to unlocking the full potential of a data science team. This section provides recommendations on fostering teamwork, encouraging knowledge sharing, and promoting open communication among team members. It also explores the benefits of creating cross-functional teams, organizing regular team meetings and brainstorming sessions, and utilizing project management tools to facilitate collaboration.

Continuous Learning and Skill Development:

The field of data science is rapidly evolving, and continuous learning is crucial for keeping the team's skills up to date. This section discusses the importance of investing in ongoing training and skill development initiatives for the team members. It explores various learning resources, such as online courses, workshops, conferences, and mentorship programs, to foster a culture of continuous learning and support the professional growth of the data science team.

Diversity and Inclusion:

Diversity and inclusion are important considerations in building a data science team. This section explores the benefits of diverse perspectives and backgrounds in driving innovation and problem-solving. It provides recommendations for promoting diversity in hiring practices, fostering an inclusive team culture, and creating equal opportunities for all team members.

Remote and Distributed Teams:

In the era of remote work, this section discusses the unique challenges and strategies for building and managing remote or distributed data science teams. It explores effective communication tools, collaboration platforms, and project management techniques to ensure seamless teamwork and productivity in a remote work environment.

By the end of this chapter, readers will have gained a comprehensive understanding of the key considerations and strategies involved in building a data science team. They will be equipped with the knowledge to attract top talent, foster collaboration, promote continuous learning, and create an inclusive environment that drives the success of data science initiatives within their organization.

Identifying Key Roles and Responsibilities

Building a successful data science team requires careful consideration of the key roles and responsibilities needed to leverage the power of data effectively. Each role brings unique skills and expertise that contribute to the team's overall capabilities. In this section, we will explore the core roles typically found in a data science team and their respective responsibilities.

Data Scientist:

Data scientists are the core members of a data science team. They possess a strong background in mathematics, statistics, and programming. Their responsibilities include:

Collecting and preprocessing data from various sources.

Applying statistical analysis and modeling techniques to extract insights and patterns from data.

Developing and implementing machine learning algorithms and predictive models.

Interpreting and communicating complex findings to stakeholders in a clear and meaningful way.

Collaborating with other team members to address specific business problems and provide data-driven recommendations.

Data Engineer:

Data engineers play a crucial role in ensuring the availability, reliability, and efficiency of data pipelines and infrastructure. Their responsibilities include:

Designing and building data infrastructure to support data collection, storage, and processing.

Developing and maintaining data pipelines to extract, transform, and load (ETL) data from various sources.

Implementing data quality checks and ensuring data integrity.

Collaborating with data scientists and analysts to understand their data needs and provide them with the necessary infrastructure support.

Machine Learning Engineer:

Machine learning engineers focus on developing and deploying machine learning models and algorithms at scale. Their responsibilities include:

Building and optimizing machine learning models and algorithms.

Integrating machine learning solutions into production systems or applications.

Optimizing model performance and scalability.

Collaborating with data scientists and data engineers to ensure seamless integration of models into the data pipeline and infrastructure.

Business Analyst:

Business analysts act as a bridge between the data science team and the business stakeholders. Their responsibilities include:

Identifying and understanding business problems and requirements.

Translating business questions into data-driven analysis and insights.

Collaborating with data scientists to define appropriate analytical approaches.

Communicating findings and recommendations to business stakeholders in a non-technical manner.

Providing input and guidance to align data initiatives with the organization's strategic objectives.

Domain Expert:

Domain experts bring industry-specific knowledge and insights to the data science team. Their responsibilities include:

Providing subject matter expertise to guide data analysis and modeling efforts.

Interpreting data findings in the context of the industry or domain.

Collaborating with data scientists to develop domain-specific models or algorithms.

Ensuring that data analysis aligns with industry standards, regulations, and best practices.

Project Manager:

A project manager oversees the planning, coordination, and execution of data science projects. Their responsibilities include:

Defining project goals, deliverables, and timelines.

Allocating resources and managing project budgets.

Monitoring project progress and ensuring timely completion.

Facilitating communication and collaboration among team members.

Identifying and mitigating project risks and challenges.

It is worth noting that the specific roles and responsibilities within a data science team can vary depending on the organization's size, industry, and objectives. Some organizations may have additional specialized roles, such as data visualization experts, data architects, or data ethics officers, depending on their specific needs and priorities.

In building a data science team, it is crucial to strike a balance between domain expertise and technical skills. Collaboration and effective communication among team members are also essential for achieving the team's goals. The roles mentioned above are often interconnected, requiring close collaboration and knowledge-sharing to maximize the impact of data-driven initiatives.

In conclusion, identifying and understanding the key roles and responsibilities within a data science team is fundamental to building a high-performing and impactful team. By recognizing the unique contributions of each role and fostering collaboration among team members, organizations can leverage the diverse skills and expertise necessary to extract valuable insights from data and drive data-driven decision-making.

Hiring and Retaining Top Talent

Building a successful data science team hinges upon hiring and retaining top talent in a competitive field. Hiring skilled and experienced professionals, and providing an environment that fosters growth and engagement, is crucial for the long-term success of the team. In this section, we will explore key considerations and strategies for hiring and retaining top talent in the data science field.

Define Clear Job Descriptions and Requirements:

To attract top talent, it is essential to have clear job descriptions that accurately reflect the skills, experience, and responsibilities required for each position. This includes outlining the technical skills (e.g., programming languages, statistical analysis, machine learning), domain knowledge (e.g., finance, healthcare, marketing), and any specific certifications or advanced degrees desired. Clear job requirements help ensure that candidates with the right expertise are targeted, increasing the likelihood of finding the best fit for the team.

Conduct Targeted Talent Searches:

Finding top talent in the data science field often requires targeted talent searches. This can involve various approaches, such as networking at industry conferences and events, leveraging professional networks, partnering with specialized recruitment agencies, or engaging with data science communities and online platforms. Proactive outreach to potential candidates can help identify individuals with exceptional skills and experience.

Technical Assessments and Interviews:

To evaluate candidates effectively, it is essential to design technical assessments and interviews that assess their proficiency in relevant technical skills and problem-solving abilities. These assessments can include coding exercises, statistical analysis challenges, or case studies that simulate real-world data science scenarios. Additionally, behavioral interviews can assess candidates' communication skills, teamwork abilities, and their ability to adapt to new challenges and learning opportunities.

Showcasing Challenging and Impactful Projects:

Top data science talent is often motivated by challenging and impactful projects. During the hiring process, organizations can highlight past or ongoing projects that demonstrate the team's potential to solve complex problems, drive innovation, and create business value. This can help attract candidates who are passionate about making a meaningful impact and who are excited about the organization's data-driven initiatives.

Competitive Compensation Packages:

Attracting top talent requires offering competitive compensation packages that align with industry standards. Compensation packages should reflect the market value of data science skills and expertise. In addition to base salary, organizations can offer benefits such as performance-based bonuses, stock options, professional development opportunities, and flexible work arrangements. Offering competitive compensation demonstrates the organization's commitment to recognizing and rewarding top talent.

Professional Growth and Learning Opportunities:

Data scientists value continuous learning and opportunities for professional growth. Organizations should provide avenues for skill development, such as training programs, access to online courses or conferences, and opportunities for collaboration and mentorship. Supporting employees' professional growth not only enhances their skills but also increases job satisfaction and retention rates. Creating a culture of learning and encouraging employees to stay up-to-date with the latest developments in the field fosters an environment that attracts and retains top talent.

Engaging Work Environment:

Creating an engaging work environment is crucial for attracting and retaining top talent. This includes fostering a collaborative and inclusive culture where individuals are encouraged to share ideas, collaborate on projects, and learn from one another. Providing access to state-of-the-art tools, technologies, and data infrastructure is also important to empower data scientists to perform their work efficiently and effectively.

Recognition and Career Advancement Opportunities:

Recognizing and appreciating the contributions of data scientists is key to retaining top talent. Organizations can implement recognition programs that acknowledge exceptional work, innovation, and achievements. Additionally, providing clear career advancement opportunities, such as promotions, leadership roles, or opportunities to lead important projects, is vital for retaining talented individuals who seek growth and upward mobility.

Regular Feedback and Performance Management:

Regular feedback and performance management processes are crucial for maintaining open lines of communication between employees and managers. Providing constructive feedback, setting clear performance goals, and conducting regular performance evaluations help employees understand their strengths and areas for improvement. This process also provides an opportunity to align individual goals with organizational objectives, fostering a sense of purpose and commitment.

Emphasizing Work-Life Balance:

Maintaining a healthy work-life balance is essential for employee satisfaction and retention. Encouraging flexible work arrangements, promoting work-life balance initiatives, and providing support for employee well-being contribute to a positive work environment. Organizations that prioritize work-life balance are more likely to attract and retain top talent, as it demonstrates a commitment to the overall well-being of their employees.

In conclusion, hiring and retaining top talent in data science requires a comprehensive and strategic approach. By defining clear job descriptions, conducting targeted talent searches, providing competitive compensation packages, fostering professional growth opportunities, creating an engaging work environment, recognizing achievements, and promoting work-life balance, organizations can attract and retain top data science talent. By investing in their data science team, organizations position themselves to excel in leveraging the power of data for innovation, growth, and competitive advantage.

Creating a Collaborative Environment

Building a collaborative environment is crucial for the success of a data science team. Collaboration fosters innovation, creativity, and knowledge sharing, allowing team members to leverage their collective skills and expertise. In this section, we will explore key strategies and considerations for creating a collaborative environment within a data science team.

Encourage Open Communication:

Open communication is the foundation of collaboration. Creating an environment where team members feel comfortable expressing their ideas, asking questions, and sharing insights is essential. Encourage regular and open discussions, both in team meetings and through digital communication channels, to facilitate the exchange of ideas and foster a culture of collaboration.

Foster Teamwork and Collaboration:

Promote teamwork and collaboration by assigning projects and tasks that require cross-functional collaboration. Encourage team members to work together on problem-solving, brainstorming, and knowledge sharing. Foster a sense of shared ownership and collective responsibility for the success of the team's projects. Recognize and reward collaborative efforts to reinforce the importance of teamwork.

Embrace Diversity and Inclusion:

Diversity of perspectives, experiences, and backgrounds enhances creativity and problem-solving. Embrace diversity and inclusion within the team by actively seeking a range of perspectives and promoting an inclusive environment. Encourage team members to respect and value different viewpoints, fostering an environment where everyone feels heard and included.

Promote Interdisciplinary Collaboration:

Data science projects often require collaboration with stakeholders from various departments, such as marketing, finance, or operations. Promote interdisciplinary collaboration by facilitating interactions between the data science team and other departments. Encourage regular meetings, joint projects, and knowledge-sharing sessions to foster a deeper understanding of each other's challenges, goals, and expertise.

Provide Shared Tools and Platforms:

Offer shared tools and platforms that facilitate collaboration and knowledge sharing. This includes collaboration software, project management tools, version control systems, and shared repositories for code and documentation. These tools enable team members to work together seamlessly, track progress, and share insights and findings.

Organize Regular Team Meetings and Discussions:

Regular team meetings and discussions are essential for maintaining open lines of communication and fostering collaboration. These meetings provide an opportunity to share project updates, discuss challenges, and solicit feedback. Consider utilizing agile methodologies, such as daily stand-ups or sprint planning, to ensure frequent and efficient communication.

Facilitate Knowledge Sharing:

Create mechanisms for sharing knowledge and expertise within the team. This can include brown bag sessions, where team members present on a specific topic of interest, or hosting internal workshops and training sessions. Encourage team members to share their learnings, best practices, and resources with their colleagues. Implement a documentation process to capture and share knowledge effectively.

Foster a Learning Culture:

Promote a culture of continuous learning within the team. Encourage team members to stay updated with the latest developments in the field, attend conferences, participate in online courses, and share their learnings with the team. Provide opportunities for professional development, such as internal training programs or support for attending external training events.

Support Remote Collaboration:

In an increasingly remote work environment, it is crucial to facilitate remote collaboration. Leverage technology tools such as video conferencing, instant messaging, and virtual collaboration platforms to ensure effective communication and collaboration among team members, regardless of their physical location. Implement remote work policies that support collaboration and create virtual spaces for informal interactions and social connections.

Lead by Example:

Leaders play a critical role in fostering a collaborative environment. Lead by example by demonstrating collaborative behaviors, actively listening to team members, and valuing diverse perspectives. Encourage collaboration, provide opportunities for growth, and recognize and reward collaborative efforts within the team. A supportive and collaborative leadership style sets the tone for the entire team.

In conclusion, creating a collaborative environment within a data science team is crucial for leveraging the collective skills and expertise of team members. By encouraging open communication, fostering teamwork and interdisciplinary collaboration, providing shared tools and platforms, organizing regular team meetings, facilitating knowledge sharing, fostering a learning culture, supporting remote collaboration, and leading by example, organizations can create an environment that nurtures collaboration and drives the success of data science initiatives.

CHAPTER 3: DEFINING OBJECTIVES AND KEY METRICS

Chapter 3 focuses on the critical step of defining objectives and key metrics in the context of data science and analytics initiatives. Establishing clear goals and metrics is essential for guiding the data-driven decision-making process and ensuring alignment with the organization's strategic objectives. In this chapter, we will explore the importance of defining objectives and key metrics, as well as strategies for effectively establishing them.

Importance of Defining Objectives:

This section emphasizes the significance of clearly defining objectives for data science and analytics initiatives. Well-defined objectives provide a clear sense of purpose, guiding the team's efforts and ensuring that data initiatives are aligned with the organization's overall goals. Objectives serve as the foundation for identifying the data needed, determining analysis methods, and measuring the success of the initiatives.

Aligning with Business Objectives:

Successful data science initiatives are closely aligned with the organization's broader business objectives. This section highlights the importance of understanding the organization's strategic goals and how data initiatives can support them. By aligning data science objectives with business objectives, organizations can ensure that data-driven insights drive tangible business outcomes and deliver value.

SMART Objectives:

SMART (Specific, Measurable, Achievable, Relevant, Time-bound) objectives provide a framework for setting meaningful goals. This section explores each aspect of the SMART framework and how it applies to data science objectives. Specific and measurable objectives ensure clarity and provide a quantifiable way to track progress. Achievable objectives are realistic and attainable within the given resources and constraints. Relevant objectives are linked to the organization's needs and priorities. Time-bound objectives establish clear deadlines for achieving the desired outcomes.

Key Performance Indicators (KPIs):

Defining key performance indicators (KPIs) is crucial for measuring the success of data science initiatives. This section explains the concept of KPIs and their significance in monitoring progress and evaluating the impact of data initiatives. It emphasizes the importance of selecting KPIs that directly reflect the objectives and provide actionable insights for decision-making. Examples of KPIs in various domains, such as customer retention, revenue growth, or operational efficiency, are provided.

Quantitative and Qualitative Metrics:

Data science initiatives often involve a combination of quantitative and qualitative metrics. This section explores the differences between quantitative and qualitative metrics and highlights their respective roles in evaluating data-driven outcomes. It discusses the importance of selecting appropriate metrics based on the nature of the objectives and the available data. Balancing quantitative metrics, such as revenue or conversion rates, with qualitative metrics, such as customer satisfaction or user feedback, provides a holistic view of the impact of data initiatives.

Establishing Baselines and Targets:

Establishing baselines and targets is crucial for measuring progress and assessing the success of data initiatives. This section explains the importance of setting baseline metrics to represent the starting point for comparison. It also emphasizes the need for realistic and challenging targets to drive continuous improvement. Baselines and targets serve as benchmarks for evaluating the effectiveness and value of data-driven decision-making.

Cascading Objectives:

Cascading objectives is a strategy to align objectives at different levels within an organization. This section explores how cascading objectives ensure that data science objectives are interconnected with broader organizational objectives. It discusses the process of breaking down high-level objectives into specific objectives at the team or individual level. Cascading objectives foster alignment, coordination, and a sense of shared purpose throughout the organization.

Monitoring and Iteration:

Defining objectives and key metrics is an iterative process that requires continuous monitoring and adjustment. This section emphasizes the importance of monitoring progress, tracking KPIs, and regularly reviewing objectives to ensure they remain relevant and aligned with the organization's evolving needs. It highlights the value of feedback loops and agile methodologies to adapt and refine objectives based on data insights and changing circumstances.

By the end of this chapter, readers will have a comprehensive understanding of the importance of defining objectives and key metrics in data science and analytics initiatives. They will be equipped with strategies and frameworks, such as SMART objectives, KPIs, quantitative and qualitative metrics, establishing baselines and targets, and cascading objectives, to effectively define objectives and measure the success of their data-driven initiatives.

Setting Clear Goals and Objectives

Setting clear goals and objectives is a critical step in driving the success of data science and analytics initiatives. Well-defined goals provide focus, clarity, and a sense of direction for the team, ensuring that efforts are aligned with the organization's strategic priorities. In this section, we will explore key strategies and considerations for setting clear goals and objectives in the context of data-driven decision-making.

Understand the Business Context:

Before setting goals and objectives, it is crucial to understand the business context and align data initiatives with the organization's overall strategic priorities. This involves gaining a deep understanding of the organization's mission, vision, and long-term goals. By aligning data science objectives with business objectives, organizations can ensure that data initiatives are directly contributing to the organization's success and generating meaningful value.

Specific and Measurable Goals:

Goals should be specific and measurable to provide clarity and enable effective monitoring of progress. Vague or ambiguous goals can lead to confusion and hinder the team's ability to track achievements. By defining specific and measurable goals, organizations can clearly communicate expectations and create a framework for evaluating success. For example, a specific and measurable goal could be to increase customer retention by 15% within the next quarter.

Align Goals with Stakeholder Needs:

Consider the needs and expectations of stakeholders when setting goals and objectives. Engage with key stakeholders, such as business leaders, department heads, and customers, to understand their priorities and requirements. This ensures that the goals are relevant and address the specific challenges or opportunities that stakeholders are concerned about.

Aligning goals with stakeholder needs increases the chances of gaining support and buy-in for data-driven initiatives.

Prioritize and Sequence Goals:

In situations where multiple goals need to be addressed, it is essential to prioritize and sequence them effectively. Prioritizing goals allows organizations to focus their efforts and resources on the most critical objectives. Sequencing goals ensures that they are pursued in a logical order, considering dependencies and interdependencies. This approach enables a step-by-step progression towards achieving broader objectives, creating a sense of accomplishment and momentum for the team.

Time-Bound Goals:

Setting time-bound goals is crucial for establishing clear deadlines and maintaining a sense of urgency. Goals without specific timelines can lack direction and fail to generate the necessary momentum for action. Time-bound goals create a sense of accountability and enable the team to monitor progress and make necessary adjustments along the way. For example, setting a goal to launch a new data-driven product within six months provides a clear timeframe for planning and execution.

Use the SMART Framework:

The SMART (Specific, Measurable, Achievable, Relevant, Time-bound) framework provides a structured approach for setting clear and effective goals. This framework ensures that goals are specific in their scope, measurable for tracking progress, achievable within the available resources, relevant to the organization's objectives, and time-bound to provide a sense of urgency. Applying the SMART framework helps refine and clarify goals, making them more actionable and attainable.

Break Down Goals into Actionable Steps:

Breaking down goals into actionable steps or sub-goals is essential for effective implementation. This involves identifying the specific tasks, milestones, or deliverables required to achieve the broader goal. Breaking down goals into smaller, manageable components provides a roadmap for the team, enhances clarity, and helps track progress more effectively. It also allows for better resource allocation and facilitates collaboration among team members.

Regularly Review and Update Goals:

Goals should not be set in stone. Regularly review and update goals to ensure they remain relevant and aligned with the organization's evolving needs and priorities. As data insights and market dynamics change, it may be necessary to adjust goals or set new objectives. Regularly reviewing and updating goals keeps the team focused on the most current and impactful initiatives, fostering agility and adaptability in the data-driven decision-making process.

Communicate Goals Clearly:

Clear communication of goals is crucial for ensuring alignment and shared understanding among team members. Clearly articulate the goals to the entire team, providing context, rationale, and desired outcomes. Use various communication channels, such as team meetings, presentations, or project management tools, to share goals and provide regular updates on progress. Effective communication promotes a shared sense of purpose, engenders enthusiasm, and fosters collaboration among team members.

Celebrate Milestones and Achievements:

Acknowledging and celebrating milestones and achievements along the way is essential for maintaining motivation and fostering a positive team spirit. Recognize and reward team members for their efforts and contributions when they achieve significant milestones or make progress towards goals. Celebrating achievements reinforces a sense of accomplishment and motivates the team to continue pursuing excellence.

In conclusion, setting clear goals and objectives is a fundamental step in driving the success of data science and analytics initiatives. By understanding the business context, setting specific and measurable goals, aligning with stakeholder needs, prioritizing and sequencing goals, using the SMART framework, breaking down goals into actionable steps, regularly reviewing and updating goals, communicating goals clearly, and celebrating milestones and achievements, organizations can create a focused and motivated team that is empowered to deliver impactful outcomes through data-driven decision-making.

Identifying Key Performance Indicators (KPIs)

Key Performance Indicators (KPIs) are essential metrics used to measure the success and progress of data science and analytics initiatives. They provide a quantifiable and objective way to assess the effectiveness and impact of data-driven decision-making. In this section, we will explore the process of identifying KPIs and highlight key considerations for selecting meaningful and actionable metrics.

Understand Business Objectives:

The first step in identifying KPIs is to gain a clear understanding of the organization's business objectives. By aligning KPIs with the broader strategic goals, organizations ensure that data initiatives are directly contributing to the desired outcomes. This involves engaging with stakeholders and decision-makers to identify the key areas where data-driven insights can drive tangible business value.

Link KPIs to Data Science Objectives:

Once the business objectives are defined, it is important to link KPIs to specific data science objectives. Data science initiatives often have multiple objectives, such as improving customer retention, optimizing resource allocation, or increasing revenue. Each objective should have one or more KPIs associated with it, which serve as measurable indicators of progress and success in achieving the objective.

Define Quantifiable Metrics:

KPIs should be quantifiable and measurable to provide clear benchmarks for evaluation. Quantifiable metrics allow for objective assessment and tracking of progress over time. This can include numerical values, percentages, counts, ratios, or other measurable indicators that align with the specific objectives. For example, if the objective is to improve customer satisfaction, the KPI could be the Net Promoter Score (NPS) or customer satisfaction ratings.

Relevance to Objectives:

KPIs should relate to the objectives they are intended to measure. They should provide meaningful insights into the performance and impact of data initiatives. It is crucial to ensure that KPIs capture the essence of the objective and reflect the specific aspect of performance that is most relevant to achieving the desired outcomes. Relevance ensures that KPIs provide actionable information for decision-making.

Data Availability and Reliability:

Consider the availability and reliability of the data required to calculate the KPIs. It is important to assess whether the necessary data sources and infrastructure are in place to collect and process the data accurately and consistently. The reliability and quality of the data are critical for ensuring the validity and integrity of the KPIs. Identify any data gaps or limitations that may affect the selection or calculation of the KPIs.

Focus on Leading and Lagging Indicators:

KPIs can be categorized as leading or lagging indicators. Leading indicators provide insights into future performance and can guide proactive decision-making. Lagging indicators, on the other hand, reflect historical performance and can be used to assess the impact of past decisions. A balanced set of KPIs should include a mix of leading and lagging indicators to provide a comprehensive view of performance and guide both short-term and long-term decision-making.

Consider Stakeholder Needs:

Take into account the needs and perspectives of various stakeholders when selecting KPIs. Different stakeholders may have different priorities and areas of interest. Engage with stakeholders to understand their information needs and preferences. By incorporating stakeholder input, organizations can ensure that the selected KPIs align with the expectations and requirements of the key decision-makers and users of the data-driven insights.

Trackable and Actionable:

KPIs should be trackable and actionable. They should be based on data that can be reliably collected and monitored over time. Organizations should have mechanisms in place to track and report on the selected KPIs regularly. Additionally, KPIs should provide actionable insights that can guide decision-making and inform strategies for improvement. They should prompt specific actions or interventions based on the insights they provide.

Set Baselines and Targets:

Establish baselines and targets for the KPIs to provide context and set expectations. Baselines represent the starting point and serve as a reference for comparison. Targets establish the desired level of performance or improvement that the organization aims to achieve. Setting baselines and targets enables organizations to monitor progress and evaluate the effectiveness of data-driven initiatives.

Regular Review and Adaptation:

KPIs should be reviewed regularly to ensure their continued relevance and effectiveness. As the business landscape changes, goals evolve, or new data sources become available, organizations should assess whether the existing KPIs still capture the desired outcomes or if adjustments are needed. Regular review and adaptation of KPIs ensure that they remain aligned with the organization's objectives and continue to provide valuable insights.

In conclusion, identifying KPIs is a crucial step in measuring the success and impact of data science and analytics initiatives. By understanding business objectives, linking KPIs to data science objectives, defining quantifiable metrics, ensuring relevance, considering data availability and reliability, focusing on leading and lagging indicators, incorporating stakeholder needs, ensuring trackability and actionability, setting baselines and targets, and regularly reviewing and adapting KPIs, organizations can select meaningful and actionable metrics that drive informed decision-making and enable continuous improvement.

Aligning Data Initiatives with Business Objectives

Aligning data initiatives with business objectives is essential for organizations to derive maximum value from their data assets and drive strategic decision-making. By ensuring that data initiatives are linked to the organization's broader goals and objectives, organizations can harness the power of data to generate actionable insights and create a competitive advantage. In this section, we will explore key strategies and considerations for aligning data initiatives with business objectives.

Understand Business Objectives:

The first step in aligning data initiatives with business objectives is to gain a deep understanding of the organization's strategic goals. This involves engaging with key stakeholders, including business leaders, department heads, and decision-makers, to identify and prioritize the strategic objectives. Understanding the organization's vision, mission, and key performance indicators (KPIs) provides the context necessary for aligning data initiatives effectively.

Identify Data-Driven Opportunities:

Once the business objectives are clear, identify the data-driven opportunities that can support and enhance the achievement of those objectives. Analyze the existing data assets, internal and external, to identify potential insights and areas where data can provide a competitive advantage. Look for gaps in data availability or quality that may need to be addressed to fully leverage the data for decision-making purposes.

Conduct a Data Audit:

Conduct a comprehensive data audit to assess the relevance, completeness, and quality of the available data. Understand the data sources, data collection methods, and data management practices within the organization.

Identify any gaps or limitations in data collection or processing that may hinder the effectiveness of data initiatives. A thorough data audit provides insights into the organization's data maturity and informs the development of a data strategy aligned with business objectives.

Establish Data Governance Framework:

Develop a robust data governance framework to ensure the effective management, security, and privacy of the data assets. Establish data governance policies and procedures that align with regulatory requirements and best practices. This framework should address data quality, data integration, data storage, data access, data privacy, and data security. A well-defined data governance framework provides the necessary foundation for aligning data initiatives with business objectives.

Define Key Performance Indicators (KPIs):

Identify and define the key performance indicators (KPIs) that align with the organization's strategic objectives. KPIs provide measurable targets for assessing the performance and impact of data initiatives. Consider both financial and non-financial KPIs that are relevant to the specific business objectives. For example, if the objective is to improve customer satisfaction, the KPI could be the Net Promoter Score (NPS) or customer retention rate.

Develop Data-Driven Strategies:

Develop data-driven strategies that leverage the insights derived from data to support the achievement of business objectives. Identify specific initiatives, projects, or actions that can capitalize on the available data and contribute to the desired outcomes. For example, data-driven strategies could involve implementing personalized marketing campaigns based on customer segmentation or optimizing supply chain operations using predictive analytics. These strategies should be directly aligned with the business objectives and provide a roadmap for implementation.

Collaborate Across Departments:

Effective alignment of data initiatives with business objectives requires collaboration across departments and functions within the organization. Engage with stakeholders from various areas, such as marketing, operations, finance, and customer service, to ensure that data initiatives address their specific needs and contribute to their respective objectives. Foster cross-functional collaboration to leverage diverse perspectives and expertise in designing and implementing data-driven solutions.

Communicate and Educate:

Effective communication and education are essential for ensuring alignment and buy-in from all stakeholders. Clearly communicate the purpose, benefits, and expected outcomes of data initiatives to gain support and participation. Educate employees on the value of data-driven decision-making and provide training or resources to enhance data literacy across the organization. Foster a data-driven culture by emphasizing the importance of data in driving strategic objectives.

Establish Feedback Loops:

Establish feedback loops to continuously monitor the progress and impact of data initiatives. Regularly review and evaluate the performance of data initiatives against the defined KPIs and objectives. Collect feedback from stakeholders and decision-makers to assess the effectiveness and identify areas for improvement. Incorporate the feedback into the refinement and evolution of data initiatives, ensuring ongoing alignment with business objectives.

Embrace Agility and Flexibility:

Business objectives may evolve over time, and market dynamics can change rapidly. Embrace agility and flexibility in data initiatives to adapt to evolving business needs. Regularly reassess the alignment between data initiatives and business objectives and make necessary adjustments. This may involve reprioritizing projects, realigning resources, or exploring new data sources and analytics approaches. Embracing agility ensures that data initiatives remain relevant and continue to provide value to the organization.

In conclusion, aligning data initiatives with business objectives is crucial for organizations to leverage their data assets effectively and drive strategic decision-making. By understanding business objectives, identifying data-driven opportunities, conducting a data audit, establishing a data governance framework, defining KPIs, developing data-driven strategies, collaborating across departments, communicating and educating stakeholders, establishing feedback loops, and embracing agility, organizations can ensure that data initiatives are directly aligned with the organization's broader goals and objectives, leading to tangible business outcomes and competitive advantage.

CHAPTER 4: DATA COLLECTION AND MANAGEMENT

Chapter 4 focuses on the crucial aspects of data collection and management in the context of data science and analytics initiatives. Effective data collection and management practices are essential for ensuring the availability, quality, and integrity of data assets, which serve as the foundation for deriving valuable insights. In this chapter, we will explore key considerations and strategies for data collection and management.

Importance of Data Collection and Management:

This section emphasizes the significance of data collection and management in data science and analytics initiatives. It highlights the role of data as a strategic asset and emphasizes the need for proper data collection and management practices to enable accurate analysis, reliable insights, and informed decision-making. Effective data collection and management processes ensure that organizations have access to the right data at the right time.

Identify Data Needs:

The first step in data collection and management is identifying the specific data needs for the intended analysis or decision-making. This involves understanding the objectives of the data initiatives and determining the types of data required to address those objectives. Identify the specific variables, attributes, or metrics that are critical for achieving the desired outcomes.

Data Sources and Acquisition:

Identify and evaluate the data sources that provide the necessary data for analysis. This may include internal data sources (e.g., transactional databases, customer relationship management systems) as well as external sources (e.g., third-party data providers, public datasets). Establish data acquisition processes, such as data extraction, data integration, and data transformation, to bring the data from various sources into a unified and usable format.

Data Quality and Integrity:

Data quality and integrity are paramount for reliable analysis and decision-making. Establish data quality standards and processes to ensure that the collected data is accurate, complete, consistent, and free from errors or biases. Implement data validation techniques, such as data profiling, data cleansing, and outlier detection, to improve the quality of the data. Implement data governance practices to maintain data integrity throughout its lifecycle.

Data Storage and Infrastructure:

Develop a robust data storage and infrastructure strategy to efficiently manage and store the collected data. This involves selecting appropriate database systems or data warehouses that can handle the volume, velocity, and variety of the data. Consider factors such as scalability, security, and performance when designing the data storage architecture. Implement backup and recovery mechanisms to ensure data resilience.

Data Privacy and Security:

Data privacy and security are critical considerations in data collection and management. Develop and implement data privacy policies and practices that comply with applicable regulations and protect sensitive or personally identifiable information. Implement robust security measures, such as encryption, access controls, and data anonymization, to safeguard the data against unauthorized access or breaches.

Data Governance:

Establish a data governance framework to ensure the effective management, control, and accountability of data assets. Define roles and responsibilities for data governance, including data stewards, data custodians, and data owners. Develop policies and procedures for data classification, data sharing, data retention, and data disposal. Data governance ensures that data is managed in a consistent, compliant, and ethical manner.

Data Documentation and Metadata:

Documenting data and maintaining metadata is essential for understanding the characteristics, context, and lineage of the collected data. Develop documentation standards and templates to capture information about data sources, data transformations, data definitions, and data relationships. Well-documented data and metadata facilitate data discovery, data integration, and knowledge sharing among data scientists and analysts.

Data Integration and Interoperability:

Ensure that the collected data can be integrated and used across different systems and applications. Implement data integration processes and tools to combine data from multiple sources and create a unified view of the data. Enable interoperability by adhering to standardized data formats, protocols, and interfaces. Data integration and interoperability enable efficient data analysis and facilitate the use of data in various applications.

Data Lifecycle Management:

Implement data lifecycle management practices to effectively manage data from its creation to its retirement. Define processes and guidelines for data ingestion, data storage, data archiving, and data disposal. Consider data retention policies, legal and regulatory requirements, and evolving business needs when managing the data lifecycle. Proper data lifecycle management ensures the availability, relevance, and accessibility of data throughout its lifespan.

In conclusion, effective data collection and management are crucial for deriving accurate and valuable insights from data science and analytics initiatives. By identifying data needs, selecting appropriate data sources, ensuring data quality and integrity, establishing robust data storage and infrastructure, addressing data privacy and security concerns, implementing data governance practices, documenting data and metadata, enabling data integration and interoperability, and implementing data lifecycle management, organizations can lay the foundation for successful data-driven decision-making.

Selecting Relevant Data Sources

Selecting relevant data sources is a crucial step in data science and analytics initiatives. The quality and relevance of the data directly impact the accuracy and validity of the insights derived from data analysis. In this section, we will explore key considerations and strategies for selecting relevant data sources to ensure the success of data-driven decision-making.

Define Data Needs and Objectives:

The first step in selecting relevant data sources is to clearly define the data needs and objectives of the project or analysis. Determine the specific information or insights that are required to address the research question or business problem at hand. Understanding the objectives helps identify the types of data that are most relevant and essential for achieving the desired outcomes.

Consider Internal Data Sources:

Start by exploring the internal data sources within your organization. Internal data sources include transactional databases, customer relationship management systems, financial records, sales data, or any other data generated or collected within the organization. Assess the availability, accessibility, and relevance of these internal data sources. They can often provide valuable insights and have the advantage of being readily accessible.

Explore External Data Sources:

Expand your search beyond internal data sources and consider external data sources that can supplement or enrich your analysis. External data sources can include public datasets, government data, industry-specific data providers, social media data, or data from third-party vendors. These sources can provide additional perspectives, context, and broader industry insights that may be relevant to your objectives.

Assess Data Quality and Reliability:

When evaluating data sources, consider the quality and reliability of the data. Assess the accuracy, completeness, consistency, and timeliness of the data. Investigate the data collection methods, data validation processes, and data governance practices of the data source to ensure the data is reliable and trustworthy. Poor-quality data can lead to inaccurate analysis and flawed insights, so it is essential to prioritize quality when selecting data sources.

Evaluate Data Relevance:

Evaluate the relevance of the data to your specific objectives and research question. Consider whether the data source provides information that relates to the variables or attributes you are interested in analyzing. Assess how well the data aligns with your research question and whether it provides insights that can contribute to answering the question or solving the problem at hand. Focus on selecting data sources that provide meaningful and actionable information.

Consider Data Granularity and Scope:

Consider the granularity and scope of the data when selecting data sources. Granularity refers to the level of detail or specificity of the data. Determine whether the data source provides the necessary granularity to address your objectives. Additionally, consider the scope of the data, whether it covers the appropriate geographic regions, time periods, or relevant segments. The data should align with the scope of your research question or business problem.

Assess Data Availability and Accessibility:

Ensure that the selected data sources are available and accessible for analysis. Evaluate whether you have the necessary permissions, licenses, or agreements to use the data. Consider the ease of obtaining and accessing the data, as well as any technical requirements or restrictions associated with the data source. Data sources that are readily available and easily accessible save time and resources during the data collection process.

Analyze Data Volume and Velocity:

Consider the volume and velocity of the data when selecting data sources. Volume refers to the amount of data available, while velocity refers to the speed at which new data is generated or collected. Assess whether the data source provides a sufficient volume of data to support your analysis. Additionally, consider whether the data source can provide real-time or near-real-time data if time-sensitive analysis is required.

Evaluate Data Cost and ROI:

Consider the cost associated with accessing or acquiring the data. Evaluate whether the potential benefits and insights derived from the data outweigh the cost of obtaining and processing the data. Assess the return on investment (ROI) of the data source in terms of the value it can provide to your analysis or decision-making process. Balancing the cost and potential benefits is important in selecting the most cost-effective data sources.

Continuous Exploration and Iteration:

Data sources evolve, and new sources become available over time. It is important to continuously explore and evaluate new data sources that may align with your objectives. Stay updated with emerging data providers, industry trends, and technological advancements that can expand your data options. Regularly re-evaluate the relevance and effectiveness of existing data sources and make adjustments as needed.

In conclusion, selecting relevant data sources is crucial for successful data-driven decision-making. By defining data needs and objectives, considering internal and external data sources, assessing data quality and relevance, evaluating data availability and accessibility, analyzing data volume and velocity, considering data granularity and scope, assessing data cost and ROI, and engaging in continuous exploration and iteration, organizations can select data sources that provide meaningful insights and support the achievement of their objectives.

Ensuring Data Quality and Reliability

Data quality and reliability are paramount for accurate analysis, reliable insights, and informed decision-making in data science and analytics initiatives. Poor-quality data can lead to incorrect conclusions, flawed insights, and misguided actions. In this section, we will explore key considerations and strategies for ensuring data quality and reliability throughout the data lifecycle.

Data Collection Process:

The data collection process is the first opportunity to ensure data quality and reliability. Design data collection procedures that are systematic, standardized, and well-documented. Clearly define the variables and attributes being collected, specify the data collection methods, and provide clear instructions to data collectors. Implement data validation checks and controls during the collection process to minimize errors and inconsistencies.

Data Validation:

Implement data validation techniques to verify the accuracy, completeness, and consistency of the collected data. This includes performing range checks, format checks, and logic checks to identify data entry errors or inconsistencies. Validate the data against predefined rules or expectations to ensure its quality and reliability. Any discrepancies or anomalies should be resolved or investigated to maintain data integrity.

Data Cleaning:

Data cleaning involves identifying and correcting errors, inconsistencies, or inaccuracies in the collected data. Implement data cleaning procedures to address missing values, outliers, duplicate entries, or other data quality issues. Use automated tools or scripts to streamline the data cleaning process and ensure consistency. Data cleaning improves the reliability and trustworthiness of the data for analysis.

Data Standardization:

Standardize the data to ensure consistency and uniformity across different sources and formats. Define and apply data standards for variables, units of measurement, formats, and naming conventions. This helps avoid discrepancies or confusion caused by inconsistent data representations. Data standardization facilitates data integration and ensures the reliability of comparative analysis across different datasets.

Data Integration:

When combining data from multiple sources, pay careful attention to data integration processes. Develop standardized procedures to integrate data from different formats, databases, or systems. Ensure that data mappings and transformations are accurately implemented, and data relationships are maintained. Data integration ensures the reliability and coherence of the combined dataset, allowing for accurate analysis and insights.

Data Documentation and Metadata:

Document the characteristics, context, and lineage of the data through metadata. Maintain detailed documentation that includes information about data sources, collection methods, transformations, data definitions, and any data-related decisions or assumptions made during the process. Well-documented data and metadata facilitate understanding, transparency, and reproducibility, which contribute to data quality and reliability.

Data Security:

Implement robust data security measures to protect data integrity and reliability. Ensure that appropriate access controls, authentication mechanisms, and encryption protocols are in place to safeguard the data from unauthorized access, tampering, or breaches. Data security measures help maintain the confidentiality, integrity, and availability of the data, ensuring its reliability for analysis and decision-making.

Data Governance:

Establish a data governance framework that governs data quality and reliability. Develop data governance policies, procedures, and guidelines that define roles, responsibilities, and accountability for maintaining data quality. Implement data quality audits and assessments to regularly evaluate and monitor data quality. Data governance ensures that data quality and reliability are prioritized throughout the organization.

Regular Data Quality Monitoring:

Implement mechanisms to regularly monitor data quality and reliability. Develop data quality metrics and key performance indicators (KPIs) to assess the accuracy, completeness, consistency, and timeliness of the data. Continuously monitor and track these metrics to identify any deviations or trends that may indicate data quality issues. Regular data quality monitoring allows for proactive identification and resolution of data quality problems.

Data Quality Improvement Initiatives:

Invest in data quality improvement initiatives to continually enhance data quality and reliability. This can involve conducting data quality assessments, training data collectors on best practices, implementing automated data validation processes, or leveraging data profiling and cleansing tools. Actively address feedback and suggestions from data users to identify areas for improvement and implement corrective measures.

In conclusion, ensuring data quality and reliability is essential for deriving accurate insights and making informed decisions. By implementing data validation, cleaning, standardization, and integration processes, maintaining comprehensive data documentation and metadata, prioritizing data security, establishing data governance, regularly monitoring data quality, and investing in data quality improvement initiatives, organizations can ensure that the data used for analysis is of high quality, reliable, and trustworthy. This enables organizations to maximize the value of their data and make data-driven decisions with confidence.

Implementing Effective Data Governance Practices

Data governance is a critical component of successful data science and analytics initiatives. It involves establishing processes, policies, and responsibilities to ensure the availability, integrity, confidentiality, and usability of data assets. Effective data governance practices facilitate data-driven decision-making, improve data quality, and mitigate risks associated with data management. In this section, we will explore key considerations and strategies for implementing effective data governance practices.

Establish Data Governance Framework:

Start by establishing a data governance framework that defines the overall structure, processes, and responsibilities for data governance within the organization. This framework should include clear roles and responsibilities, governance policies, and guidelines for data management, data quality, data security, and compliance. The framework should be aligned with organizational objectives and strategies.

Appoint Data Stewards and Data Owners:

Appoint data stewards and data owners who are responsible for managing and ensuring the quality of specific data assets or domains. Data stewards are responsible for data governance implementation, data policy enforcement, and data quality monitoring. Data owners are responsible for making data-related decisions, ensuring data availability, and determining access rights. Clearly define their roles, responsibilities, and decision-making authority.

Develop Data Policies and Procedures:

Develop data policies and procedures that govern data management, data quality, data security, and data privacy. These policies should outline the guidelines and best practices for data collection, storage, sharing, retention, and disposal. Ensure that the policies are aligned with relevant regulations, industry standards, and organizational requirements. Document the procedures and communicate them to all stakeholders.

Data Classification and Categorization:

Classify and categorize data based on its sensitivity, criticality, and business impact. Establish a data classification framework that defines different levels of data classification, such as confidential, sensitive, or public data. This helps in determining appropriate access controls, encryption requirements, and data handling procedures. Categorizing data based on its purpose and context enables better data management and supports compliance efforts.

Data Quality Management:

Implement data quality management practices to ensure the accuracy, completeness, consistency, and reliability of data assets. Define data quality standards and metrics that align with the organization's objectives. Establish data quality monitoring processes and conduct regular data quality assessments. Implement data validation, profiling, and cleansing techniques to address data quality issues and maintain high-quality data.

Data Security and Privacy:

Ensure that data governance practices incorporate robust data security and privacy measures. Develop data security policies that outline procedures for data access controls, authentication mechanisms, encryption, and data masking. Implement privacy policies that comply with relevant regulations, such as GDPR or CCPA, and protect personally identifiable information. Regularly assess and monitor data security measures to ensure ongoing compliance and data protection.

Data Lifecycle Management:

Implement data lifecycle management processes to effectively manage data from creation to disposal. Define data retention policies that specify how long data should be retained based on legal, regulatory, and business requirements. Establish procedures for archiving, backup, and secure data destruction. Consider the environmental impact of data storage and disposal methods to align with sustainability goals.

Data Governance Communication and Training:

Communicate data governance policies, processes, and guidelines to all stakeholders in the organization. Ensure that employees understand their roles and responsibilities related to data governance. Provide training on data governance practices, data handling, and compliance requirements. Regularly communicate updates, changes, and successes related to data governance to foster a culture of data governance awareness and participation.

Collaborate Across Departments:

Effective data governance requires collaboration across departments and functions within the organization. Establish cross-functional data governance committees or teams to promote collaboration, knowledge sharing, and alignment of data governance practices. Involve stakeholders from different departments, such as IT, legal, compliance, and business units, to ensure that data governance practices address their specific needs and requirements.

Continuous Improvement and Evaluation:

Regularly evaluate and refine data governance practices to ensure their effectiveness and alignment with evolving business needs. Establish mechanisms for feedback collection and analysis to identify areas for improvement. Conduct audits and assessments to assess the adherence to data governance policies and identify potential risks or gaps. Embrace a culture of continuous improvement and learning in data governance practices.

In conclusion, implementing effective data governance practices is essential for organizations to leverage their data assets efficiently, ensure data quality and security, and make informed decisions. By establishing a data governance framework, appointing data stewards and owners, developing data policies and procedures, implementing data classification and categorization, managing data quality, prioritizing data security and privacy, practicing data lifecycle management, communicating and training stakeholders, fostering collaboration, and embracing continuous improvement, organizations can establish a strong foundation for data governance and unlock the full potential of their data assets.

CHAPTER 5: DATA EXPLORATION AND VISUALIZATION

Chapter 5 delves into the crucial aspects of data exploration and visualization in the context of data science and analytics. Data exploration involves examining and understanding the characteristics, patterns, and relationships within the data. Visualization, on the other hand, enables the effective communication of insights through graphical representations. In this chapter, we will explore key strategies and considerations for data exploration and visualization.

Importance of Data Exploration:

This section emphasizes the significance of data exploration as a fundamental step in the data analysis process. Data exploration helps uncover patterns, trends, and anomalies within the data, providing valuable insights that drive decision-making. By examining the data from different perspectives, data exploration aids in formulating hypotheses, identifying variables of interest, and refining the research question or business problem.

Data Cleaning and Preparation:

Before embarking on data exploration, it is crucial to clean and prepare the data. This involves addressing missing values, outliers, data inconsistencies, and other data quality issues. Implement data cleaning techniques, such as imputation, outlier detection, and data transformation, to ensure the accuracy and reliability of the data. Data cleaning and preparation lay the foundation for meaningful data exploration and visualization.

Selecting Data Exploration Techniques:

Choose appropriate data exploration techniques based on the characteristics of the data and the objectives of the analysis. This may involve summary statistics, data profiling, data aggregation, correlation analysis, clustering, or dimensionality reduction techniques. Select techniques that allow for the discovery of patterns, relationships, and trends within the data. Combine multiple techniques to gain a comprehensive understanding of the data.

Exploratory Data Analysis (EDA):

Perform exploratory data analysis to gain insights into the distribution, central tendencies, variability, and relationships within the data. Utilize descriptive statistics, data visualization, and graphical representations to summarize and explore the data. EDA techniques, such as histograms, box plots, scatter plots, and correlation matrices, help uncover patterns, identify outliers, and guide further analysis.

Feature Engineering:

During data exploration, consider feature engineering techniques to create new variables or transform existing ones. Feature engineering involves creating meaningful features that capture relevant information or enhance the predictive power of the data. This may include variable transformations, creating interaction terms, or deriving new variables based on domain knowledge. Feature engineering enriches the dataset and enables deeper insights during data exploration.

Interactive Data Visualization:

Leverage interactive data visualization tools and techniques to effectively communicate insights and patterns within the data. Interactive visualizations allow users to explore the data dynamically, zoom in on specific areas, filter data based on different criteria, and interact with the visual representation. This enhances the understanding and interpretation of complex datasets, enabling users to uncover hidden insights.

Choosing Visualization Techniques:

Select visualization techniques that are appropriate for the data attributes and the objectives of the analysis. This can include bar charts, line graphs, scatter plots, heatmaps, treemaps, network graphs, or geospatial visualizations, among others. Consider the type of data being visualized (categorical, numerical, temporal), the relationships to be conveyed, and the audience for the visualization. Choose techniques that effectively represent the data and facilitate meaningful insights.

Designing Effective Visualizations:

Design visualizations that are clear, concise, and visually appealing. Emphasize simplicity, ensuring that the main message is easily understood. Use appropriate color schemes, labels, and annotations to enhance comprehension. Apply effective data encoding principles, such as position, length, and color, to represent data accurately. Consider the context and audience when designing visualizations to ensure they effectively communicate the intended insights.

Storytelling with Data Visualization:

Data visualization can be a powerful storytelling tool. Use data visualization to create narratives and communicate compelling stories that drive understanding and engagement. Structure visualizations in a logical sequence, guiding the audience through the data insights. Incorporate annotations, titles, and captions to provide context and highlight key findings. Effective storytelling with data visualization helps stakeholders grasp complex concepts and make informed decisions.

Iterative Exploration and Visualization:

Data exploration and visualization are iterative processes that evolve as insights are gained and analysis progresses. Continuously refine and iterate the exploration and visualization techniques based on the emerging insights and feedback. Consider additional variables, refine visual representations, or apply advanced analysis techniques to delve deeper into the data. Iterative exploration and visualization ensure a thorough understanding of the data and support the generation of valuable insights.

In conclusion, data exploration and visualization are vital steps in the data analysis process. By leveraging appropriate data exploration techniques, conducting exploratory data analysis, performing feature engineering, using interactive and effective visualization techniques, designing clear and compelling visualizations, and employing storytelling principles, organizations can uncover patterns, trends, and insights within the data, effectively communicate findings, and drive informed decision-making.

Exploring and Understanding the Data

Exploring and understanding the data is a crucial step in the data science and analytics process. It involves examining the characteristics, patterns, and relationships within the data to gain insights and inform subsequent analysis. By thoroughly exploring and understanding the data, analysts can make informed decisions, identify meaningful variables, and generate accurate and reliable results. In this section, we will explore key strategies and considerations for effectively exploring and understanding the data.

Data Familiarization:

Begin by familiarizing yourself with the dataset. Understand the structure of the data, including the variables or features, their types (categorical, numerical, text), and their relationships. Review any available documentation or data dictionaries that provide insights into the data sources, collection methods, and variable definitions. Familiarizing yourself with the data helps establish a foundation for subsequent exploration and analysis.

Summary Statistics:

Calculate summary statistics to gain a high-level understanding of the data. This includes measures such as mean, median, standard deviation, minimum, and maximum. Summary statistics provide insights into the central tendency, variability, and range of the data. They help identify any initial patterns, outliers, or potential issues that may require further investigation.

Data Visualization:

Utilize data visualization techniques to explore and visualize the data. Graphical representations, such as histograms, box plots, scatter plots, and heatmaps, provide visual insights into the distribution, relationships, and patterns within the data. Visualization facilitates the identification of trends, outliers, clusters, or correlations that may not be immediately apparent in tabular form. Visual exploration enhances the understanding and interpretation of the data.

Univariate Analysis:

Conduct univariate analysis to examine individual variables in isolation. Analyze the distribution of each variable, exploring measures such as frequency counts, proportions, or histograms. Identify any outliers, missing values, or unexpected patterns. Univariate analysis provides insights into the characteristics and behavior of individual variables and helps identify variables of interest for subsequent analysis.

Bivariate Analysis:

Perform bivariate analysis to explore the relationships between pairs of variables. This involves examining the correlations, associations, or dependencies between variables. Use techniques such as scatter plots, correlation matrices, or cross-tabulations to identify potential relationships or patterns. Bivariate analysis helps uncover dependencies or interactions between variables, guiding the selection of variables for further analysis.

Multivariate Analysis:

Extend the analysis to multivariate techniques to explore relationships among multiple variables simultaneously. Use techniques such as cluster analysis, factor analysis, or principal component analysis to identify groups, latent factors, or underlying dimensions in the data. Multivariate analysis uncovers complex relationships and provides a comprehensive understanding of the data, enabling more advanced analysis and modeling.

Data Segmentation:

Consider segmenting the data based on relevant categorical variables or factors. This involves dividing the dataset into subsets based on specific characteristics or groupings. By examining subsets separately, you can identify variations, trends, or patterns that may be obscured in the overall dataset. Data segmentation provides deeper insights into different segments of the data, enabling more targeted analysis.

Data Sampling:

If working with large datasets, consider using data sampling techniques to explore subsets of the data. Random sampling or stratified sampling can help reduce computational complexity while still providing representative insights. By exploring a sample, you can gain an understanding of the overall data characteristics and verify the feasibility of analysis techniques before applying them to the entire dataset.

Domain Knowledge and Hypothesis Testing:

Leverage domain knowledge and formulate hypotheses to guide the exploration and understanding of the data. Use your expertise and subject matter knowledge to identify variables or relationships that are likely to be meaningful or relevant. Develop hypotheses and test them against the data to validate or refute initial assumptions. Incorporating domain knowledge adds context and depth to the exploration process.

Iterative Exploration and Documentation:

Data exploration is an iterative process that evolves as insights are gained and analysis progresses. Continuously refine and iterate the exploration techniques based on emerging findings and feedback. Document your exploration process, including the steps taken, observations made, and insights gained. Comprehensive documentation facilitates reproducibility, knowledge sharing, and the ability to return to previous findings.

In conclusion, exploring and understanding the data are essential steps in data science and analytics. By familiarizing yourself with the data, calculating summary statistics, employing data visualization techniques, conducting univariate and multivariate analysis, segmenting the data, considering sampling techniques, leveraging domain knowledge, and engaging in iterative exploration, analysts can gain a comprehensive understanding of the data, identify meaningful patterns and relationships, and make informed decisions for subsequent analysis. Thorough exploration and understanding of the data lay the foundation for accurate and reliable insights.

Choosing Appropriate Visualization Techniques

Choosing appropriate visualization techniques is crucial for effectively communicating insights and patterns within the data. Visualization enables analysts to present complex information in a visually appealing and easily interpretable manner. By selecting the right visualization techniques, analysts can enhance understanding, reveal trends, highlight relationships, and facilitate data-driven decision-making. In this section, we will explore key considerations and strategies for choosing appropriate visualization techniques.

Understand Data Types:

Start by understanding the types of data you are working with. Data can be categorized into three main types: categorical, numerical, and temporal. Categorical data represents distinct categories or groups, while numerical data consists of measurable quantities. Temporal data represents values recorded over time. Understanding the data types helps determine the appropriate visualization techniques that best represent the underlying information.

Identify Variables of Interest:

Identify the variables or dimensions of the data that you want to visualize. Consider the purpose of the visualization and the specific insights you want to convey. Determine whether you are interested in comparing categories, examining distributions, highlighting relationships, or showing trends over time. Identifying the variables of interest guides the selection of visualization techniques that effectively highlight the desired information.

Consider Data Relationships:

Consider the relationships between variables when choosing visualization techniques. Determine whether you want to explore correlations, dependencies, or associations between variables. Scatter plots, correlation matrices, network graphs, or heatmaps are useful for visualizing relationships and dependencies. Choosing techniques that effectively represent data relationships enables a deeper understanding of the underlying patterns and interactions.

Choose Visualization Formats:

Select appropriate visualization formats based on the characteristics of the data and the insights you want to convey. Common visualization formats include bar charts, line graphs, scatter plots, pie charts, area charts, histograms, treemaps, and geospatial maps. Each format has its strengths and is suitable for different types of data and objectives. Consider the nature of the data and the message you want to convey when choosing visualization formats.

Consider Data Distribution:

Consider the distribution of the data when selecting visualization techniques. If the data is continuous and follows a normal distribution, line graphs or histograms may be suitable. If the data is categorical, bar charts or pie charts can effectively represent proportions or frequencies. Box plots are useful for displaying the distribution, variability, and outliers within data. Understanding the distribution of the data helps in selecting appropriate visualization techniques that accurately represent the data characteristics.

Scale and Size of the Data:

Consider the scale and size of the data when choosing visualization techniques. Large datasets may require techniques such as aggregation, sampling, or summarization to manage the volume of data. Line plots or area charts can effectively display trends over time for large datasets. For geospatial data, choropleth maps or bubble maps can be used to visualize regional variations. Adapting visualization techniques to accommodate large or small-scale data ensures clarity and readability.

Interactivity and User Engagement:

Evaluate the need for interactivity and user engagement in visualization. Interactive visualizations allow users to explore and interact with the data, enabling a more personalized and engaging experience. Techniques such as zooming, filtering, or drilling down into specific data subsets enhance user engagement and facilitate deeper insights. Consider the level of interactivity required to effectively communicate the message and engage the target audience.

Context and Audience:

Consider the context in which the visualization will be presented and the characteristics of the target audience. Different visualization techniques may be more suitable for specific contexts or audiences. Consider factors such as the level of data literacy, domain knowledge, and preferences of the audience. Tailor the visualization to effectively communicate with the intended audience, ensuring that the visualization resonates with their needs and understanding.

Balance Simplicity and Complexity:

Strike a balance between simplicity and complexity when choosing visualization techniques. Aim for simplicity to ensure that the main message or insights are easily understood. Avoid cluttering the visualization with unnecessary elements or excessive details that may confuse or distract the audience. However, balance simplicity with providing enough information and context to convey the intended message effectively.

Experiment and Iterate:

Experiment with different visualization techniques and iterate based on feedback and insights gained. Explore alternative approaches and variations to find the most suitable representation for the data and objectives. Be open to adjusting and refining the visualization based on the emerging needs or new insights obtained during the analysis process. The iterative approach allows for continuous improvement and ensures that the chosen visualization techniques effectively communicate the desired insights.

In conclusion, choosing appropriate visualization techniques is essential for effective communication and understanding of data insights. By understanding data types, identifying variables of interest, considering data relationships, choosing suitable visualization formats, accounting for data distribution and scale, evaluating interactivity and user engagement, considering context and audience, balancing simplicity and complexity, and embracing an iterative approach, analysts can select visualization techniques that enhance understanding, reveal patterns, and effectively convey insights for data-driven decision-making.

Communicating Insights Effectively

Effective communication of insights is a crucial aspect of data science and analytics. It involves presenting complex findings and patterns in a clear, concise, and compelling manner that resonates with the intended audience. Effective communication enables stakeholders to understand and act upon the insights derived from data analysis, ultimately driving informed decision-making. In this section, we will explore key strategies and considerations for communicating insights effectively.

Know Your Audience:

Understanding your audience is fundamental to effective communication. Consider the background, expertise, and level of familiarity with data analysis concepts of your audience. Adapt your communication style, language, and level of technical detail to match their needs and knowledge. Tailoring the message to the audience ensures that insights are conveyed in a manner that is accessible and meaningful to them.

Focus on the Key Message:

Identify the key message or main takeaway from the analysis. Distill the insights into a clear, concise, and actionable statement. Avoid overwhelming the audience with excessive information or irrelevant details. By focusing on the key message, you ensure that the most important findings are highlighted and resonate with the audience.

Tell a Story:

Frame your insights within a narrative to engage and captivate the audience. Use storytelling techniques to create a compelling narrative that guides the audience through the insights. Structure the story with a clear beginning, middle, and end, presenting the problem or question, the analysis process, and the resulting insights. A well-crafted story adds context, emotion, and relatability, making the insights more memorable and impactful.

Use Clear and Simple Language:

Communicate insights using clear and simple language, avoiding jargon or technical terms that may confuse or alienate the audience. Explain complex concepts or statistical terms in plain language, using analogies or examples to enhance understanding. Use visuals, such as charts, graphs, or infographics, to supplement and reinforce the message. Clear and simple language ensures that the insights are easily comprehensible to a wide range of stakeholders.

Visualize the Data:

Utilize data visualization techniques to present insights visually. Visualizations, such as charts, graphs, and maps, help communicate complex patterns and relationships in an easily digestible format. Choose the most appropriate visualization type for the data and the message you want to convey. Ensure that the visuals are well-designed, with clear labels, titles, and annotations, to enhance comprehension and engagement.

Highlight Key Findings:

Emphasize the most important and relevant findings in your communication. Highlight key insights, trends, or patterns that are critical to understanding the implications and recommendations derived from the analysis. Use visual cues, color coding, or annotations to draw attention to these key findings. By highlighting the most significant insights, you ensure that they are not lost within the larger context of the analysis.

Provide Context:

Contextualize the insights by providing relevant background information or benchmarks. Explain the significance of the findings within the broader business or industry context. Help the audience understand the implications of the insights and how they relate to their specific goals or challenges. Providing context allows stakeholders to better grasp the relevance and impact of the insights on decision-making.

Use Real-World Examples:

Illustrate the insights with real-world examples or case studies that resonate with the audience. Relate the findings to tangible scenarios, challenges, or success stories that the audience can connect with. Real-world examples make the insights more relatable and applicable to their own context, increasing the likelihood of action and adoption.

Address Limitations and Uncertainty:

Acknowledge the limitations and uncertainties associated with the analysis. Be transparent about the data quality, assumptions, or potential biases that may affect the findings. Clearly communicate any areas where further investigation or data collection may be required. Addressing limitations and uncertainties builds trust and credibility, ensuring that stakeholders have a realistic understanding of the insights and their potential implications.

Seek Feedback and Engagement:

Encourage feedback and engage in a dialogue with stakeholders to foster a collaborative and iterative approach to communication. Actively listen to their questions, concerns, and perspectives. Adjust and refine the communication based on their feedback. By seeking feedback and promoting engagement, you create a shared understanding and ownership of the insights, fostering a data-driven culture within the organization.

In conclusion, effective communication of insights is essential for driving action and decision-making based on data analysis. By knowing your audience, focusing on the key message, telling a compelling story, using clear and simple language, visualizing the data, highlighting key findings, providing context, using real-world examples, addressing limitations and uncertainty, and seeking feedback and engagement, you can effectively communicate insights and empower stakeholders to leverage data for informed decision-making. Effective communication bridges the gap between data analysis and action, unlocking the full value of data-driven insights.

CHAPTER 6: STATISTICAL ANALYSIS AND MACHINE LEARNING

Chapter 6 explores the application of statistical analysis and machine learning techniques in data science and analytics. Statistical analysis and machine learning provide powerful tools for extracting insights, making predictions, and uncovering patterns within data. This chapter covers key concepts, methodologies, and considerations for conducting statistical analysis and applying machine learning algorithms.

Introduction to Statistical Analysis:

The chapter begins with an introduction to statistical analysis, highlighting its role in data science. Statistical analysis involves applying statistical techniques to analyze and interpret data. It includes descriptive statistics to summarize data, inferential statistics for drawing conclusions, hypothesis testing to make statistical inferences, and regression analysis to examine relationships between variables. Understanding the fundamentals of statistical analysis is essential for conducting meaningful data analysis.

Exploratory Data Analysis (EDA):

Exploratory Data Analysis is a crucial step in statistical analysis. EDA involves visualizing and summarizing data to understand its distribution, identify patterns, detect outliers, and explore relationships between variables. EDA techniques, such as scatter plots, histograms, box plots, and correlation matrices, help analysts gain insights into the data and guide further statistical analysis.

Hypothesis Testing:

Hypothesis testing is a statistical technique used to make inferences about population parameters based on sample data. It involves formulating null and alternative hypotheses, selecting an appropriate statistical test, and calculating p-values to determine the significance of the findings.

Hypothesis testing allows analysts to draw conclusions about the data and make informed decisions based on statistical evidence.

Regression Analysis:

Regression analysis is a statistical method for modeling the relationship between a dependent variable and one or more independent variables. It helps assess the impact of independent variables on the dependent variable, make predictions, and identify significant predictors. Regression analysis techniques include linear regression, logistic regression, and multiple regression. Regression analysis is widely used in various fields, such as finance, marketing, and social sciences.

Machine Learning Basics:

The chapter introduces the basics of machine learning, which involves using algorithms to automatically learn patterns and make predictions from data. It covers supervised learning, unsupervised learning, and reinforcement learning. Supervised learning algorithms use labeled data to train models for prediction or classification tasks. Unsupervised learning algorithms discover patterns and structures in unlabeled data. Reinforcement learning involves training agents to make decisions and learn from feedback in an environment.

Machine Learning Algorithms:

The chapter provides an overview of commonly used machine learning algorithms. This includes decision trees, random forests, support vector machines (SVM), k-nearest neighbors (KNN), naive Bayes, and neural networks. Each algorithm has its strengths and weaknesses, and the choice depends on the nature of the data, the problem at hand, and the desired outcome. Understanding the characteristics and capabilities of different machine learning algorithms is crucial for selecting the appropriate approach.

Model Evaluation and Validation:

Model evaluation and validation are essential steps in the machine learning process. Evaluating models involves assessing their performance and generalization capabilities. Common evaluation metrics include accuracy, precision, recall, F1 score, and area under the receiver operating characteristic curve (AUC-ROC). Cross-validation techniques, such as k-fold cross-validation, help estimate the model's performance on unseen data. Proper model evaluation and validation ensure reliable and robust predictions.

Feature Selection and Engineering:

Feature selection and engineering play a crucial role in both statistical analysis and machine learning. Feature selection involves identifying the most relevant variables or features that contribute to the analysis or prediction. Feature engineering involves transforming or creating new features to enhance the model's performance. These techniques help improve the accuracy and interpretability of statistical models and machine learning algorithms.

Overfitting and Regularization:

Overfitting is a common challenge in machine learning where the model performs well on the training data but fails to generalize to new data. Regularization techniques, such as L1 regularization (Lasso) and L2 regularization (Ridge), help prevent overfitting by adding penalty terms to the model's objective function. Understanding and addressing overfitting are crucial for building reliable and robust statistical models and machine learning algorithms.

Ethical Considerations in Statistical Analysis and Machine Learning:

The chapter concludes by addressing ethical considerations in statistical analysis and machine learning. Ethical considerations include privacy protection, fairness, transparency, accountability, and bias mitigation. It is essential to consider the potential impact of data analysis and machine learning algorithms on individuals, society, and decision-making processes. Adhering to ethical principles ensures responsible and ethical use of statistical analysis and machine learning techniques.

In conclusion, Chapter 6 provides an overview of statistical analysis and machine learning techniques in data science and analytics. By understanding statistical analysis concepts, conducting exploratory data analysis, performing hypothesis testing and regression analysis, applying machine learning algorithms, evaluating and validating models, conducting feature selection and engineering, addressing overfitting, and considering ethical considerations, analysts can effectively leverage statistical analysis and machine learning to derive meaningful insights, make accurate predictions, and inform decision-making processes.

Introduction to Statistical Analysis and Modeling

Statistical analysis and modeling play a fundamental role in data science and analytics. They provide powerful tools for extracting insights, making predictions, and understanding patterns within data. Statistical analysis involves applying statistical techniques to analyze and interpret data, while statistical modeling focuses on building mathematical models to represent relationships and make predictions. In this section, we will explore the key concepts and methodologies involved in statistical analysis and modeling.

Purpose of Statistical Analysis:

The primary purpose of statistical analysis is to uncover patterns, relationships, and insights within data. It helps analysts understand the underlying structure, characteristics, and distributions of the data. Statistical analysis enables researchers and practitioners to draw conclusions, make inferences, and support decision-making based on evidence derived from data.

Descriptive and Inferential Statistics:

Statistical analysis encompasses two main branches: descriptive statistics and inferential statistics. Descriptive statistics involve summarizing and describing the main features of the data, such as measures of central tendency (mean, median, mode) and measures of variability (standard deviation, range). Descriptive statistics provide a snapshot of the data and help identify general patterns and trends.

Inferential statistics, on the other hand, involve drawing conclusions and making inferences about a population based on a sample. Inferential statistics utilize techniques such as hypothesis testing and confidence intervals to estimate population parameters, compare groups, and assess the significance of relationships. Inferential statistics enable analysts to generalize findings from a sample to a larger population.

Statistical Modeling:

Statistical modeling involves building mathematical models that represent relationships and patterns observed in the data. Models are constructed based on statistical principles and techniques. Statistical models can be linear or nonlinear, parametric or nonparametric, depending on the nature of the data and the assumptions made. Models capture the systematic components and random variations within the data, allowing for prediction and inference.

Regression Analysis:

Regression analysis is a widely used statistical modeling technique that explores the relationship between a dependent variable and one or more independent variables. It helps determine the impact of independent variables on the dependent variable and make predictions. Linear regression, one of the most common regression techniques, assumes a linear relationship between the variables. Nonlinear regression models capture more complex relationships.

Regression analysis provides insights into the strength and direction of relationships, significance of predictors, and predictive accuracy. It allows for hypothesis testing, model evaluation, and forecasting. Regression analysis is widely applied in fields such as economics, social sciences, finance, and marketing.

Hypothesis Testing:

Hypothesis testing is a statistical technique used to make inferences about population parameters based on sample data. It involves formulating a null hypothesis (H0) and an alternative hypothesis (Ha). The null hypothesis represents no significant effect or difference, while the alternative hypothesis represents the presence of a significant effect or difference.

Hypothesis testing involves selecting an appropriate statistical test, calculating test statistics (e.g., t-test, z-test), and determining the p-value—the probability of obtaining results as extreme as observed, assuming the null hypothesis is true. If the p-value is below a predefined significance level (often 0.05), the null hypothesis is rejected in favor of the alternative hypothesis.

Hypothesis testing allows analysts to draw conclusions and make inferences about the data. It provides a systematic framework for assessing the significance of relationships, comparing groups, and evaluating the effectiveness of interventions or treatments.

Time Series Analysis:

Time series analysis is a statistical modeling technique used for analyzing and forecasting data that is observed sequentially over time. Time series data often exhibits temporal dependencies and trends, making it different from cross-sectional data. Time series analysis involves techniques such as autoregressive integrated moving average (ARIMA) models, exponential smoothing models, and seasonal decomposition.

Time series analysis helps identify patterns, seasonal variations, trends, and forecasting future values. It is widely used in finance, economics, weather forecasting, and other domains where data is collected over time.

Model Evaluation and Validation:

Model evaluation and validation are crucial steps in statistical analysis and modeling. It involves assessing the performance and reliability of the model. Various metrics are used to evaluate models, including goodness-of-fit measures, such as R-squared (coefficient of determination), mean squared error (MSE), and root mean squared error (RMSE).

Validation techniques, such as cross-validation, are employed to estimate the model's performance on unseen data. Model evaluation and validation ensure that the model accurately represents the underlying patterns in the data and can be trusted for prediction and inference.

Assumptions and Limitations:

Statistical analysis and modeling rely on certain assumptions and have limitations that need to be considered. Assumptions include the independence of observations, linearity, normality, and homoscedasticity. Violations of these assumptions can impact the validity of the results.

Additionally, statistical analysis and modeling cannot account for all factors and variables influencing a phenomenon. They provide insights based on the available data but may not capture the entire complexity of the real-world situation. Analysts must be mindful of the limitations and interpret the results in context.

In conclusion, statistical analysis and modeling are essential components of data science and analytics. They enable the extraction of insights, prediction, and inference from data. By employing descriptive and inferential statistics, regression analysis, hypothesis testing, time series analysis, and model evaluation techniques, analysts can understand the data, test hypotheses, make predictions, and support decision-making processes. Understanding the underlying principles and considerations of statistical analysis and modeling is crucial for conducting meaningful and reliable data analysis.

Understanding Machine Learning Algorithms

Machine learning algorithms form the backbone of data science and analytics. They enable the extraction of patterns, relationships, and insights from data, leading to accurate predictions and informed decision-making. Understanding the different types of machine learning algorithms and their characteristics is essential for effectively applying them to solve complex problems. In this section, we will explore key machine learning algorithms and their functionalities.

Supervised Learning Algorithms:

Supervised learning algorithms are trained on labeled data, where the input features and corresponding output labels are known. They learn patterns from the labeled data and use that knowledge to make predictions on new, unseen data. Two common types of supervised learning algorithms are:

Classification Algorithms: These algorithms predict categorical or discrete labels. Examples include logistic regression, support vector machines (SVM), decision trees, random forests, and naive Bayes. Classification algorithms are used in various applications such as image recognition, sentiment analysis, and fraud detection.

Regression Algorithms: These algorithms predict continuous numerical values. Linear regression, polynomial regression, and support vector regression are examples of regression algorithms. Regression algorithms are employed in predicting housing prices, stock market trends, and demand forecasting.

Unsupervised Learning Algorithms:

Unsupervised learning algorithms are used when the data is unlabeled or lacks explicit output labels. These algorithms explore the underlying structure and patterns within the data without any prior knowledge. Two common types of unsupervised learning algorithms are:

Clustering Algorithms: Clustering algorithms group similar data points together based on their inherent similarities. Examples include k-means clustering, hierarchical clustering, and DBSCAN. Clustering algorithms are used in customer segmentation, image segmentation, and anomaly detection.

Dimensionality Reduction Algorithms: Dimensionality reduction algorithms reduce the number of input features while preserving important information. Principal Component Analysis (PCA), t-SNE, and LLE (Locally Linear Embedding) are commonly used dimensionality reduction techniques. Dimensionality reduction is beneficial in visualizing high-dimensional data and removing irrelevant features.

Ensemble Learning Algorithms:

Ensemble learning algorithms combine multiple individual models to improve prediction accuracy and robustness. They leverage the wisdom of the crowd by aggregating the predictions of different models. Ensemble learning algorithms include:

Random Forest: Random forest combines multiple decision trees to form a robust and accurate model. Each tree is trained on a random subset of features and data samples, resulting in a diverse set of predictions that are averaged to make the final prediction.

Gradient Boosting: Gradient boosting builds a sequence of models, where each model corrects the mistakes made by the previous model. It combines weak learners (usually decision trees) into a strong predictive model.

AdaBoost: AdaBoost assigns weights to data points, focusing more on misclassified instances in each iteration. It iteratively trains weak models and combines their predictions to make the final prediction.

Deep Learning Algorithms:

Deep learning algorithms are a subset of neural network algorithms designed to mimic the functioning of the human brain. They are particularly effective in processing large amounts of complex data and extracting intricate patterns. Deep learning algorithms include:

Convolutional Neural Networks (CNN): CNNs are primarily used for image classification, object detection, and image recognition tasks. They utilize convolutional layers to extract hierarchical features from images.

Recurrent Neural Networks (RNN): RNNs are suited for sequential data, such as text, speech, and time series data. They have memory units that can capture dependencies between data points.

Generative Adversarial Networks (GAN): GANs consist of two neural networks, a generator and a discriminator, which compete with each other.

GANs are used for generating synthetic data, image synthesis, and data augmentation.

Reinforcement Learning Algorithms:

Reinforcement learning algorithms involve training an agent to make decisions in an environment. The agent interacts with the environment and receives rewards or penalties based on its actions. Over time, the agent learns to take actions that maximize its cumulative rewards. Reinforcement learning algorithms are used in robotics, game playing, and optimization tasks.

Understanding the characteristics, strengths, and weaknesses of different machine learning algorithms is crucial for selecting the appropriate algorithm for a given problem. Consider factors such as the type of data, the nature of the problem (classification, regression, clustering), the interpretability of the model, and the available computing resources. It is also important to consider algorithmic complexity, scalability, and the need for interpretability when choosing the right machine learning algorithm.

In conclusion, machine learning algorithms provide powerful tools for extracting insights and making predictions from data. By understanding the various types of machine learning algorithms, including supervised learning, unsupervised learning, ensemble learning, deep learning, and reinforcement learning, analysts can choose the most appropriate algorithm to solve specific problems. Applying the right machine learning algorithm contributes to accurate predictions, improved decision-making, and the discovery of valuable insights from data.

Applying Advanced Analytics Techniques

Advanced analytics techniques enable organizations to gain deeper insights, make more accurate predictions, and derive actionable recommendations from their data. These techniques go beyond traditional statistical analysis and basic machine learning algorithms, incorporating sophisticated methodologies to handle complex data structures and uncover hidden patterns. In this section, we will explore several advanced analytics techniques and their applications.

Time Series Analysis:

Time series analysis is a technique used to analyze data that is collected sequentially over time. It involves identifying patterns, trends, and seasonality within the data. Time series analysis is commonly employed in forecasting future values and understanding the dynamics of data. Techniques such as autoregressive integrated moving average (ARIMA), exponential smoothing, and state space models are applied to time series data in various domains, including finance, sales forecasting, and demand planning.

Text Mining and Natural Language Processing (NLP):

Text mining and NLP techniques are used to extract valuable information from unstructured textual data. By applying techniques such as sentiment analysis, topic modeling, named entity recognition, and text classification, organizations can gain insights from large volumes of text data. Text mining and NLP are widely used in social media analysis, customer feedback analysis, and content analysis for market research and competitive intelligence.

Network Analysis:

Network analysis focuses on understanding the relationships and interactions between entities in a network. It involves analyzing the structure, centrality, and connectivity of nodes and edges in a network graph. Network analysis is employed in social network analysis, transportation planning, fraud detection, and supply chain optimization. Techniques such as social network analysis, community detection, and graph algorithms are utilized to extract insights from complex networks.

Geospatial Analysis:

Geospatial analysis combines geographic data with analytical techniques to understand patterns and relationships in spatial data. It involves analyzing and visualizing data based on their geographic location. Geospatial analysis is used in fields such as urban planning, logistics optimization, and environmental monitoring. Techniques such as geographic information systems (GIS), spatial clustering, and spatial regression are applied to geospatial data to uncover spatial patterns and make informed decisions.

Anomaly Detection:

Anomaly detection techniques identify rare events, outliers, or patterns that deviate significantly from the norm within a dataset. Anomaly detection is crucial for fraud detection, cybersecurity, network monitoring, and predictive maintenance. Techniques such as statistical modeling, machine learning algorithms, and unsupervised learning approaches, including clustering and outlier detection, are employed to detect anomalies and ensure data integrity.

Recommendation Systems:

Recommendation systems provide personalized recommendations to users based on their preferences, behavior, and past interactions. These systems are widely used in e-commerce, streaming services, and content recommendation. Collaborative filtering, content-based filtering, and hybrid approaches are employed to generate accurate and relevant recommendations. Recommendation systems leverage techniques such as matrix factorization, association rules, and deep learning architectures.

Predictive Analytics and Prescriptive Analytics:

Predictive analytics uses historical data and statistical models to make predictions about future outcomes. It helps organizations forecast customer behavior, demand, and financial performance. Techniques such as regression analysis, time series forecasting, and machine learning algorithms are used to build predictive models.

Prescriptive analytics takes predictive analytics a step further by recommending optimal actions to achieve desired outcomes. It combines optimization techniques, simulation, and decision analysis to provide actionable insights and recommendations. Prescriptive analytics is applied in supply chain optimization, resource allocation, and strategic decision-making.

Ensemble Techniques:

Ensemble techniques combine multiple models or algorithms to improve prediction accuracy and robustness. Techniques such as bagging, boosting, and stacking are used to aggregate predictions from diverse models. Ensemble techniques reduce the impact of model bias, increase generalization capabilities, and address overfitting issues. Ensemble models, such as random forests, gradient boosting machines (GBM), and stacked models, are widely used in various domains.

Deep Reinforcement Learning:

Deep reinforcement learning combines deep learning and reinforcement learning to enable agents to learn optimal actions through trial and error. It has been successfully applied in areas such as autonomous driving, robotics, and game playing. Deep reinforcement learning leverages deep neural networks and reinforcement learning algorithms to learn complex decision-making policies in dynamic environments.

In conclusion, applying advanced analytics techniques enhances organizations' ability to derive meaningful insights, make accurate predictions, and drive informed decision-making. By utilizing techniques such as time series analysis, text mining and NLP, network analysis, geospatial analysis, anomaly detection, recommendation systems, predictive analytics, prescriptive analytics, ensemble techniques, and deep reinforcement learning, organizations can extract valuable insights from complex data and gain a competitive edge in their respective industries. Advanced analytics techniques empower organizations to unlock the full potential of their data and navigate the complexities of today's data-driven world.

CHAPTER 7: IMPLEMENTING PREDICTIVE ANALYTICS

Chapter 7 focuses on the implementation of predictive analytics, which involves using historical data and statistical models to make predictions about future outcomes. Predictive analytics is a powerful tool for organizations to gain insights into customer behavior, optimize operations, and drive informed decision-making. This chapter provides an overview of the key steps and considerations involved in implementing predictive analytics successfully.

Defining Business Objectives:

The chapter begins by emphasizing the importance of defining clear business objectives for the implementation of predictive analytics. Organizations need to identify the specific questions they want to answer or the problems they aim to solve using predictive analytics. This step ensures that the predictive analytics efforts are aligned with the overall strategic goals of the organization.

Data Collection and Preparation:

The next step in implementing predictive analytics is to gather and prepare the relevant data for analysis. This includes identifying the necessary data sources, collecting the data, cleaning and transforming the data to ensure its quality and consistency, and integrating disparate data sources if required. Data preparation is a critical step as the quality of the input data directly impacts the accuracy and effectiveness of the predictive models.

Feature Selection and Engineering:

Feature selection and engineering involve identifying the most relevant variables or features that contribute to the predictive models. This step may include analyzing the correlations between variables, conducting exploratory data analysis, and employing techniques such as dimensionality reduction to remove irrelevant features. Feature engineering may also involve creating new variables that capture additional information or insights.

Model Selection:

Choosing the appropriate predictive modeling techniques is crucial for accurate predictions. The chapter explores various modeling approaches, such as regression analysis, decision trees, support vector machines, neural networks, and ensemble techniques. The selection of the modeling technique depends on the nature of the data, the complexity of the problem, the interpretability of the model, and the available resources. Evaluating multiple models and comparing their performance helps identify the most suitable model for the specific application.

Model Training and Validation:

Once the model is selected, it needs to be trained on the historical data. The chapter discusses the importance of dividing the data into training and validation sets to assess the model's performance. Training involves using the historical data to estimate the model's parameters or to learn the underlying patterns. Validation allows for assessing how well the model generalizes to unseen data and ensures that it is not overfitting the training data.

Model Evaluation and Performance Metrics:

Measuring the performance of predictive models is crucial to assess their accuracy and reliability. The chapter explains common evaluation metrics such as accuracy, precision, recall, F1 score, and area under the receiver operating characteristic curve (AUC-ROC). Choosing the appropriate metrics depends on the specific application and the nature of the problem being addressed. Regular model evaluation allows for continuous improvement and refinement of the predictive models.

Deployment and Integration:

After the model is trained, validated, and evaluated, it is ready for deployment and integration into the organization's operational systems. The chapter discusses the challenges and considerations involved in deploying predictive models, including scalability, computational resources, data privacy, and interpretability. Integration ensures that the predictions generated by the models can be seamlessly incorporated into decision-making processes and workflow automation.

Monitoring and Maintenance:

The final step in implementing predictive analytics is to establish a system for monitoring the performance of the predictive models over time. Monitoring allows organizations to track the accuracy and reliability of the models and detect any deviations or changes in their performance. Regular maintenance, including updating the models with new data and retraining as needed, ensures that the predictive analytics capabilities remain up-to-date and effective.

In conclusion, Chapter 7 provides a comprehensive overview of the key steps involved in implementing predictive analytics successfully. By defining clear business objectives, collecting and preparing relevant data, selecting appropriate modeling techniques, training and validating models, evaluating performance, deploying and integrating models, and establishing monitoring and maintenance practices, organizations can effectively leverage predictive analytics to gain valuable insights, optimize operations, and drive data-driven decision-making. The implementation of predictive analytics empowers organizations to unlock the potential of their data and gain a competitive advantage in the marketplace.

Forecasting Future Trends and Outcomes

Forecasting future trends and outcomes is a critical component of data science and analytics. It enables organizations to anticipate changes, make informed decisions, and plan for the future. Forecasting techniques leverage historical data and statistical models to project future patterns, behaviors, and outcomes. In this section, we will delve into the details of forecasting, including key techniques, considerations, and best practices.

Time Series Forecasting:

Time series forecasting is a widely used technique for predicting future trends based on historical data collected over time. It is particularly effective when analyzing data with temporal dependencies, such as stock prices, sales data, or weather patterns. Time series forecasting models capture patterns, trends, and seasonality in the data to generate future predictions.

Common time series forecasting methods include:

Moving Averages: Moving averages calculate the average of a specified number of past observations to predict future values. Simple moving averages (SMA) and exponential moving averages (EMA) are commonly used techniques.

Autoregressive Integrated Moving Average (ARIMA): ARIMA models capture both autoregressive (AR) and moving average (MA) components, along with differencing to account for non-stationarity in the data.

Exponential Smoothing: Exponential smoothing techniques, such as Simple Exponential Smoothing (SES), Holt's Linear Exponential Smoothing, and Holt-Winters' Seasonal Exponential Smoothing, assign exponentially decreasing weights to past observations.

Prophet: Prophet is a popular forecasting tool developed by Facebook, which handles various components of time series data, including seasonality, trends, and outliers.

Regression-Based Forecasting:

Regression-based forecasting leverages statistical regression models to predict future outcomes based on the relationship between predictor variables and the target variable. This approach is useful when historical data contains multiple explanatory variables that influence the outcome.

Linear Regression: Linear regression models establish a linear relationship between the predictor variables and the target variable. They estimate the coefficients that represent the slope and intercept of the regression line.

Multiple Regression: Multiple regression extends linear regression by considering multiple predictor variables. It accounts for the collective impact of these variables on the outcome.

Polynomial Regression: Polynomial regression models capture non-linear relationships by introducing polynomial terms in the regression equation. They can fit curves and capture more complex patterns in the data.

Machine Learning-Based Forecasting:

Machine learning algorithms can also be employed for forecasting tasks, leveraging their ability to capture intricate patterns and relationships in the data. Supervised learning algorithms, such as decision trees, random forests, support vector machines, and neural networks, can be adapted for forecasting by training them on historical data and using them to make future predictions.

Support Vector Machines (SVM): SVM algorithms can be used for regression tasks, estimating the continuous target variable based on the input features.

Neural Networks: Neural networks, particularly recurrent neural networks (RNNs), are well-suited for sequence data and time series forecasting. Long

Short-Term Memory (LSTM) networks, a type of RNN, are widely used for their ability to capture temporal dependencies.

Considerations and Best Practices for Forecasting:

When conducting forecasting, it is crucial to keep in mind the following considerations and best practices:

Data Quality: Ensure that the historical data used for forecasting is accurate, consistent, and representative of the underlying patterns. Address missing values, outliers, and data inconsistencies before performing the analysis.

Feature Selection: Select the most relevant features or predictor variables for the forecasting task. Conduct exploratory data analysis and feature engineering to identify the variables that have the most significant impact on the outcome.

Model Selection and Evaluation: Choose an appropriate forecasting model based on the data characteristics, the problem at hand, and the desired level of accuracy. Evaluate the model's performance using suitable metrics, such as mean absolute error (MAE), mean squared error (MSE), or root mean squared error (RMSE).

Validation and Testing: Split the historical data into training and testing sets to validate the performance of the forecasting models. Use the training set to estimate the model parameters and the testing set to evaluate the model's ability to generalize to new, unseen data.

Time Horizon: Determine the time horizon for the forecasting task. Are you interested in short-term predictions or long-term projections? Different techniques may be more suitable depending on the desired time frame.

Monitoring and Updating: Continuously monitor the accuracy and performance of the forecasting models. Update the models regularly with new data to ensure that the predictions remain relevant and accurate over time.

Consideration of External Factors: Consider external factors that may influence the forecasted outcomes. This could include macroeconomic indicators, social trends, policy changes, or industry-specific factors. Incorporating external factors can enhance the accuracy and relevance of the forecasts.

In conclusion, forecasting future trends and outcomes is a vital component of data science and analytics. By leveraging techniques such as time series forecasting, regression-based forecasting, and machine learning-based forecasting, organizations can anticipate changes, make informed decisions, and plan for the future. Considerations such as data quality, feature selection, model selection and evaluation, validation, time horizon, monitoring, and consideration of external factors are crucial for accurate and reliable forecasting. By applying these best practices, organizations can harness the power of forecasting to gain a competitive edge and navigate the complexities of an ever-changing business landscape.

Building Predictive Models

Building predictive models is a key aspect of data science and analytics. Predictive models leverage historical data and statistical techniques to make accurate predictions about future outcomes. These models enable organizations to gain valuable insights, make informed decisions, and optimize their operations. In this section, we will delve into the details of building predictive models, including key steps, considerations, and best practices.

Define the Problem and Objectives:

The first step in building predictive models is to clearly define the problem and the objectives. Identify the specific question you want to answer or the outcome you want to predict. For example, you may want to predict customer churn, forecast sales, or classify fraudulent transactions. Defining the problem and objectives helps guide the subsequent steps and ensures that the modeling efforts are focused and aligned with the organization's goals.

Data Collection and Preparation:

To build predictive models, you need high-quality data. Collect relevant data from various sources, ensuring that it is comprehensive, accurate, and representative of the problem domain. The data may include numerical variables, categorical variables, text data, or time series data, depending on the problem at hand.

Next, preprocess and clean the data to ensure its quality and consistency. Handle missing values, outliers, and data inconsistencies appropriately. Perform data transformations, such as normalization or scaling, if necessary. Feature engineering may also be performed to create new variables or derive meaningful features from the existing ones. Data preparation is crucial as it directly affects the performance and accuracy of the predictive models.

Feature Selection:

Feature selection involves identifying the most relevant variables or features that contribute to the predictive models. Select features that have a strong impact on the outcome variable and are independent of each other to avoid multicollinearity. Techniques such as correlation analysis, feature importance ranking, and domain expertise can guide the feature selection process. Feature selection reduces model complexity, enhances interpretability, and improves model performance.

Model Selection:

Choose an appropriate modeling technique based on the nature of the problem, the type of data, and the desired outcome. Consider whether the problem requires classification, regression, or clustering. Commonly used predictive modeling techniques include:

Linear Regression: Linear regression models establish a linear relationship between the input variables and the target variable. They are suitable for problems where the outcome is continuous.

Decision Trees: Decision trees use a tree-like structure to make predictions by splitting the data based on the input features. They are intuitive, interpretable, and handle both categorical and numerical variables.

Random Forest: Random forest combines multiple decision trees to create a more robust and accurate predictive model. It addresses overfitting and improves generalization by aggregating the predictions of multiple trees.

Support Vector Machines (SVM): SVMs find an optimal hyperplane that separates different classes in the data. They work well for both linear and non-linear classification problems.

Neural Networks: Neural networks, particularly deep learning models, can capture complex patterns in the data. They are suitable for problems with large amounts of data and intricate relationships.

Gradient Boosting: Gradient boosting algorithms, such as XGBoost or LightGBM, sequentially build models that correct the mistakes of previous models, resulting in a highly accurate predictive model.

Consider the strengths, limitations, and assumptions of different models, and select the one that best fits the problem and data characteristics.

Model Training and Evaluation:

Split the data into training and testing sets. Use the training set to train the predictive model, estimating its parameters or learning the underlying patterns. Evaluate the model's performance using appropriate evaluation metrics such as accuracy, precision, recall, F1 score, or area under the curve (AUC).

Fine-tune the model by adjusting hyperparameters to optimize its performance. Techniques such as cross-validation and grid search can help find the optimal hyperparameters for the model.

Model Validation and Testing:

Validate the model's performance on an independent validation set or through cross-validation. This ensures that the model can generalize well to unseen data and is not overfitting the training data.

After validation, test the model on a separate testing set that closely represents the real-world data distribution. This final evaluation provides an unbiased assessment of the model's performance and its ability to make accurate predictions.

Deployment and Monitoring:

Once the predictive model has been trained, validated, and tested, it can be deployed in a production environment. Integrate the model into operational systems or workflows to make predictions on new, unseen data.

Regularly monitor the model's performance and recalibrate it, as necessary. Monitoring ensures that the model continues to make accurate predictions as data patterns or distributions change over time.

Interpretability and Explainability:

Consider the interpretability and explainability of the predictive model. Some models, such as linear regression or decision trees, offer a clear understanding of the variables and their impact on the outcome. Other models, such as neural networks, may be more complex and require additional techniques to interpret their predictions, such as feature importance analysis or model-agnostic interpretability methods.

In conclusion, building predictive models involves a series of steps that begin with defining the problem and collecting and preparing the data. Feature selection, model selection, training, evaluation, validation, and testing are crucial stages in the model-building process. Deployment, monitoring, and interpretability of the model ensure its effectiveness and usability in real-world scenarios. By following these steps and best practices, organizations can build accurate and reliable predictive models that drive data-driven decision-making and provide valuable insights.

Evaluating and Refining Predictions

Evaluating and refining predictions is a critical step in the data science and analytics process. It ensures that the predictive models are accurate, reliable, and effective in making informed decisions. Evaluation involves assessing the performance of the models against the actual outcomes, while refinement focuses on improving the models based on the evaluation results. In this section, we will explore the details of evaluating and refining predictions, including key evaluation metrics, techniques, and best practices.

Evaluation Metrics:

Evaluation metrics measure the performance of predictive models by quantifying the accuracy and quality of their predictions. The choice of evaluation metrics depends on the specific problem and the nature of the data. Some commonly used evaluation metrics include:

Accuracy: Accuracy measures the proportion of correct predictions over the total number of predictions. It is suitable for balanced datasets but may be misleading for imbalanced datasets.

Precision and Recall: Precision measures the proportion of true positive predictions among all positive predictions, while recall measures the proportion of true positive predictions among all actual positive instances. Precision and recall are useful in classification problems, especially when the class distribution is imbalanced.

F1 Score: The F1 score is the harmonic mean of precision and recall. It provides a balanced measure that takes into account both precision and recall, particularly useful when the class distribution is imbalanced.

Mean Absolute Error (MAE) and Mean Squared Error (MSE): MAE and MSE are common metrics for regression problems. MAE measures the average absolute difference between predicted and actual values, while

MSE measures the average squared difference. Root Mean Squared Error (RMSE) is the square root of MSE and is often used for interpretability.

Area Under the Curve (AUC): AUC measures the performance of classification models based on the trade-off between true positive rate and false positive rate. It provides a single scalar value that summarizes the model's discrimination power.

Cross-Validation:

Cross-validation is a technique used to evaluate the performance of predictive models by splitting the data into multiple subsets. The model is trained on a portion of the data and then tested on the remaining portion. This process is repeated several times with different splits to obtain an average performance measure. Cross-validation helps assess the model's ability to generalize to unseen data and provides a more robust evaluation of its performance.

Common cross-validation methods include k-fold cross-validation, stratified k-fold cross-validation, and leave-one-out cross-validation. The choice of cross-validation technique depends on the size of the dataset, the available computing resources, and the specific requirements of the problem.

Overfitting and Underfitting:

Overfitting occurs when a predictive model performs extremely well on the training data but fails to generalize to new, unseen data. Underfitting, on the other hand, occurs when the model is too simple to capture the underlying patterns in the data. Both overfitting and underfitting result in poor predictive performance.

To address overfitting, techniques such as regularization, cross-validation, and early stopping can be applied. Regularization methods, like L1 and L2 regularization, add penalty terms to the model's objective function, reducing the complexity of the model. Cross-validation helps identify overfitting by assessing the model's performance on unseen data. Early stopping stops the training process when the model's performance on a validation set starts deteriorating.

To address underfitting, more complex models can be considered, additional features can be engineered, or the model's hyperparameters can be adjusted. It is essential to strike a balance between model complexity and generalization capabilities.

Model Refinement:

Refining predictive models involves improving their performance based on the evaluation results. Several techniques can be employed to refine the models:

Feature Engineering: Feature engineering involves creating new features or transforming existing ones to capture more relevant information. It may involve selecting important features, creating interaction terms, or encoding categorical variables effectively.

Hyperparameter Tuning: Adjusting the hyperparameters of the model can significantly impact its performance. Hyperparameters are parameters that define the model's behavior but are not learned from the data. Techniques like grid search, random search, or Bayesian optimization can be used to find the optimal combination of hyperparameters.

Ensemble Methods: Ensemble methods combine multiple models to make predictions, leveraging the wisdom of the crowd. Techniques such as bagging, boosting, or stacking can improve predictive performance by aggregating the predictions of diverse models.

Model Selection: If multiple models are considered, evaluation results can guide the selection of the most suitable model. Model selection involves comparing the performance of different models and selecting the one that provides the best balance between accuracy, interpretability, and generalization.

Validation on Unseen Data:

Once the models have been refined, it is essential to validate their performance on a completely independent set of data. This unseen data represents real-world scenarios and ensures that the models can generalize beyond the training and validation data. By testing the models on unseen data, organizations can gain confidence in their predictive capabilities and assess their performance in practical applications.

Iterative Process:

Evaluating and refining predictions is an iterative process. As new data becomes available or the problem evolves, it is necessary to reassess and refine the models. Monitoring the models' performance over time and updating them with new data ensures that the predictions remain accurate and relevant.

In conclusion, evaluating and refining predictions is a crucial step in the data science and analytics process. By employing appropriate evaluation metrics, cross-validation techniques, addressing overfitting and underfitting, and refining the models through feature engineering, hyperparameter tuning, ensemble methods, and model selection, organizations can improve the accuracy and reliability of their predictive models. It is important to remember that evaluation and refinement are iterative processes that require continuous monitoring, updating, and adaptation to changing data and business requirements.

CHAPTER 8: DATA-DRIVEN DECISION-MAKING

Chapter 8 focuses on the concept of data-driven decision-making, which emphasizes using data and analytics to drive informed and effective decision-making processes within organizations. Data-driven decision-making is essential for leveraging the full potential of data and transforming it into actionable insights. This chapter provides an overview of the key principles, benefits, and challenges of data-driven decision-making.

Principles of Data-Driven Decision-Making:

The chapter begins by introducing the principles that guide data-driven decision-making:

Decision-Making Based on Evidence: Data-driven decision-making relies on empirical evidence and facts rather than intuition or gut feelings. Decisions are supported by thorough data analysis and interpretation.

Analytical Thinking: Data-driven decision-making requires analytical thinking skills to uncover patterns, relationships, and insights within the data. Analytical thinking enables organizations to move beyond descriptive analysis and delve into predictive and prescriptive analytics.

Continuous Learning: Data-driven decision-making promotes a culture of continuous learning and improvement. Organizations embrace feedback, monitor performance, and use insights gained from data to refine decision-making processes.

Collaboration: Collaboration between data scientists, analysts, and decision-makers is crucial in data-driven decision-making. Effective collaboration ensures that data insights are effectively communicated, understood, and integrated into the decision-making process.

Benefits of Data-Driven Decision-Making:

The chapter explores the numerous benefits that organizations can gain from adopting data-driven decision-making practices:

Improved Accuracy and Reliability: Data-driven decision-making reduces reliance on subjective judgment and enhances decision accuracy and reliability. Decisions are based on robust data analysis and evidence, reducing the impact of bias and guesswork.

Faster Decision-Making: Access to real-time data and advanced analytics tools enables organizations to make faster decisions. Data-driven decision-making eliminates lengthy manual processes and provides timely insights for effective action.

Enhanced Efficiency and Cost Reduction: By leveraging data and analytics, organizations can identify inefficiencies, optimize processes, and reduce costs. Data-driven insights help allocate resources more effectively and identify areas for improvement.

Better Risk Management: Data-driven decision-making enables organizations to assess risks more accurately. By analyzing historical data and using predictive modeling, organizations can anticipate potential risks, mitigate them, and make informed risk management decisions.

Improved Customer Experience: Data-driven decision-making allows organizations to gain insights into customer behavior, preferences, and needs. By understanding customer patterns and trends, organizations can personalize products, services, and experiences, leading to improved customer satisfaction and loyalty.

Challenges of Data-Driven Decision-Making:

While data-driven decision-making offers numerous benefits, organizations may encounter several challenges during its implementation:

Data Quality and Availability: Data-driven decision-making relies on high-quality data. Organizations need to ensure data accuracy, completeness, and reliability. Data availability and accessibility can also be a challenge, requiring effective data governance and integration processes.

Data Privacy and Security: With increased reliance on data, organizations must prioritize data privacy and security. They need to implement robust data protection measures to safeguard sensitive information and comply with privacy regulations.

Change Management: Shifting to a data-driven decision-making culture may require significant organizational change. It involves embracing data-driven practices, building data literacy, and overcoming resistance to change.

Talent and Skill Gaps: Organizations need skilled data scientists, analysts, and decision-makers who understand data and analytics. Bridging talent and skill gaps through training, recruitment, and upskilling programs is essential.

Best Practices for Data-Driven Decision-Making:

The chapter concludes by providing best practices for successful data-driven decision-making:

Define Clear Objectives: Clearly define the decision-making objectives and align them with the organization's strategic goals.

Establish Data Governance: Implement robust data governance practices to ensure data quality, accessibility, privacy, and security.

Cultivate Data Literacy: Foster a culture of data literacy throughout the organization. Provide training and education to enhance data literacy skills among employees.

Encourage Collaboration: Foster collaboration between data scientists, analysts, and decision-makers to effectively leverage data insights in decision-making processes.

Embrace Agile Decision-Making: Adopt agile decision-making methodologies that emphasize iterative and adaptive approaches. Use data to inform decisions, evaluate outcomes, and refine strategies.

Monitor and Evaluate: Continuously monitor and evaluate the impact of data-driven decisions. Assess the accuracy, effectiveness, and efficiency of decision-making processes.

In conclusion, Chapter 8 highlights the significance of data-driven decision-making in modern organizations. By adhering to the principles of data-driven decision-making, organizations can benefit from improved accuracy, faster decision-making, enhanced efficiency, better risk management, and improved customer experience. Although challenges exist, organizations can overcome them through effective data governance, talent development, and change management strategies. Implementing best practices such as defining clear objectives, fostering data literacy, encouraging collaboration, and embracing agile decision-making are key to successful data-driven decision-making and realizing the full potential of data.

Integrating Data Insights into Decision-Making Processes

Integrating data insights into decision-making processes is a critical step in leveraging the power of data to drive informed and effective decisions. Data insights provide valuable information and evidence that can inform and guide decision-making, leading to improved outcomes and organizational success. In this section, we will delve into the details of integrating data insights into decision-making processes, including key considerations, strategies, and best practices.

Establishing a Data-Driven Culture:

Integrating data insights into decision-making requires fostering a data-driven culture within the organization. This involves:

Leadership Support: Leadership should actively promote and support data-driven decision-making, emphasizing its importance and demonstrating its value through their actions.

Data Literacy: Promoting data literacy among employees is crucial. Providing training and resources to improve data literacy skills enables individuals to understand, interpret, and effectively utilize data insights in decision-making.

Communication and Collaboration: Encouraging open communication and collaboration between data professionals, analysts, and decision-makers fosters a collaborative environment for sharing insights, discussing findings, and integrating data into decision-making processes.

Aligning Data Insights with Decision-Making Needs:

To effectively integrate data insights into decision-making, it is essential to align the data insights with the specific needs of decision-makers. This involves:

Understanding Decision-Making Context: Gaining a deep understanding of the decision-making context, including the problem at hand, the desired outcomes, and the decision-makers' information needs.

Identifying Relevant Data: Identifying the most relevant data sources and variables that can provide insights into the decision-making context. This may involve analyzing historical data, conducting surveys, or collecting real-time data.

Customizing Data Analysis: Tailoring the data analysis approach to address the specific decision-making needs. This may include applying statistical techniques, data visualization, or advanced analytics algorithms to extract meaningful insights.

Data-Driven Decision-Making Framework:

Implementing a structured data-driven decision-making framework can streamline the integration of data insights into the decision-making process. Key components of such a framework include:

Define Decision Objectives: Clearly articulate the decision objectives, desired outcomes, and key performance indicators (KPIs) that will guide the decision-making process.

Gather and Analyze Data: Collect, preprocess, and analyze relevant data to extract insights. Use techniques such as exploratory data analysis, statistical modeling, and machine learning to uncover patterns, correlations, and predictions.

Interpretation and Visualization: Interpret the data insights and communicate them effectively through data visualization techniques. Visual representations such as charts, graphs, and dashboards can make complex data more accessible and facilitate understanding.

Evaluation and Validation: Validate the data insights by comparing them with real-world outcomes or expert judgment. Assess the accuracy, reliability, and relevance of the insights to ensure their suitability for decision-making.

Decision Integration: Incorporate the data insights into the decision-making process. Decision-makers should consider the data insights alongside other relevant factors, such as domain knowledge, experience, and stakeholder input.

Real-Time Data Integration:

Integrating real-time data into decision-making processes enhances their timeliness and relevance. Real-time data sources, such as sensors, social media feeds, or customer feedback systems, can provide up-to-date information for decision-making. Strategies for real-time data integration include:

Data Infrastructure: Establish a robust data infrastructure that can capture, store, and process real-time data effectively. This may involve implementing technologies like data streaming, event-driven architectures, or cloud-based data platforms.

Automation and Alerts: Implement automated processes and alerts that notify decision-makers of critical real-time data changes or anomalies. This enables proactive decision-making based on real-time insights.

Dynamic Decision-Making: Adapt decision-making processes to accommodate the availability of real-time data. This may involve agile decision-making methodologies that emphasize flexibility, responsiveness, and quick feedback loops.

Monitoring and Iterative Improvement:

To ensure continuous improvement and effectiveness of data-driven decision-making, it is important to:

Monitor Decision Outcomes: Continuously monitor the outcomes of decisions and evaluate their alignment with the expected results. Assess whether the data insights provided accurate guidance and identify opportunities for improvement.

Feedback Loop: Establish a feedback loop between decision-making and data analysis. Decision outcomes and feedback should inform the refinement of data analysis techniques, models, and approaches to improve their relevance and accuracy.

Iterative Learning: Embrace a culture of iterative learning and experimentation. Use data insights to inform hypothesis testing, A/B testing, or pilot projects that can provide valuable insights for future decision-making.

In conclusion, integrating data insights into decision-making processes is a key component of leveraging the power of data. By establishing a data-driven culture, aligning data insights with decision-making needs, implementing a structured framework, integrating real-time data, and embracing monitoring and iterative improvement, organizations can effectively integrate data insights into decision-making. This enables informed, evidence-based decision-making that leads to improved outcomes, increased efficiency, and competitive advantage in today's data-driven world.

Communicating Results to Stakeholders

Effective communication of data-driven results to stakeholders is crucial for the successful implementation of data science and analytics initiatives. Clear and compelling communication ensures that stakeholders understand the insights, value, and implications of the data-driven findings, leading to informed decision-making and organizational success. In this section, we will delve into the details of communicating results to stakeholders, including key considerations, strategies, and best practices.

Know Your Audience:

Understanding the needs, preferences, and knowledge level of your stakeholders is essential for effective communication. Consider the following factors:

Background and Expertise: Adapt your communication style and terminology based on the stakeholders' level of familiarity with data and analytics concepts. Avoid jargon and technical details if the audience is not well-versed in the subject matter.

Decision-Making Roles: Tailor the communication to the specific roles and responsibilities of the stakeholders. Executives may require a high-level summary, while analysts may seek more technical details and methodologies.

Interests and Goals: Identify the stakeholders' interests, concerns, and goals. Frame the communication in a way that highlights the relevance and benefits of the data-driven insights to their specific needs.

Simplify and Visualize:

Complex data and technical analysis can be challenging to grasp for stakeholders who are not data experts. Simplify the message and use visualizations to convey the insights effectively:

Storytelling: Frame the communication as a compelling story that captures the stakeholders' attention and connects with their experiences. Use narratives, anecdotes, and examples to bring the insights to life and make them relatable.

Data Visualization: Utilize charts, graphs, infographics, and other visual representations to convey complex data and insights in a concise and intuitive manner. Visualizations make it easier for stakeholders to understand patterns, trends, and relationships within the data.

Key Messages: Identify and emphasize the key messages or takeaways from the data-driven results. Focus on the most important insights that are relevant to the stakeholders' goals and decision-making processes.

Contextualize and Relate to Business Objectives:

Relating the data-driven insights to the stakeholders' business objectives and challenges enhances their understanding and relevance:

Business Impact: Clearly articulate the business impact of the data-driven insights. Demonstrate how the findings align with organizational goals, address specific challenges, or provide opportunities for improvement.

ROI and Value Proposition: Quantify and communicate the potential return on investment (ROI) or value proposition associated with the data-driven insights. Show how the insights can drive cost savings, revenue growth, improved customer satisfaction, or other tangible benefits.

Actionable Recommendations: Provide actionable recommendations based on the insights. Help stakeholders understand how they can translate the findings into practical actions and decision-making processes.

Transparency and Interpretability:

Promote transparency and facilitate understanding by explaining the data sources, methodologies, and limitations of the analysis:

Methodology Explanation: Provide a clear and concise explanation of the data analysis techniques and methodologies used. Describe the assumptions, data quality considerations, and any limitations that stakeholders should be aware of.

Uncertainty and Risks: Acknowledge and communicate the uncertainties and risks associated with the data-driven insights. Discuss the confidence level, the margin of error, or any assumptions made during the analysis.

Opportunities for Further Analysis: Identify areas where further analysis or data exploration can provide additional insights. Encourage stakeholders to ask questions, seek clarification, and explore related topics that may enhance decision-making.

Engage in Two-Way Communication:

Promote an interactive and collaborative communication approach that encourages stakeholders to ask questions, provide feedback, and actively participate in the dialogue:

Q&A Sessions: Organize question-and-answer sessions or workshops to address stakeholders' queries, clarify any ambiguities, and ensure their understanding of the insights.

Collaborative Discussions: Facilitate discussions where stakeholders can share their perspectives, insights, and concerns related to the data-driven results. Encourage open dialogue and collaboration to foster a deeper understanding and a sense of ownership.

Tailored Communication Channels: Choose communication channels that are appropriate for the stakeholders. This could include presentations, reports, dashboards, workshops, or one-on-one meetings.

Continuous Communication and Follow-Up:

Data-driven insights are not a one-time deliverable. Establish a process for ongoing communication and follow-up:

Regular Updates: Provide regular updates to stakeholders on the progress, updates, and new insights derived from data analysis. Ensure that stakeholders are kept informed of any changes or updates that may impact their decision-making.

Feedback Incorporation: Actively seek feedback from stakeholders on the usefulness and relevance of the data-driven insights. Incorporate feedback into future analysis and communication to continuously improve the value and impact of the insights.

Evaluation and Impact Assessment: Conduct periodic evaluations to assess the impact of the data-driven insights on decision-making and organizational outcomes. Use the evaluation results to refine communication strategies and ensure the continuous improvement of data-driven initiatives.

In conclusion, effectively communicating data-driven results to stakeholders is vital for driving informed decision-making. By understanding the audience, simplifying complex information, relating insights to business objectives, promoting transparency, engaging in two-way communication, and establishing continuous communication channels, organizations can ensure that stakeholders understand and value the insights derived from data analysis. This, in turn, leads to more effective decision-making, improved organizational performance, and a culture that embraces data-driven approaches.

Implementing Feedback Loops for Continuous Improvement

Implementing feedback loops is a crucial component of a successful data science and analytics initiative. Feedback loops provide a mechanism for organizations to gather insights, learn from past experiences, and continuously improve their data-driven processes and outcomes. In this section, we will delve into the details of implementing feedback loops for continuous improvement, including key considerations, strategies, and best practices.

Define Clear Objectives and Key Performance Indicators (KPIs):

To establish effective feedback loops, it is essential to define clear objectives and identify relevant KPIs that align with the organization's goals. Clear objectives provide a basis for evaluating the success of data-driven initiatives, while KPIs serve as measurable indicators of performance.

Objectives: Clearly define the specific goals and objectives that the data-driven initiative aims to achieve. This could include improving efficiency, increasing revenue, enhancing customer satisfaction, or optimizing processes.

KPIs: Identify the key metrics or indicators that will be used to measure progress towards the defined objectives. KPIs should be specific, measurable, achievable, relevant, and time-bound (SMART). For example, KPIs could include conversion rates, customer retention rates, or cost savings.

Establish Data Collection and Analysis Processes:

To implement effective feedback loops, organizations need to establish robust data collection and analysis processes. This involves:

Data Collection: Identify the relevant data sources and define the methods for collecting and storing data. This could involve integrating data from various systems, setting up data pipelines, or utilizing APIs to collect data from external sources.

Data Analysis: Implement data analysis techniques to derive insights from the collected data. This could involve descriptive analysis, predictive modeling, or advanced machine learning algorithms depending on the objectives and requirements.

Performance Tracking: Set up systems to track and monitor the defined KPIs. This could involve developing dashboards, reports, or visualizations that provide real-time or periodic updates on performance.

Regular Evaluation and Review:

Regular evaluation and review are essential components of feedback loops. This involves assessing the performance of data-driven initiatives against the defined objectives and KPIs:

Evaluation Criteria: Establish the criteria and benchmarks against which the performance will be evaluated. This could involve comparing actual performance against predefined targets or industry benchmarks.

Review Frequency: Determine the frequency of evaluation and review sessions. This could be weekly, monthly, quarterly, or based on the specific needs and timeframes of the initiative.

Stakeholder Involvement: Engage relevant stakeholders in the evaluation and review process. This ensures that different perspectives are considered and that insights are gathered from those directly involved in the initiative.

Actionable Insights and Recommendations:

Effective feedback loops should provide actionable insights and recommendations based on the evaluation and review. This helps organizations identify areas for improvement and take appropriate actions:

Insights Generation: Analyze the evaluation results and derive meaningful insights. Identify patterns, trends, and areas of underperformance or success that can guide decision-making and improvement efforts.

Actionable Recommendations: Based on the insights, provide actionable recommendations for improvement. These recommendations should be specific, practical, and aligned with the identified areas for enhancement.

Prioritization and Resource Allocation: Prioritize the recommendations based on their potential impact and feasibility. Allocate resources, such as budget, personnel, or technology, to implement the identified improvements effectively.

Continuous Learning and Adaptation:

Implementing feedback loops necessitates a culture of continuous learning and adaptation. This involves:

Knowledge Sharing: Encourage knowledge sharing and collaboration among team members involved in data-driven initiatives. Facilitate regular discussions, meetings, or workshops to share insights, lessons learned, and best practices.

Documentation: Document the insights, recommendations, and actions taken as part of the feedback loops. This ensures that valuable knowledge is captured, shared, and available for future reference.

Experimentation and Innovation: Foster a culture of experimentation and innovation. Encourage teams to explore new approaches, test hypotheses, and learn from failures and successes to drive continuous improvement.

Feedback Incorporation and Iterative Process:

Feedback loops should be iterative in nature, allowing organizations to incorporate feedback and make adjustments over time:

Feedback Incorporation: Actively seek feedback from stakeholders involved in the data-driven initiatives. This could include feedback from decision-makers, end-users, customers, or other relevant parties. Incorporate the feedback into the evaluation, insights generation, and recommendation processes.

Iterative Improvements: Use the feedback and evaluation results to drive iterative improvements in data collection, analysis, decision-making processes, and overall data-driven initiatives. Continuously refine and optimize the systems and processes to enhance their effectiveness.

In conclusion, implementing feedback loops is crucial for continuous improvement in data-driven initiatives. By defining clear objectives and KPIs, establishing robust data collection and analysis processes, conducting regular evaluations and reviews, providing actionable insights and recommendations, fostering a culture of continuous learning, and incorporating feedback in an iterative process, organizations can drive ongoing improvement in their data-driven decision-making processes and outcomes. Implementing effective feedback loops allows organizations to adapt, optimize, and maximize the value and impact of their data-driven initiatives over time.

CHAPTER 9: DATA PRIVACY AND SECURITY

Chapter 9 focuses on the critical aspects of data privacy and security in data science and analytics initiatives. As organizations handle large volumes of data and leverage advanced technologies, ensuring the privacy and security of sensitive information becomes paramount. This chapter provides an overview of the key considerations, challenges, and best practices related to data privacy and security.

Importance of Data Privacy and Security:

The chapter begins by highlighting the importance of data privacy and security in data science and analytics initiatives. The increasing digitization of data, advancements in data collection technologies, and regulatory requirements necessitate robust measures to protect sensitive information. Data privacy and security are crucial for maintaining customer trust, complying with regulations, mitigating the risk of data breaches, and safeguarding the organization's reputation.

Understanding Data Privacy:

The chapter explores the concept of data privacy and the principles that guide its implementation. Key aspects include:

Personally Identifiable Information (PII): Understanding what constitutes PII and recognizing the types of data that require special protection. PII includes information such as names, addresses, social security numbers, financial data, or any data that can be used to identify an individual.

Legal and Regulatory Frameworks: Familiarizing oneself with the applicable data privacy laws and regulations in the relevant jurisdictions. Examples include the General Data Protection Regulation (GDPR) in the European Union, the California Consumer Privacy Act (CCPA) in the United States, and other industry-specific regulations.

Consent and Data Subjects' Rights: Recognizing the importance of obtaining informed consent for data collection and processing activities. Understanding the rights of data subjects, such as the right to access, rectify, or erase their personal data.

Ensuring Data Security:

The chapter addresses the critical aspect of data security in data science and analytics. It covers various considerations for safeguarding data:

Data Access Control: Implementing strong access control mechanisms to ensure that only authorized individuals have access to sensitive data. This involves user authentication, role-based access control (RBAC), and encryption of data in transit and at rest.

Data Encryption: Implementing encryption techniques to protect sensitive data from unauthorized access or breaches. This includes encrypting data at the database level, during transmission, and when stored in cloud services.

Data Anonymization and Pseudonymization: Employing techniques such as data anonymization and pseudonymization to protect privacy while still allowing data analysis. These techniques remove or obfuscate personally identifiable information, reducing the risk of re-identification.

Incident Response and Recovery: Establishing incident response plans to address data breaches or security incidents promptly. This involves defining roles and responsibilities, implementing monitoring systems, and conducting regular security audits.

Ethical Considerations:

The chapter emphasizes the importance of ethical considerations in data science and analytics. Ethical practices include:

Transparency and Informed Consent: Ensuring transparency in data collection and processing activities. Organizations should provide clear and concise information to individuals about how their data will be used and obtain their informed consent.

Data Minimization: Adopting the principle of data minimization, which involves collecting only the necessary data required for the intended purpose. Minimizing data collection reduces the risk of unauthorized access or misuse of sensitive information.

Bias and Fairness: Addressing biases in data collection and analysis to ensure fair treatment of individuals. Organizations should be aware of potential biases in algorithms, models, or data sources and take steps to mitigate them.

Accountability and Governance: Establishing robust governance frameworks and mechanisms to ensure compliance with ethical standards. This includes appointing data protection officers, conducting privacy impact assessments, and establishing clear policies and procedures.

Best Practices for Data Privacy and Security:

The chapter concludes by providing best practices for ensuring data privacy and security in data science and analytics initiatives:

Privacy by Design: Implement privacy measures from the outset of data collection and processing activities. Consider privacy implications in the design of systems, algorithms, and processes.

Data Protection Impact Assessments (DPIAs): Conduct DPIAs to assess the potential privacy risks and impacts of data processing activities. This helps identify and mitigate risks proactively.

Regular Training and Awareness: Provide regular training and awareness programs to employees involved in data science and analytics. Educate them about data privacy and security best practices, regulations, and the importance of ethical considerations.

Secure Infrastructure and Systems: Implement robust security measures for data storage, data transmission, and computing systems. This includes using secure cloud services, regularly patching and updating software, and implementing firewalls and intrusion detection systems.

Third-Party Data Processing: Ensure that third-party vendors or partners handling data adhere to robust privacy and security practices. Establish clear data processing agreements and conduct due diligence to verify their compliance.

In conclusion, Chapter 9 emphasizes the significance of data privacy and security in data science and analytics initiatives. Understanding data privacy principles, ensuring data security, and addressing ethical considerations are crucial for maintaining trust, compliance, and the protection of sensitive information. By implementing best practices such as privacy by design, conducting DPIAs, providing regular training, securing infrastructure and systems, and vetting third-party data processors, organizations can safeguard data privacy and security throughout their data-driven initiatives.

Ensuring Compliance with Data Protection Regulations

Compliance with data protection regulations is essential for organizations engaged in data science and analytics. As the volume and complexity of data continue to grow, regulatory frameworks have been established to protect individuals' privacy rights and ensure responsible handling of personal data. This section provides a detailed exploration of the key considerations, challenges, and best practices for ensuring compliance with data protection regulations.

Understanding Data Protection Regulations:

The first step in ensuring compliance is to understand the applicable data protection regulations. Some prominent regulations include:

General Data Protection Regulation (GDPR): The GDPR, implemented in the European Union (EU), sets strict guidelines for the collection, processing, storage, and transfer of personal data. It grants individuals greater control over their data and imposes obligations on organizations to protect personal information.

California Consumer Privacy Act (CCPA): The CCPA, enacted in California, USA, provides consumers with greater control over their personal information held by businesses. It requires businesses to disclose data collection practices, honor consumer rights, and implement security measures.

Other Regional and Industry-Specific Regulations: Various countries and industries have additional data protection regulations, such as the Personal Information Protection and Electronic Documents Act (PIPEDA) in Canada and the Health Insurance Portability and Accountability Act (HIPAA) in the United States.

Data Mapping and Inventory:

To ensure compliance, organizations must have a comprehensive understanding of the personal data they collect, process, store, and share. This involves:

Data Mapping: Identify the sources, types, and flows of personal data within the organization. Determine how data is collected, stored, accessed, and transferred, including any third-party involvement.

Data Inventory: Maintain a detailed inventory of the personal data held by the organization. This includes categories of data, purposes of processing, legal basis, retention periods, and any data transfers to external parties.

Consent and Lawful Basis for Processing:

Data protection regulations often require organizations to obtain individuals' consent or establish a lawful basis for processing personal data. Best practices include:

Consent Management: Implement mechanisms to obtain valid consent from individuals for data processing activities. This involves providing clear and specific information about the purposes, recipients, and rights associated with data processing.

Lawful Basis Determination: Identify and document the lawful basis for processing personal data. This can include contractual necessity, legal obligation, legitimate interests, vital interests, consent, or performance of a task carried out in the public interest.

Data Subject Rights and Privacy Notices:

Data protection regulations grant individuals certain rights over their personal data. To ensure compliance, organizations should:

Establish Privacy Notices: Develop clear, concise, and transparent privacy notices that inform individuals about their rights, data processing activities, and how to exercise their rights.

Enable Data Subject Rights: Establish processes to handle data subject requests, such as access, rectification, erasure, restriction, and data portability. Ensure that these requests are addressed promptly and in accordance with regulatory requirements.

Data Transfers and Cross-Border Compliance:

When transferring personal data across borders, organizations must ensure compliance with regulations that govern international data transfers. Considerations include:

Adequacy Decisions: Transfer personal data to countries or organizations that are deemed to provide an adequate level of data protection according to regulatory assessments.

Standard Contractual Clauses (SCCs): Implement SCCs, which are model contractual clauses approved by regulatory authorities, when transferring data to countries without adequacy decisions.

Binding Corporate Rules (BCRs): Establish BCRs for intra-organizational data transfers to ensure compliance when sharing data across different entities within the organization.

Data Protection Impact Assessments (DPIAs):

DPIAs help organizations identify and mitigate privacy risks associated with specific data processing activities. Key considerations include:

Conducting DPIAs: Perform DPIAs for high-risk processing activities, such as large-scale data processing, use of sensitive data, or systematic monitoring of individuals.

Privacy Risk Mitigation: Assess the potential risks to individuals' privacy and implement measures to mitigate those risks. This may involve implementing privacy-enhancing technologies, pseudonymization techniques, or conducting data protection training.

Data Breach Management:

Organizations must have robust processes in place to detect, respond to, and report data breaches. Key steps include:

Incident Response Plan: Develop an incident response plan that outlines the steps to be taken in the event of a data breach. This includes identifying responsible parties, establishing communication protocols, and conducting impact assessments.

Notification and Reporting: Comply with regulatory requirements for notifying affected individuals, data protection authorities, or other relevant parties in the event of a data breach.

Regular Audits and Monitoring:

To ensure ongoing compliance, organizations should conduct regular audits and monitoring of their data protection practices. This includes:

Data Protection Officer (DPO): Designate a DPO responsible for overseeing data protection activities, ensuring compliance, and serving as a point of contact for data protection authorities and individuals.

Privacy Impact Assessments: Conduct regular assessments to evaluate the impact of new projects, systems, or processes on data privacy. This helps identify and address privacy risks before implementation.

Compliance Audits: Regularly audit data protection practices to assess compliance with regulations, internal policies, and industry standards. This includes reviewing data handling processes, data security measures, and ongoing training programs.

In conclusion, ensuring compliance with data protection regulations is critical for organizations engaged in data science and analytics. By understanding the applicable regulations, conducting data mapping and inventory, obtaining valid consent, respecting data subject rights, implementing appropriate safeguards for data transfers, conducting DPIAs, establishing breach management processes, and conducting regular audits and monitoring, organizations can navigate the complex landscape of data protection regulations and maintain compliance. Compliance not only helps organizations avoid penalties and reputational damage but also builds trust with customers and stakeholders, ensuring responsible and ethical data practices.

Safeguarding Sensitive Information

Safeguarding sensitive information is of utmost importance in data science and analytics initiatives. Organizations handle vast amounts of data, including personal, financial, or proprietary information, and must take robust measures to protect it from unauthorized access, breaches, or misuse. This section provides a detailed exploration of key considerations, challenges, and best practices for safeguarding sensitive information.

Risk Assessment:

Conducting a comprehensive risk assessment is the first step in safeguarding sensitive information. This involves:

Identifying Sensitive Data: Determine the types of sensitive information your organization collects, processes, or stores. This may include personal information, financial data, health records, or proprietary business information.

Assessing Threats and Vulnerabilities: Identify potential threats and vulnerabilities that could compromise the security of sensitive information. This may include cyberattacks, physical theft, insider threats, or inadequate access controls.

Evaluating Impact and Likelihood: Assess the potential impact and likelihood of risks materializing. This helps prioritize security measures and allocate resources effectively.

Implementing Access Controls:

Effective access controls ensure that only authorized individuals can access sensitive information. Key considerations include:

User Authentication: Implement strong user authentication mechanisms, such as passwords, two-factor authentication, or biometric authentication, to verify the identity of individuals accessing sensitive data.

Role-Based Access Control (RBAC): Assign access rights based on job roles and responsibilities. Grant individuals the minimum level of access necessary to perform their tasks effectively.

Regular Access Reviews: Conduct periodic reviews of user access rights to ensure they align with current job roles and responsibilities. Remove or modify access privileges promptly when individuals change roles or leave the organization.

Data Encryption:

Encryption is a fundamental technique for protecting sensitive information, both at rest and in transit. Considerations include:

Data-at-Rest Encryption: Encrypt sensitive data stored on servers, databases, or other storage devices. This ensures that even if the data is compromised, it remains unreadable without the encryption key.

Data-in-Transit Encryption: Use secure communication protocols, such as SSL/TLS, to encrypt data during transmission over networks. This prevents unauthorized interception or eavesdropping.

Encryption Key Management: Implement secure key management practices to safeguard encryption keys. This includes proper storage, rotation, and access control to prevent unauthorized use or disclosure of keys.

Secure Data Storage and Destruction:

Proper data storage and destruction practices are vital for safeguarding sensitive information. Consider the following:

Data Retention Policies: Establish clear policies for data retention, specifying the duration for which sensitive data will be stored. Regularly review and dispose of data that is no longer necessary.

Secure Disposal: Implement secure procedures for disposing of sensitive data. This may involve shredding physical documents, securely erasing data from storage media, or using specialized data destruction services.

Data Backup and Recovery: Implement regular data backup procedures to ensure the availability and integrity of sensitive information. Store backups securely and test data recovery processes periodically.

Employee Training and Awareness:

Employees play a critical role in safeguarding sensitive information. Provide comprehensive training and awareness programs to ensure a security-conscious culture:

Security Policies and Procedures: Educate employees about security policies, procedures, and best practices for handling sensitive data. Emphasize the importance of data protection and their role in maintaining it.

Phishing and Social Engineering Awareness: Train employees to recognize and report phishing attempts or social engineering techniques that can lead to unauthorized access or data breaches.

Incident Reporting and Response: Establish clear procedures for employees to report security incidents or suspicious activities. Train employees on the appropriate response, including whom to contact and how to preserve evidence.

Regular Security Audits and Monitoring:

Regular security audits and monitoring are essential for identifying vulnerabilities and detecting potential breaches. Consider the following:

Vulnerability Assessments: Conduct regular vulnerability assessments to identify weaknesses in systems, networks, or applications. Remediate vulnerabilities promptly to mitigate the risk of unauthorized access.

Intrusion Detection and Prevention Systems: Implement intrusion detection and prevention systems that monitor network traffic, detect anomalies, and block unauthorized access attempts.

Security Incident Monitoring: Establish systems for monitoring and logging security incidents. Analyze logs and investigate any suspicious activities promptly to detect and respond to potential breaches.

Third-Party Risk Management:

When working with third-party vendors or partners, ensure they have appropriate security measures in place to protect sensitive information:

Due Diligence: Conduct due diligence to assess the security practices and controls of third parties before sharing sensitive information. This may involve reviewing their security policies, conducting audits, or obtaining certifications.

Contractual Agreements: Establish clear contractual agreements that outline the responsibilities and expectations regarding the protection of sensitive data. Include provisions for security assessments, data breach notification, and data handling requirements.

In conclusion, safeguarding sensitive information is a critical aspect of data science and analytics initiatives. By conducting risk assessments, implementing access controls, encrypting data, ensuring secure storage and destruction, providing employee training and awareness, conducting regular security audits and monitoring, and managing third-party risks, organizations can significantly mitigate the risk of data breaches and protect sensitive information. Prioritizing data security helps maintain customer trust, comply with regulations, and safeguard organizational reputation.

Implementing Robust Security Measures

Implementing robust security measures is essential for protecting data and ensuring the integrity, confidentiality, and availability of sensitive information in data science and analytics initiatives. Organizations must proactively address potential threats and vulnerabilities to safeguard their data assets. This section provides a detailed exploration of key considerations, challenges, and best practices for implementing robust security measures.

Security Framework and Policies:

Establishing a comprehensive security framework and policies provides a foundation for implementing robust security measures. Consider the following:

Security Governance: Define the roles, responsibilities, and accountability for security within the organization. Establish a clear governance structure that ensures effective oversight and decision-making regarding security initiatives.

Security Policies: Develop and communicate security policies that address key areas such as access control, data classification, incident response, remote access, and employee awareness. Ensure that policies are aligned with industry best practices and regulatory requirements.

Regular Policy Reviews: Conduct regular reviews of security policies to ensure their relevance and effectiveness in addressing emerging threats and evolving regulatory landscapes.

Risk Assessment and Management:

Performing risk assessments and implementing risk management processes is crucial for identifying and mitigating potential security risks. Consider the following:

Risk Identification: Identify and assess potential risks and vulnerabilities to sensitive data. This includes evaluating risks related to physical security, technology infrastructure, human factors, and external threats.

Risk Prioritization: Prioritize risks based on their potential impact and likelihood. This helps allocate resources effectively and focus efforts on addressing high-priority risks.

Risk Mitigation: Develop and implement risk mitigation strategies, including the selection and deployment of appropriate security controls and countermeasures. Regularly monitor and update these controls to address emerging threats.

Access Control and Authentication:

Implementing robust access control and authentication mechanisms is vital for preventing unauthorized access to sensitive data. Consider the following:

User Authentication: Utilize strong authentication methods such as multi-factor authentication (MFA), biometrics, or digital certificates to verify user identities.

Role-Based Access Control (RBAC): Assign access rights based on job roles and responsibilities. Grant users the least privilege necessary to perform their tasks effectively.

Privileged Access Management (PAM): Implement controls and monitoring mechanisms for privileged accounts to prevent misuse and unauthorized access.

Data Encryption:

Data encryption is a critical security measure for protecting sensitive information both at rest and in transit. Consider the following:

Encryption at Rest: Utilize encryption algorithms to protect data stored on servers, databases, or other storage devices. Encryption ensures that even if the data is compromised, it remains unreadable without the encryption key.

Encryption in Transit: Implement secure communication protocols such as SSL/TLS to encrypt data during transmission over networks. This prevents unauthorized interception or eavesdropping.

Key Management: Implement robust key management practices to safeguard encryption keys. This includes secure key storage, key rotation, and access control to prevent unauthorized use or disclosure of keys.

Security Monitoring and Incident Response:

Establishing robust monitoring and incident response processes allows for the timely detection and response to security incidents. Consider the following:

Security Information and Event Management (SIEM): Implement SIEM systems to collect and analyze security logs and events from various systems and applications. This allows for the timely detection of suspicious activities or security breaches.

Intrusion Detection and Prevention Systems (IDS/IPS): Deploy IDS/IPS solutions to monitor network traffic, detect potential intrusions, and block or mitigate malicious activities.

Incident Response Plan: Develop a comprehensive incident response plan that outlines the steps to be taken in the event of a security incident. This includes establishing communication protocols, defining roles and responsibilities, and conducting post-incident analysis and remediation.

Regular Security Assessments and Audits:

Conducting regular security assessments and audits helps identify vulnerabilities and ensure the effectiveness of security measures. Consider the following:

Vulnerability Assessments: Perform regular vulnerability scans and assessments to identify weaknesses in systems, networks, or applications. Address identified vulnerabilities promptly to mitigate risks.

Penetration Testing: Conduct periodic penetration testing to simulate real-world attacks and identify potential security weaknesses. This helps uncover vulnerabilities and validates the effectiveness of security controls.

Compliance Audits: Conduct internal or external audits to assess compliance with security policies, regulatory requirements, and industry best practices. Identify any gaps or non-compliance and take corrective actions.

Security Awareness and Training:

Building a security-conscious culture through employee awareness and training is vital. Consider the following:

Security Awareness Programs: Provide regular training and awareness programs to educate employees about security risks, best practices, and their role in safeguarding sensitive information.

Phishing Awareness: Train employees to recognize and report phishing attempts or social engineering techniques that can lead to unauthorized access or data breaches.

Ongoing Education: Continuously educate employees about emerging security threats, new attack vectors, and evolving security practices to foster a culture of vigilance and proactive security measures.

In conclusion, implementing robust security measures is critical for protecting sensitive information in data science and analytics initiatives. By establishing a security framework, performing risk assessments, implementing access control mechanisms, encrypting data, establishing monitoring and incident response processes, conducting regular security assessments and audits, and promoting security awareness and training, organizations can effectively mitigate security risks and safeguard their data assets. Prioritizing security ensures the integrity, confidentiality, and availability of sensitive information, building trust with customers and stakeholders while protecting organizational reputation.

CHAPTER 10: SCALING DATA SCIENCE PROJECTS

Chapter 10 focuses on the challenges and strategies for scaling data science projects to handle larger datasets, increased complexity, and higher demands. As organizations grow and invest in data science and analytics capabilities, the need to scale projects becomes crucial for achieving broader impact and maximizing the value of data-driven initiatives. This chapter provides an overview of key considerations, best practices, and techniques for effectively scaling data science projects.

Understanding the Need for Scaling:

The chapter begins by highlighting the importance of scaling data science projects. Scaling is necessary when organizations aim to process larger datasets, handle more complex analytics tasks, accommodate higher user demands, or expand the application of data-driven insights across different departments or business functions.

Infrastructure and Computing Resources:

Scaling data science projects requires appropriate infrastructure and computing resources. Consider the following:

Distributed Computing: Implement distributed computing frameworks such as Apache Hadoop or Apache Spark to process and analyze large volumes of data across multiple machines or clusters.

Cloud Computing: Leverage cloud computing platforms such as Amazon Web Services (AWS), Google Cloud Platform (GCP), or Microsoft Azure to scale computing resources dynamically based on project needs.

High-Performance Computing: Utilize high-performance computing (HPC) environments or dedicated hardware accelerators, such as graphics processing units (GPUs) or field-programmable gate arrays (FPGAs), to accelerate computationally intensive tasks.

Data Storage and Management:

As datasets grow in size and complexity, efficient data storage and management become essential. Consider the following:

Distributed File Systems: Implement distributed file systems like Hadoop Distributed File System (HDFS) or object storage systems like Amazon S3 to store and manage large-scale data across multiple nodes or cloud storage.

Data Warehousing: Utilize data warehousing solutions, such as Amazon Redshift or Google BigQuery, to efficiently store and query structured data for analytics purposes.

Data Lakes: Set up data lakes that can handle various types of data, including structured, semi-structured, and unstructured data. Data lakes provide a flexible and scalable approach to store and analyze diverse data sources.

Scalable Analytics and Machine Learning:

Scaling data science projects involves ensuring scalability in analytics and machine learning processes. Consider the following:

Distributed Processing: Leverage distributed computing frameworks and parallel processing techniques to distribute analytical workloads across multiple nodes or computing resources.

Stream Processing: Implement stream processing frameworks, such as Apache Kafka or Apache Flink, to handle real-time or near-real-time data streams and enable scalable analytics on streaming data.

Model Parallelism: Apply model parallelism techniques to scale the training and deployment of machine learning models across distributed computing resources or GPU clusters.

Automation and Workflow Management:

Automation and workflow management are essential for scaling data science projects efficiently. Consider the following:

Workflow Automation: Utilize workflow management tools, such as Apache Airflow or Kubernetes, to automate data pipelines, task scheduling, and dependency management.

DevOps Practices: Implement DevOps practices to automate deployment, monitoring, and management of data science applications, ensuring consistency and scalability across environments.

Collaboration and Knowledge Sharing:

As data science projects scale, collaboration and knowledge sharing become crucial. Consider the following:

Collaboration Platforms: Implement collaboration platforms, such as project management tools or data science notebooks, to facilitate communication, documentation, and knowledge sharing among team members.

Version Control: Utilize version control systems, such as Git, to track code changes, collaborate on code repositories, and enable seamless collaboration and code sharing within the team.

Knowledge Sharing Initiatives: Encourage knowledge sharing through regular team meetings, code reviews, technical documentation, and internal presentations. Foster a culture of learning and collaboration to leverage collective expertise.

Monitoring and Performance Optimization:

Monitoring project performance and optimizing resource utilization are key to scaling data science projects. Consider the following:

Performance Monitoring: Implement monitoring and logging systems to track project performance, identify bottlenecks, and detect anomalies or performance degradation.

Resource Optimization: Continuously optimize resource allocation and utilization to ensure efficient scaling. This includes monitoring computing resource usage, optimizing algorithms, and tuning system configurations.

In conclusion, scaling data science projects is crucial for organizations to effectively handle larger datasets, complex analytics tasks, and increased demands. By considering infrastructure and computing resources, efficient data storage and management, scalable analytics and machine learning techniques, automation and workflow management, collaboration and knowledge sharing, and monitoring and performance optimization, organizations can successfully scale their data science projects. Scaling enables organizations to harness the full potential of their data, drive impactful insights, and deliver valuable outcomes across various business functions and domains.

Handling Large-Scale Data Processing

In data science and analytics, handling large-scale data processing is essential for extracting valuable insights from vast amounts of information. As organizations collect and generate increasingly large datasets, it becomes critical to implement efficient and scalable techniques to process and analyze this data effectively. This section provides a detailed exploration of key considerations, challenges, and best practices for handling large-scale data processing.

Distributed Computing:

Distributed computing is a fundamental approach for handling large-scale data processing. It involves breaking down data processing tasks into smaller subtasks that can be executed simultaneously across multiple computing resources. Key considerations include:

Distributed File Systems: Utilize distributed file systems, such as Hadoop Distributed File System (HDFS), to store and manage large volumes of data across a cluster of machines. Distributed file systems provide fault tolerance, scalability, and efficient data processing capabilities.

MapReduce Paradigm: Implement the MapReduce programming model to distribute data processing tasks across the computing cluster. The Map phase performs data transformation and filtering, while the Reduce phase aggregates and summarizes the results.

Frameworks like Apache Hadoop and Apache Spark: Leverage distributed computing frameworks like Apache Hadoop and Apache Spark to execute data processing tasks in parallel across multiple nodes. These frameworks provide built-in support for distributed file systems, fault tolerance, and high-level abstractions for data manipulation and analysis.

Stream Processing:

Stream processing is designed to handle real-time or near-real-time data streams and enables efficient processing of continuous data. Key considerations include:

Streaming Platforms: Utilize streaming platforms such as Apache Kafka, Apache Flink, or Apache Storm to ingest, process, and analyze streaming data. These platforms provide fault tolerance, scalability, and support for real-time analytics.

Windowing and Time-based Operations: Employ windowing techniques to process data streams in fixed time intervals or sliding windows. Time-based operations allow for analyzing data within specific time windows, enabling timely insights and event-driven processing.

Complex Event Processing (CEP): Use CEP techniques to identify patterns or detect complex events in streaming data. CEP enables real-time analysis of high-velocity data streams and can trigger actions or alerts based on defined rules.

Parallel Processing and Optimization:

To achieve efficient large-scale data processing, parallel processing and optimization techniques are crucial. Key considerations include:

Data Partitioning: Partition large datasets into smaller subsets to enable parallel processing. Divide the data based on key attributes or a hashing function to distribute the workload evenly across multiple processing units.

Task and Resource Scheduling: Implement intelligent task scheduling algorithms to assign processing tasks to available computing resources. Optimize resource allocation to ensure efficient utilization and minimize processing time.

Data Compression and Serialization: Apply compression and serialization techniques to reduce data storage requirements and optimize data transmission between nodes. Compressed and serialized data reduces I/O overhead and improves overall processing efficiency.

Scalable Algorithms and Techniques:

Implementing scalable algorithms and techniques is essential for large-scale data processing. Key considerations include:

Sampling and Approximation: Utilize sampling techniques to extract representative subsets of data for analysis, reducing the computational requirements. Approximation algorithms allow for trading off accuracy for faster processing when dealing with massive datasets.

Incremental Processing: Design algorithms that can process data incrementally, rather than requiring the entire dataset to be loaded into memory. Incremental processing reduces memory requirements and allows for processing streaming or dynamically changing data.

Distributed Machine Learning: Employ distributed machine learning algorithms, such as distributed gradient descent or model-parallel training, to train models using large-scale datasets. Distributing the computation across multiple nodes or machines enables efficient model training and scalability.

Resource Management and Scaling:

Efficient resource management and scaling strategies are crucial for handling large-scale data processing. Key considerations include:

Dynamic Resource Allocation: Implement dynamic resource allocation techniques to scale computing resources based on workload demand. This may involve automatically provisioning additional computing nodes or cloud resources when processing requirements increase.

Containerization and Orchestration: Utilize containerization technologies, such as Docker, and container orchestration platforms, such as Kubernetes, to deploy and manage distributed processing environments. Containerization provides portability and scalability while simplifying resource management.

Auto-Scaling: Leverage auto-scaling capabilities provided by cloud service providers to automatically adjust computing resources based on workload patterns. Auto-scaling ensures optimal resource utilization and avoids overprovisioning or under provisioning.

Data Quality and Cleansing:

Maintaining data quality is essential for accurate and meaningful analysis, particularly when dealing with large-scale datasets. Key considerations include:

Data Validation and Cleaning: Implement data validation and cleaning processes to identify and correct errors, inconsistencies, or missing values in the dataset. Data cleaning techniques ensure the reliability and accuracy of the data used for analysis.

Outlier Detection: Apply outlier detection techniques to identify and handle anomalous data points that may adversely affect analysis results. Outliers can skew statistical measures or machine learning models and should be appropriately managed.

Data Integration and Fusion: Address challenges related to data integration, including resolving conflicts, handling missing data, or integrating data from different sources. Ensure that data fusion techniques are employed to merge heterogeneous datasets and maintain data integrity.

In conclusion, handling large-scale data processing is critical for extracting valuable insights from massive datasets. By leveraging distributed computing, stream processing, parallel processing, scalable algorithms, resource management, and data quality techniques, organizations can efficiently process and analyze large volumes of data. Effective large-scale data processing enables organizations to gain deeper insights, make informed decisions, and unlock the full potential of their data assets.

Leveraging Cloud Computing and Distributed Systems

Cloud computing and distributed systems play a vital role in enabling organizations to handle large-scale data processing and analytics. These technologies provide the infrastructure, scalability, and flexibility needed to efficiently process and analyze vast amounts of data. This section explores the benefits, considerations, and best practices for leveraging cloud computing and distributed systems in data science and analytics initiatives.

Benefits of Cloud Computing:

Cloud computing offers several advantages for data processing and analytics projects:

Scalability: Cloud platforms, such as Amazon Web Services (AWS), Microsoft Azure, or Google Cloud Platform (GCP), provide on-demand scalability. Organizations can easily scale computing resources up or down based on the workload, ensuring efficient processing of large datasets.

Elasticity: Cloud services allow for automatic resource provisioning and deprovisioning, enabling organizations to dynamically adjust computing resources as needed. This elasticity ensures optimal resource utilization and cost efficiency.

Cost Savings: Cloud computing offers a pay-as-you-go model, where organizations only pay for the resources and services they consume. This eliminates the need for upfront infrastructure investments and allows for cost optimization through resource scaling.

Flexibility: Cloud platforms provide a wide range of services, including data storage, processing, analytics, and machine learning. Organizations can leverage these services based on their specific requirements, reducing the need for managing complex infrastructure.

Global Accessibility: Cloud services are accessible from anywhere with an internet connection. This enables collaboration among geographically dispersed teams and allows for real-time data access and analysis.

Distributed Computing:

Distributed computing involves dividing data processing tasks across multiple machines or nodes to achieve faster and more efficient processing. Consider the following distributed computing concepts:

Parallel Processing: Splitting data processing tasks into smaller subtasks and executing them simultaneously across multiple computing resources improves processing speed. Parallel processing techniques, such as MapReduce or data parallelism, enable efficient distributed computing.

Distributed File Systems: Distributed file systems, like Hadoop Distributed File System (HDFS) or Amazon S3, store and manage large volumes of data across a cluster of machines. Data is divided into smaller chunks and distributed across nodes, allowing for parallel processing.

Distributed Data Processing Frameworks: Distributed computing frameworks, such as Apache Hadoop or Apache Spark, provide high-level abstractions and APIs for distributed data processing. These frameworks handle data distribution, task scheduling, fault tolerance, and result aggregation.

Considerations for Cloud Computing and Distributed Systems:

When leveraging cloud computing and distributed systems, consider the following key considerations:

Data Storage and Transfer: Determine the appropriate storage solutions for data, considering factors such as volume, velocity, and variety. Evaluate options like object storage, databases, or data lakes based on the specific needs of the project. Additionally, optimize data transfer between storage and computing resources to minimize latency and maximize processing efficiency.

Security and Compliance: Address security and compliance requirements when utilizing cloud services and distributed systems. Implement robust security measures, including encryption, access controls, and regular security audits. Ensure compliance with data protection regulations and industry standards to protect sensitive information.

Cost Optimization: Monitor and optimize costs associated with cloud computing and distributed systems. Leverage resource auto-scaling, spot instances, or reserved instances to optimize resource allocation. Regularly review and adjust the usage of cloud services to minimize costs while meeting project requirements.

Data Locality and Network Bandwidth: Consider the location of data and computing resources to minimize data transfer time and latency. Co-locating data and computing resources within the same region or availability zone reduces network overhead and enhances processing performance.

Fault Tolerance and Resilience: Design fault-tolerant systems that can handle failures in distributed environments. Implement techniques such as data replication, fault detection, and automatic recovery mechanisms to ensure system resilience and data availability.

Best Practices for Cloud Computing and Distributed Systems:

To effectively leverage cloud computing and distributed systems, follow these best practices:

Architecture Design: Design an architecture that leverages distributed computing principles, considering factors such as data partitioning, workload distribution, and fault tolerance. Utilize well-established patterns and frameworks to optimize performance and scalability.

Performance Monitoring: Implement robust monitoring and logging mechanisms to track performance, identify bottlenecks, and optimize resource utilization. Monitor metrics such as CPU utilization, memory usage, and network traffic to ensure efficient data processing.

Automation and Orchestration: Utilize automation and orchestration tools, such as Kubernetes or Apache Airflow, to manage distributed resources, automate workflows, and streamline data processing pipelines. This improves efficiency, reduces manual effort, and enhances repeatability.

Data Pipeline Management: Build robust data pipelines to manage the flow of data from ingestion to processing and analysis. Implement proper data validation, cleansing, and transformation steps to ensure data quality throughout the pipeline.

Continuous Integration and Deployment: Adopt continuous integration and deployment practices to streamline development processes and enable rapid iterations. This facilitates the deployment of updates and enhancements to cloud-based applications or distributed systems.

In conclusion, leveraging cloud computing and distributed systems provides organizations with scalable infrastructure, elastic resource allocation, and flexibility for large-scale data processing and analytics. By considering factors such as data storage and transfer, security, cost optimization, data locality, and fault tolerance, organizations can effectively harness the power of cloud computing and distributed systems. This empowers them to handle massive datasets, process data efficiently, and derive valuable insights for informed decision-making.

Managing Infrastructure and Scalability Challenges

Managing infrastructure and scalability challenges is crucial for successful data science and analytics projects. As data volumes and processing requirements increase, organizations must effectively manage their infrastructure to ensure efficient and scalable operations. This section explores the key considerations, challenges, and best practices for managing infrastructure and addressing scalability challenges in data science and analytics initiatives.

Scalable Infrastructure Design:

Designing a scalable infrastructure lays the foundation for managing large-scale data processing and analytics. Consider the following:

Modular Architecture: Adopt a modular and component-based architecture that allows for easy scalability. Break down the system into loosely coupled components, enabling independent scaling of different parts of the infrastructure.

Cloud Infrastructure: Leverage cloud computing platforms, such as Amazon Web Services (AWS), Microsoft Azure, or Google Cloud Platform (GCP), to take advantage of their elastic and scalable infrastructure. Cloud platforms offer flexible resource provisioning, auto-scaling capabilities, and managed services that can handle increased workloads.

Containerization: Utilize containerization technologies, such as Docker or Kubernetes, to encapsulate application components and dependencies. Containers provide portability, scalability, and facilitate the deployment of applications across different environments.

Microservices Architecture: Implement a microservices architecture, where complex applications are built as a collection of small, independent services. This allows for individual scalability of services based on demand and promotes flexibility and maintainability.

Resource Provisioning and Auto-Scaling:

Efficient resource provisioning and auto-scaling are essential for managing infrastructure scalability. Consider the following:

Resource Monitoring: Implement robust monitoring systems to track resource utilization, performance metrics, and workload patterns. This enables informed decision-making for resource provisioning and scaling.

Auto-Scaling Policies: Define auto-scaling policies that automatically adjust resources based on predefined thresholds or workload patterns. Auto-scaling can be based on metrics such as CPU utilization, memory usage, or request rates.

Horizontal and Vertical Scaling: Utilize horizontal scaling by adding more instances of resources, such as adding more servers or containers, to distribute the workload. Vertical scaling involves increasing the capacity of existing resources, such as upgrading CPU or memory, to handle increased demand.

Load Balancing: Implement load balancing mechanisms to distribute incoming requests across multiple servers or containers. Load balancers ensure efficient utilization of resources and improve system performance and availability.

Data Storage and Database Scalability:

Managing data storage and database scalability is critical for handling large volumes of data. Consider the following:

Distributed File Systems: Utilize distributed file systems, such as Hadoop Distributed File System (HDFS) or Amazon S3, for storing and managing large-scale data. Distributed file systems offer scalability, fault tolerance, and support for parallel data processing.

NoSQL Databases: Consider using NoSQL databases, such as Apache Cassandra or MongoDB, for scalable and flexible data storage. NoSQL databases provide horizontal scalability, allowing for distributed storage and efficient data retrieval.

Sharding and Partitioning: Implement sharding or partitioning techniques to distribute data across multiple nodes or servers. This ensures data is evenly distributed and facilitates parallel processing and query performance.

Database Replication: Configure database replication to ensure high availability and fault tolerance. Replication allows for data redundancy and load balancing across multiple database instances.

Performance Optimization and Caching:

Optimizing performance and implementing caching strategies are essential for managing scalability challenges. Consider the following:

Query Optimization: Optimize database queries, indexing, and data retrieval mechanisms to improve query performance and reduce response times. Analyze query execution plans, eliminate bottlenecks, and use appropriate indexing techniques.

Caching Mechanisms: Implement caching mechanisms to store frequently accessed data in memory. Caching reduces the need for repetitive data retrieval from storage, improving response times and overall system performance.

Content Delivery Networks (CDNs): Utilize CDNs to cache and deliver static content, such as images or files, to users from geographically distributed edge servers. CDNs minimize latency and reduce the load on origin servers.

Continuous Monitoring and Capacity Planning:

Continuous monitoring and capacity planning help ensure efficient infrastructure management. Consider the following:

Infrastructure Monitoring: Implement robust monitoring systems to continuously track infrastructure performance, resource utilization, and system health. Monitor metrics such as CPU, memory, network traffic, and response times to identify bottlenecks or capacity constraints.

Capacity Planning: Use historical data, workload projections, and growth trends to plan for future infrastructure needs. Conduct capacity planning exercises to identify potential resource shortages, determine optimal scaling thresholds, and anticipate infrastructure upgrades or additions.

Performance Testing: Perform regular performance testing to evaluate the system's behavior under various load conditions. Load testing and stress testing help identify performance bottlenecks, validate scalability, and ensure the system can handle anticipated workloads.

Disaster Recovery and High Availability:

Maintaining disaster recovery capabilities and high availability is critical for managing infrastructure challenges. Consider the following:

Backup and Recovery: Implement regular backups of critical data and establish reliable data recovery mechanisms. Backup strategies should consider data integrity, retention policies, and off-site storage options.

Redundancy and Failover: Configure redundant systems and failover mechanisms to ensure high availability. Implement load balancers, clustering, or redundant components to handle hardware failures or disruptions.

Disaster Recovery Planning: Develop and test disaster recovery plans to address potential infrastructure failures, data loss, or natural disasters. Define recovery objectives, establish recovery procedures, and regularly update and test the plans to ensure effectiveness.

In conclusion, managing infrastructure and addressing scalability challenges is vital for successful data science and analytics projects. By focusing on scalable infrastructure design, resource provisioning, data storage scalability, performance optimization, continuous monitoring, capacity planning, and disaster recovery, organizations can effectively manage infrastructure and ensure efficient and scalable operations. Proper infrastructure management facilitates the handling of large-scale data processing, enables scalability as needs grow, and supports the delivery of valuable insights and outcomes.

CHAPTER 11: REAL-TIME ANALYTICS AND STREAM PROCESSING

Chapter 11 delves into the world of real-time analytics and stream processing, highlighting the importance of analyzing data as it is generated and exploring techniques for processing streaming data in real time. In today's fast-paced and data-driven world, organizations need to make immediate decisions based on up-to-date information. Real-time analytics and stream processing enable organizations to derive actionable insights from data as it flows in, enabling quick response times and proactive decision-making. This chapter provides an overview of the concepts, challenges, and best practices related to real-time analytics and stream processing.

Understanding Real-Time Analytics:

Real-time analytics involves processing and analyzing data as it is generated or received, allowing organizations to gain immediate insights and take timely actions. Key concepts and considerations include:

Data Velocity: Real-time analytics focuses on high-velocity data streams that require immediate processing and analysis. This data can be generated from various sources such as sensors, social media feeds, transactional systems, or IoT devices.

Event-Driven Architecture: Implementing event-driven architectures enables organizations to capture and process events in real time. Events can be defined as significant occurrences or changes in the data stream that trigger actions or analytics processes.

Low Latency: Real-time analytics aims to minimize the time between data generation and insights. Low-latency processing and analysis enable organizations to react quickly to changing conditions and make timely decisions.

Stream Processing Frameworks:

Stream processing frameworks are designed to handle continuous data streams and enable real-time analytics. Key considerations include:

Apache Kafka: Apache Kafka is a popular distributed streaming platform that provides high-throughput, fault-tolerance, and scalable messaging capabilities. It allows organizations to ingest, store, and process streaming data efficiently.

Apache Flink: Apache Flink is a powerful stream processing framework that supports event-time processing, fault tolerance, and exactly-once processing semantics. Flink enables complex analytics operations, including windowing, aggregations, and pattern detection.

Apache Storm: Apache Storm is a real-time distributed computing framework that processes streaming data in a fault-tolerant and scalable manner. Storm provides low-latency processing capabilities and is well-suited for real-time analytics use cases.

Stream Processing Concepts and Techniques:

Stream processing involves applying various concepts and techniques to analyze and process streaming data effectively. Key considerations include:

Windowing: Windowing allows for dividing the continuous data stream into smaller segments, enabling analysis and aggregation over fixed or sliding time intervals. Windowing techniques facilitate computations on data subsets and support time-based analytics.

State Management: Stream processing frameworks maintain state information to enable contextual analysis and aggregations over the streaming data. State management techniques ensure that computations can access and update relevant information in real time.

Event Time vs. Processing Time: Stream processing frameworks handle data in either event time or processing time. Event time refers to the time when an event actually occurred, while processing time refers to the time when an event is processed. Understanding and handling event time correctly is essential for accurate analysis and windowing operations.

Use Cases for Real-Time Analytics:

Real-time analytics has numerous applications across various industries. Some common use cases include:

Fraud Detection: Real-time analytics helps organizations detect and respond to fraudulent activities as they occur, preventing financial losses and protecting customer interests.

Predictive Maintenance: By analyzing real-time data from sensors and equipment, organizations can detect anomalies and predict potential failures, allowing for proactive maintenance and reducing downtime.

Sentiment Analysis: Real-time sentiment analysis of social media feeds or customer interactions enables organizations to gauge public sentiment, identify emerging trends, and respond promptly to customer feedback.

Supply Chain Optimization: Real-time analytics helps organizations optimize their supply chains by monitoring inventory levels, tracking shipments, and identifying bottlenecks or delays in real time.

Personalized Marketing: Real-time analytics enables organizations to deliver personalized marketing offers or recommendations based on immediate customer behavior or preferences.

Challenges and Considerations:

Implementing real-time analytics and stream processing comes with certain challenges that organizations must address. Key considerations include:

Data Volume and Velocity: High-volume and high-velocity data streams require robust infrastructure and efficient processing techniques to handle the continuous flow of data.

Data Quality and Cleansing: Real-time analytics requires accurate and clean data for meaningful insights. Implementing data quality checks and cleansing techniques ensures the reliability of real-time analysis.

Scalability and Resilience: Real-time analytics systems must be designed to scale horizontally and handle fluctuations in data volume and processing requirements. Fault tolerance and resilience mechanisms should be in place to ensure system availability and continuity.

Integration with Batch Processing: Integrating real-time analytics with existing batch processing systems or data warehouses may require careful planning and synchronization to ensure consistent and coherent insights across different data processing paradigms.

Best Practices for Real-Time Analytics:

To successfully implement real-time analytics and stream processing, organizations should consider the following best practices:

Define Clear Objectives: Clearly define the business objectives and use cases for real-time analytics to ensure that the analysis focuses on delivering actionable insights aligned with organizational goals.

Architect for Scalability: Design an architecture that can scale horizontally to handle increasing data volume and processing requirements. Leverage cloud computing or distributed computing frameworks to achieve scalability and fault tolerance.

Ensure Data Quality: Implement data quality checks and validation mechanisms to ensure the accuracy and reliability of real-time data. Address issues such as missing data, outliers, or data inconsistencies to maintain data integrity.

Monitor Performance and Latency: Continuously monitor the performance of real-time analytics systems, tracking latency and processing times.

Optimize system configurations and algorithms to minimize latency and ensure timely insights.

Embrace DevOps and Automation: Adopt DevOps practices to automate deployments, testing, and monitoring of real-time analytics systems. Continuous integration and continuous delivery (CI/CD) pipelines ensure efficient and reliable updates and enhancements.

In conclusion, real-time analytics and stream processing empower organizations to derive immediate insights from high-velocity data streams, enabling timely decision-making and proactive actions. By understanding the concepts, leveraging stream processing frameworks, addressing challenges, and following best practices, organizations can harness the power of real-time analytics to gain a competitive edge, drive operational efficiency, and deliver superior customer experiences.

Understanding Real-Time Analytics Concepts

Real-time analytics is a discipline within data science and analytics that focuses on processing and analyzing data as it is generated or received, enabling organizations to gain immediate insights and make timely decisions. In today's fast-paced and data-driven world, the ability to analyze data in real time has become increasingly critical for businesses to stay competitive and responsive to rapidly changing conditions. This section explores the key concepts and components of real-time analytics.

Data Velocity:

Data velocity refers to the speed at which data is generated, received, and processed. Real-time analytics is particularly concerned with high-velocity data streams that require immediate analysis. This data can be sourced from various channels, including sensors, social media feeds, web applications, transactional systems, or Internet of Things (IoT) devices. Understanding data velocity is crucial for designing effective real-time analytics systems.

Event-Driven Architecture:

Real-time analytics often relies on event-driven architecture, which is centered around capturing and processing events as they occur. Events can be defined as significant occurrences or changes in the data stream that trigger actions or analytics processes. An event-driven architecture allows organizations to react to events in real time, enabling immediate analysis and response. Common event-driven technologies include publish/subscribe messaging systems, message queues, or event streaming platforms like Apache Kafka.

Low Latency:

One of the fundamental characteristics of real-time analytics is low latency, which refers to the minimal delay between data generation and the availability of actionable insights. Low-latency processing is achieved through efficient data ingestion, rapid analysis, and immediate response times. Real-time analytics systems are designed to minimize latency by optimizing data processing pipelines, implementing distributed computing, and leveraging scalable infrastructure.

Streaming Data Processing:

Real-time analytics heavily relies on stream processing, which involves processing and analyzing continuous data streams in real time. Stream processing techniques enable organizations to handle the velocity and volume of data by breaking it down into smaller, manageable chunks. Stream processing frameworks like Apache Kafka, Apache Flink, or Apache Storm facilitate the ingestion, transformation, and analysis of streaming data, often incorporating windowing, aggregation, and filtering operations.

Event Time vs. Processing Time:

When dealing with real-time analytics, it is essential to differentiate between event time and processing time. Event time refers to the time when an event actually occurred in the real world, while processing time refers to the time when an event is processed by the analytics system. Event time is critical for accurate analysis and enables windowing and aggregation based on the actual timing of events. On the other hand, processing time allows for real-time analysis based on the system's clock, ensuring timely insights.

Windowing:

Windowing is a key concept in stream processing that allows for dividing the continuous data stream into smaller segments or windows. Windowing enables analysis and aggregation operations over fixed or sliding time intervals. Fixed windows group events within a specific time period, while sliding windows continuously slide over the stream, allowing for continuous analysis. Windowing is useful for computing rolling averages, time-based aggregations, or detecting patterns within specific time frames.

State Management:

State management is essential in real-time analytics, as it involves maintaining and updating state information about the data stream. State can include relevant contextual information, intermediate results, or aggregations. Real-time analytics systems employ various techniques to manage state efficiently, such as in-memory data stores, key-value databases, or distributed computing frameworks that provide fault tolerance and scalability.

Real-Time Dashboards and Alerts:

Real-time analytics often involves the visualization of insights through real-time dashboards and alerts. Dashboards provide a visual representation of key performance indicators (KPIs), trends, or anomalies in real time, enabling users to monitor the data stream and make informed decisions. Alerts notify users when predefined thresholds or conditions are met, allowing for immediate action.

Continuous Monitoring and Feedback Loops:

Real-time analytics requires continuous monitoring to ensure the effectiveness of the analytics system and the accuracy of insights. Monitoring metrics such as system performance, data quality, latency, or response times helps identify bottlenecks, detect anomalies, and optimize the system. Feedback loops enable organizations to continuously improve their real-time analytics processes by incorporating insights into iterative model training, data validation, or system enhancements.

In conclusion, understanding the key concepts of real-time analytics is essential for organizations seeking to derive immediate insights and make timely decisions. By grasping the principles of data velocity, event-driven architecture, low latency, streaming data processing, windowing, state management, real-time dashboards, continuous monitoring, and feedback loops, organizations can harness the power of real-time analytics to gain a competitive advantage, drive operational efficiency, and provide superior customer experiences.

Implementing Stream Processing Frameworks

Stream processing frameworks play a crucial role in enabling organizations to implement real-time analytics and process high-velocity data streams efficiently. These frameworks provide the necessary infrastructure and tools to ingest, transform, and analyze streaming data in real time, allowing organizations to derive timely insights and make immediate decisions. This section explores the key considerations, steps, and best practices for implementing stream processing frameworks.

Choosing the Right Stream Processing Framework:

The first step in implementing a stream processing framework is to select the right one for your organization's needs. Consider the following factors when choosing a framework:

Scalability: Ensure that the framework can handle the expected volume and velocity of data. Look for distributed stream processing frameworks that can scale horizontally by adding more computing resources.

Fault Tolerance: Look for frameworks that provide built-in fault tolerance mechanisms, such as data replication and automatic recovery, to ensure data integrity and system reliability.

Processing Guarantees: Consider the processing guarantees offered by the framework. For example, frameworks that support exactly-once processing semantics ensure that each event is processed only once, eliminating duplicates and ensuring accurate results.

Integration Capabilities: Evaluate how well the framework integrates with your existing infrastructure, data sources, and downstream systems. Consider compatibility with popular messaging systems, storage platforms, and analytics tools.

Ecosystem and Community Support: Assess the ecosystem and community around the framework. A vibrant community ensures ongoing support, frequent updates, and a rich ecosystem of connectors, libraries, and extensions.

Designing Stream Processing Pipelines:

Once you have selected a stream processing framework, the next step is to design your stream processing pipeline. Consider the following components:

Data Ingestion: Define how you will ingest data from various sources into the stream processing framework. This may involve connectors or adapters to interact with message queues, event hubs, databases, or data streaming platforms.

Data Transformation: Determine the necessary transformations and operations to apply to the incoming data stream. This includes filtering, aggregating, enriching, joining, or cleansing the data to prepare it for analysis.

Analytics and Insights: Identify the analytics techniques, algorithms, or models you will apply to the streaming data. This may include real-time aggregations, pattern detection, machine learning algorithms, or complex event processing (CEP) techniques.

Output and Action: Decide how to present the results and insights derived from the stream processing pipeline. This could involve generating alerts, updating real-time dashboards, triggering notifications, or writing results to databases or data warehouses.

Developing Stream Processing Applications:

Developing stream processing applications involves writing the necessary code or configurations to implement the designed pipeline using the chosen framework. Consider the following:

Programming Model: Understand the programming model and APIs provided by the stream processing framework. Common programming models include event-driven programming, functional programming, or SQL-like query languages.

Data Serialization: Define how data will be serialized and deserialized within the stream processing application. Choose a suitable serialization format, such as Avro, JSON, or Protobuf, that balances performance, efficiency, and compatibility.

State Management: Determine how to manage and maintain state information within the stream processing application. This involves defining how to store and update intermediate results, aggregations, or contextual information required for real-time analytics.

Testing and Debugging: Implement comprehensive testing strategies to ensure the correctness and reliability of the stream processing application. Develop unit tests, integration tests, and end-to-end tests to validate the functionality and performance of the pipeline.

Deployment and Scaling:

Once the stream processing application is developed, it needs to be deployed and scaled to handle the data streams efficiently. Consider the following:

Infrastructure Requirements: Provision the necessary computing resources, including CPU, memory, and storage, to accommodate the expected data volume and processing load. Cloud computing platforms provide scalability and flexibility for stream processing deployments.

Monitoring and Observability: Implement robust monitoring and observability mechanisms to track the health, performance, and resource utilization of the stream processing application. Monitor metrics such as throughput, latency, errors, and system-level indicators.

Scalability and Elasticity: Design the deployment architecture to handle scaling requirements. Consider horizontal scaling by adding more instances or nodes to distribute the workload and ensure responsiveness to changes in data volume and processing demands.

Fault Tolerance and Recovery: Configure the stream processing framework to provide fault tolerance and recovery mechanisms. This may involve data replication, checkpointing, or transactional guarantees to ensure the reliability of the stream processing application.

Performance Optimization:

To optimize the performance of stream processing frameworks, consider the following best practices:

Data Partitioning: Distribute the data across multiple partitions or shards to enable parallel processing and load balancing. Partitioning ensures that the workload is evenly distributed across the processing resources.

Windowing and Time-Based Operations: Leverage windowing techniques to aggregate and analyze data within specific time intervals. Windowing allows for real-time aggregations, sliding windows, or tumbling windows to derive meaningful insights.

Watermarking and Event Time Processing: Implement techniques such as watermarking to handle out-of-order events and event time processing. This ensures accurate analysis based on the actual timing of events, enabling correct windowing and temporal operations.

Memory Management and State Size: Optimize memory usage by carefully managing the size of state information, intermediate results, or cached data. Avoid excessive state accumulation, which can impact performance and scalability.

Benchmarking and Profiling: Continuously benchmark and profile the performance of the stream processing application to identify bottlenecks, optimize resource usage, and fine-tune the application's performance.

In conclusion, implementing stream processing frameworks involves choosing the right framework, designing the stream processing pipeline, developing the stream processing application, deploying and scaling the application, and optimizing its performance. By following best practices and considering factors such as scalability, fault tolerance, data serialization, state management, and performance optimization, organizations can successfully implement stream processing frameworks to derive real-time insights and make data-driven decisions.

Building Real-Time Dashboards and Alerts

Real-time dashboards and alerts play a vital role in enabling organizations to monitor and visualize data in real time, allowing for immediate insights and timely decision-making. These tools provide a visual representation of key performance indicators (KPIs), trends, and anomalies, empowering users to track data streams, identify patterns, and take action as events unfold. This section explores the key considerations, steps, and best practices for building real-time dashboards and alerts.

Define Dashboard Objectives:

Before building a real-time dashboard, it is essential to define its objectives and purpose. Consider the following:

Identify Key Metrics: Determine the most critical metrics that need to be monitored in real time. These metrics should align with the organization's goals and provide actionable insights for decision-making.

Define User Roles: Understand the target audience and the specific needs of different user roles. Tailor the dashboard's design and content to cater to the requirements of executives, managers, analysts, or operational teams.

Set Alerting Criteria: Define the criteria that will trigger alerts and notifications. These criteria can be based on predefined thresholds, anomalies, or specific events that require immediate attention.

Choose the Right Visualization Tools:

Selecting the appropriate visualization tools is crucial for building effective real-time dashboards. Consider the following:

Dashboard Platforms: Choose a dashboard platform that provides real-time capabilities, supports live data streaming, and offers a wide range of visualization options. Popular dashboard platforms include Tableau, Power BI, QlikView, or Grafana.

Visualization Techniques: Select visualization techniques that best represent the data and provide insights at a glance. Consider using charts, graphs, gauges, heatmaps, or geographic maps to convey information effectively.

Real-Time Data Integration: Ensure that the dashboard platform supports real-time data integration. This may involve connecting to streaming data sources, APIs, or message queues to ingest and display data in real time.

Data Ingestion and Integration:

To build real-time dashboards, organizations need to ingest and integrate data from various sources. Consider the following:

Streaming Data Sources: Connect to streaming data sources such as message queues, event hubs, or IoT platforms to receive real-time data updates. Use connectors or adapters provided by the dashboard platform to establish the data pipeline.

APIs and Webhooks: Integrate with external APIs or webhooks to retrieve real-time data from external systems. This could include social media platforms, transactional systems, or third-party services that provide real-time data feeds.

Data Transformation and Preparation: Transform and prepare the data to match the requirements of the dashboard visualization. This may involve data cleansing, aggregation, filtering, or enrichment to ensure data accuracy and quality.

Designing the Dashboard Layout:

The design of the real-time dashboard is crucial for providing a clear and intuitive user experience. Consider the following:

Focus on Key Metrics: Highlight the most important metrics or KPIs that users need to monitor in real time. Place them prominently on the dashboard to draw immediate attention.

Visual Hierarchy: Organize the dashboard elements in a logical and intuitive manner, using visual hierarchy principles. Group related metrics, use color coding for significance, and arrange elements based on priority.

Responsive Design: Ensure that the dashboard layout is responsive and adapts to different screen sizes and devices. This allows users to access the dashboard from desktops, laptops, or mobile devices, providing flexibility and accessibility.

Drill-Down and Interactivity: Provide interactivity features that allow users to drill down into specific metrics, explore data details, and filter the dashboard based on specific criteria. This enhances the user's ability to uncover insights and perform ad-hoc analysis.

Real-Time Alerts and Notifications:

Real-time dashboards should be complemented by alerts and notifications that notify users of critical events or anomalies. Consider the following:

Define Alerting Criteria: Establish the criteria that will trigger alerts based on predefined thresholds, anomalies, or specific conditions. Ensure that the thresholds are set appropriately to avoid unnecessary alerts or missing critical events.

Notification Channels: Determine the appropriate channels for delivering alerts and notifications. This can include email, SMS, instant messaging, or integration with collaboration platforms like Slack or Microsoft Teams.

Escalation and Routing: Define escalation and routing rules for alerts that require immediate attention. Ensure that alerts are sent to the appropriate individuals or teams based on the severity or nature of the event.

Actionable Alerts: Make alerts actionable by providing contextual information, suggested actions, or links to relevant dashboards or reports. This helps users quickly understand the situation and take necessary steps.

Testing and Iteration:

Regular testing and iteration are crucial for building effective real-time dashboards and alerts. Consider the following:

User Feedback: Gather feedback from dashboard users to identify usability issues, data discrepancies, or missing features. Incorporate user feedback into the dashboard design and functionality.

Performance Testing: Perform performance testing to ensure that the dashboard can handle real-time data updates and user interactions without latency or performance degradation.

Continuous Improvement: Continuously monitor and analyze the usage patterns and effectiveness of the dashboard. Use data-driven insights to identify areas of improvement and iterate on the design and content to better serve user needs.

In conclusion, building real-time dashboards and alerts requires careful planning, data integration, visualization techniques, and user-centric design. By defining objectives, selecting the right visualization tools, integrating real-time data sources, designing intuitive layouts, implementing real-time alerts, and iterating based on user feedback, organizations can build effective dashboards that provide immediate insights, facilitate timely decision-making, and empower users with real-time awareness of key metrics and events.

CHAPTER 12: ETHICAL CONSIDERATIONS IN DATA SCIENCE

Chapter 12 focuses on the ethical considerations that accompany data science practices. As data science continues to evolve and organizations rely more heavily on data-driven decision-making, it is crucial to address the ethical implications associated with collecting, analyzing, and utilizing data. This chapter explores the ethical challenges and provides guidelines for ethical data science practices.

Importance of Ethical Data Science:

Ethical data science ensures that data is collected, analyzed, and used in a responsible and ethical manner. It promotes transparency, fairness, privacy, and accountability, addressing potential biases, discrimination, and misuse of data. Ethical data science practices build trust among stakeholders, protect individuals' rights, and contribute to positive societal impacts.

Data Privacy and Consent:

Data privacy is a fundamental ethical consideration. Organizations must obtain informed consent from individuals when collecting and using their personal data. This involves clearly communicating the purpose of data collection, the types of data being collected, how it will be used, and any third parties involved. Organizations should comply with relevant data protection regulations, implement robust data security measures, and respect individuals' rights to control their personal information.

Fairness and Bias:

Ensuring fairness in data science is crucial to avoid discriminatory outcomes. Data scientists must be aware of biases in data and algorithms that can result in unfair treatment or discrimination against certain individuals or groups. Steps should be taken to identify and mitigate bias, such as diverse representation in data collection, regular audits of algorithms, and ongoing monitoring of system outputs to detect and rectify any unfair impacts.

Transparency and Explainability:

Transparency is key to ethical data science practices. Organizations should strive to be transparent about their data collection, processing, and analysis methods. This includes providing clear explanations of the algorithms used, the data sources involved, and the reasoning behind the decisions made based on the data. Transparent practices foster trust, enable scrutiny, and allow for meaningful engagement with stakeholders.

Data Governance and Accountability:

Ethical data science requires robust data governance frameworks and mechanisms for accountability. Organizations should establish clear policies and procedures for data handling, access, sharing, and retention. They should appoint responsible individuals or teams to oversee data governance, monitor compliance with ethical standards, and handle any breaches or ethical concerns that may arise. Accountability ensures that individuals and organizations are held responsible for their data science practices.

Impact on Society and Public Interest:

Data science has the potential to shape society and influence public interest. Ethical data science takes into account the broader societal impacts of data analysis and decision-making. Organizations should consider the potential consequences of their actions on individuals, communities, and society as a whole. They should strive to use data science for positive social outcomes, consider the needs and perspectives of diverse populations, and avoid harmful or exploitative practices.

Responsible Use of Artificial Intelligence:

Artificial Intelligence (AI) technologies, such as machine learning algorithms, pose ethical challenges that require careful consideration. Organizations should ensure that AI systems are developed and deployed responsibly, with a focus on transparency, fairness, and accountability. Regular audits of AI systems, monitoring for unintended consequences, and addressing potential biases or risks are essential for ethical AI practices.

Ethical Decision-Making Frameworks:

Organizations should adopt ethical decision-making frameworks to guide data science practices. These frameworks provide a systematic approach to identifying and addressing ethical considerations throughout the data science lifecycle. Ethical frameworks may include principles such as beneficence, non-maleficence, autonomy, justice, and integrity. They assist in evaluating the potential ethical implications of data science projects and aid in making informed and responsible decisions.

Continuous Education and Ethical Awareness:

Ethical data science requires ongoing education and awareness among data scientists and professionals involved in data-driven decision-making. Organizations should provide training programs, workshops, and resources to enhance ethical awareness, promote ethical decision-making, and keep professionals informed about evolving ethical standards and regulations.

In conclusion, ethical considerations are integral to data science practices. By prioritizing data privacy and consent, addressing bias and fairness, fostering transparency and explainability, implementing effective data governance, considering societal impact, and adopting ethical decision-making frameworks, organizations can ensure ethical data science practices that respect individuals' rights, promote fairness, and contribute to positive societal outcomes. Ethical data science builds trust, protects stakeholders, and ensures the responsible use of data for the benefit of individuals and society as a whole.

Addressing Bias and Fairness in Algorithms

Algorithms play a critical role in data science and analytics, driving automated decision-making processes and influencing outcomes in various domains. However, algorithms can be prone to biases that perpetuate unfair treatment and discrimination against certain individuals or groups. Addressing bias and promoting fairness in algorithms is essential to ensure ethical data science practices. This section explores the key considerations, challenges, and strategies for addressing bias and promoting fairness in algorithms.

Understanding Bias in Algorithms:

Bias in algorithms refers to systematic and unfair treatment of certain individuals or groups based on protected characteristics such as race, gender, age, or ethnicity. Bias can arise at various stages of the algorithmic lifecycle, including data collection, preprocessing, feature engineering, model training, and decision-making. Common types of bias include:

Sampling Bias: Data used to train algorithms may not be representative of the population, leading to skewed results.

Prejudice Bias: Algorithms may reflect or reinforce existing prejudices and discriminatory practices present in the training data.

Measurement Bias: Biased or inaccurate measurements may lead to biased algorithmic outputs.

Proxy Bias: Algorithms may use proxies that are correlated with sensitive attributes, resulting in indirect discrimination.

Feedback Loop Bias: Biased algorithmic decisions can perpetuate unfair outcomes, creating a feedback loop that amplifies the bias over time.

Data Collection and Preprocessing:

Addressing bias in algorithms starts with careful data collection and preprocessing. Consider the following strategies:

Diverse and Representative Data: Ensure that the training data includes diverse representation of individuals and groups to avoid under- or over-representation. Collect data from various sources and use sampling techniques that capture the true distribution of the population.

Data Cleaning and Quality Assessment: Thoroughly clean and assess the quality of the data to eliminate biases or inaccuracies. Remove or mitigate biased or misleading data points that could influence the algorithm's behavior.

Attribute Selection: Select attributes or features for training that are relevant to the task at hand and avoid using attributes that may introduce bias or discrimination.

Anonymization and De-identification: Protect individuals' privacy by anonymizing or de-identifying sensitive attributes in the data to prevent discriminatory patterns from emerging.

Model Training and Validation:

During the model training and validation phase, specific steps can be taken to address bias and promote fairness. Consider the following strategies:

Bias-Aware Model Selection: Choose models that are known to be less susceptible to bias or have built-in mechanisms for fairness, such as causal inference models or models that explicitly optimize for fairness metrics.

Fairness Constraints and Regularization: Introduce fairness constraints or regularization terms during model training to explicitly control and minimize the impact of sensitive attributes on the model's predictions.

Bias Detection and Mitigation: Implement techniques to detect and mitigate bias in the model. This can include analyzing the model's outputs for disparate impact, evaluating fairness metrics, and adjusting model weights or features to reduce bias.

Model Interpretability and Explainability: Use interpretable models that allow for better understanding of the decision-making process and provide explanations for the model's predictions. This transparency helps identify potential biases and address fairness concerns.

Evaluation and Monitoring:

Ongoing evaluation and monitoring are crucial to identify and address biases that may emerge during the deployment and usage of algorithms. Consider the following strategies:

Fairness Metrics: Define appropriate fairness metrics that capture the desired notions of fairness for the specific context. Evaluate the algorithm's performance against these metrics to ensure fairness throughout its lifecycle.

Bias and Error Analysis: Conduct thorough analysis of the algorithm's outputs to identify instances of bias or discriminatory patterns. Evaluate the impact of the algorithm's decisions across different subgroups to ensure fairness across all segments of the population.

User Feedback and Auditing: Encourage user feedback and incorporate external audits to detect biases and address fairness concerns. Engage with stakeholders to understand the impact of the algorithm on different groups and incorporate their perspectives in the decision-making process.

Ethical Considerations and Human Oversight:

While algorithmic approaches are important for addressing bias, human oversight and ethical considerations are equally crucial. Consider the following strategies:

Ethical Review Boards: Establish ethical review boards or committees to assess the potential biases and fairness implications of algorithmic systems. These boards can provide guidance, review algorithms, and ensure ethical decision-making.

Diversity and Inclusion in Development Teams: Foster diverse and inclusive development teams that bring different perspectives and experiences to the table. Diverse teams are better equipped to identify and mitigate bias, ensuring fairness in algorithm design and development.

Regulatory Compliance: Ensure compliance with relevant regulations and guidelines, such as anti-discrimination laws or data protection regulations. Stay informed about emerging regulatory frameworks that address algorithmic bias and fairness.

Continuous Learning and Improvement: Embrace a culture of continuous learning and improvement. Stay updated with the latest research, best practices, and advancements in addressing bias and fairness. Foster collaboration and knowledge sharing among data scientists and researchers working on these issues.

In conclusion, addressing bias and promoting fairness in algorithms is a crucial aspect of ethical data science practices. By focusing on diverse and representative data collection, careful preprocessing, bias-aware model training, fairness evaluation, ongoing monitoring, human oversight, and regulatory compliance, organizations can mitigate bias, promote fairness, and ensure that algorithms contribute to equitable decision-making processes. Striving for fairness in algorithms fosters trust, protects individuals' rights, and upholds ethical principles in data-driven decision-making.

Ensuring Ethical Use of Data

In today's data-driven world, it is essential for organizations to prioritize the ethical use of data. Ethical considerations encompass various aspects, including data privacy, consent, transparency, fairness, accountability, and societal impact. This section explores the key strategies and practices for ensuring the ethical use of data.

Data Privacy and Consent:

Data privacy is a fundamental aspect of ethical data use. Organizations must prioritize the protection of individuals' personal information. Consider the following strategies:

Data Protection Policies: Establish clear policies and procedures for data protection, outlining how personal data should be collected, stored, processed, and shared. Ensure compliance with relevant data protection regulations, such as the General Data Protection Regulation (GDPR) or the California Consumer Privacy Act (CCPA).

Informed Consent: Obtain informed consent from individuals before collecting and using their personal data. Clearly communicate the purpose of data collection, the types of data being collected, how it will be used, and any third parties involved. Allow individuals to exercise their right to withdraw consent or request the deletion of their data.

Privacy by Design: Incorporate privacy considerations from the early stages of data projects. Implement privacy-enhancing technologies, anonymization techniques, and data minimization practices to minimize the collection and storage of personally identifiable information.

Transparency and Explainability:

Transparency is crucial for ensuring the ethical use of data. Organizations should strive to be transparent about their data practices and decision-making processes. Consider the following strategies:

Clear Data Policies: Clearly communicate data policies, including data collection practices, data processing methods, and the purposes for which the data will be used. Make these policies easily accessible to individuals through privacy notices or data protection statements.

Explainability of Algorithms: Ensure that algorithms used for data analysis or decision-making are explainable. Provide clear explanations of the logic, inputs, and outputs of the algorithms to allow individuals to understand how their data is being used.

Auditability and Documentation: Maintain detailed records and documentation of data processing activities, including the sources of data, the steps taken for data transformation, and the decisions made based on the data. This documentation aids in accountability and transparency.

Fairness and Avoidance of Bias:

Promoting fairness and avoiding bias in data analysis and decision-making is crucial. Consider the following strategies:

Bias Detection and Mitigation: Regularly assess data and algorithms for potential biases. Use techniques such as fairness metrics, bias testing, and impact assessments to identify and mitigate biases that may arise during data collection, preprocessing, modeling, or decision-making processes.

Diverse and Representative Data: Ensure that the data used for analysis represents the diversity of the population. Collect data from various sources and strive to include underrepresented groups to avoid bias and ensure fairness.

Regular Evaluation and Monitoring: Continuously evaluate the impact of data analysis and decision-making processes on different groups. Monitor for disparate impacts, unintended consequences, and potential biases. Take corrective actions when biases or unfair outcomes are identified.

Responsible Data Sharing:

Responsible data sharing involves ensuring that data is shared securely, ethically, and with proper consent. Consider the following strategies:

Data Anonymization and Aggregation: Before sharing data, anonymize or aggregate it to protect individuals' privacy and prevent re-identification. Remove or modify personally identifiable information to minimize the risk of data breaches or unauthorized access.

Data Sharing Agreements: Establish clear data sharing agreements with third parties that outline the purposes, limitations, and safeguards for data usage. Include provisions to ensure that shared data is used ethically, securely, and in compliance with relevant regulations.

Secure Data Infrastructure: Implement robust data security measures to protect data during sharing. This includes encryption, access controls, secure data transfer protocols, and regular security audits to safeguard against unauthorized access or breaches.

Ethical Use of Artificial Intelligence (AI) and Machine Learning (ML):

AI and ML technologies pose unique ethical challenges. Consider the following strategies:

Algorithmic Fairness: Develop AI and ML models that are designed to be fair and unbiased. Incorporate fairness metrics, conduct bias testing, and implement techniques such as equal opportunity or demographic parity to ensure fairness.

Human Oversight and Accountability: Maintain human oversight and accountability in AI and ML systems. Avoid fully automated decision-making processes that lack human intervention and review. Ensure that decisions made by AI and ML systems are transparent and explainable.

Ethical AI Frameworks: Adopt ethical AI frameworks and guidelines, such as those developed by organizations like the Partnership on AI, IEEE, or the

European Commission. These frameworks provide guidance on the responsible and ethical use of AI and ML technologies.

Continuous Education and Ethical Awareness:

Promoting ethical data use requires continuous education and awareness among employees and stakeholders. Consider the following strategies:

Ethical Training Programs: Provide comprehensive training programs on ethical data use, data protection, privacy, and responsible decision-making. Educate employees about the ethical implications of data collection, analysis, and usage.

Ethical Guidelines and Codes of Conduct: Develop and communicate clear ethical guidelines and codes of conduct that outline the expected behaviors and practices related to data use. Encourage employees to adhere to these guidelines and ensure a culture of ethical data use within the organization.

Stakeholder Engagement: Engage with stakeholders, including customers, partners, and the broader community, to understand their expectations, concerns, and feedback regarding the ethical use of data. Incorporate their perspectives in decision-making processes.

In conclusion, ensuring the ethical use of data is crucial for maintaining trust, protecting individuals' privacy, promoting fairness, and avoiding unintended negative consequences. By prioritizing data privacy and consent, transparency, fairness, responsible data sharing, ethical use of AI and ML technologies, continuous education, and stakeholder engagement, organizations can uphold ethical data practices and foster a culture of responsible data use. Ethical data use not only protects individuals' rights but also contributes to positive societal impacts and sustainable business practices.

Promoting Transparency and Accountability

Transparency and accountability are key principles that underpin ethical data practices. Organizations that prioritize transparency and accountability build trust with stakeholders, demonstrate responsible behavior, and ensure that their actions align with ethical standards. This section explores the strategies and practices for promoting transparency and accountability in the context of data-driven decision-making.

Clear Communication of Data Practices:

Transparency begins with clear and comprehensive communication about an organization's data practices. Consider the following strategies:

Data Policies and Privacy Notices: Develop and communicate data policies that outline how data is collected, stored, processed, and shared. Provide privacy notices or data protection statements that clearly explain the purposes and legal basis for data collection, the types of data collected, and how individuals can exercise their rights.

Plain Language Explanations: Avoid using technical jargon or complex language when communicating about data practices. Use plain language to ensure that individuals can easily understand how their data is being used and what choices they have.

Data Usage Examples: Provide practical examples of how data is used within the organization. This helps individuals grasp the tangible implications of data usage and promotes transparency about the value and benefits derived from data-driven decision-making.

Access to Personal Data:

Granting individuals access to their personal data is a crucial aspect of transparency and accountability. Consider the following strategies:

Data Subject Access Requests: Establish processes for individuals to request access to their personal data held by the organization. Respond to these requests promptly and provide individuals with a copy of their data in a commonly used format.

User-Friendly Data Portals: Develop user-friendly online portals where individuals can easily access and manage their personal data. Such portals provide transparency and empower individuals to exercise control over their data.

Data Retention Policies: Clearly communicate the organization's data retention policies, specifying how long personal data is retained and the criteria used for retention. This ensures that individuals are aware of how their data is handled and for how long it will be retained.

Explainability of Algorithms and Decision-Making Processes:

Promoting transparency in algorithmic decision-making is crucial to build trust and ensure accountability. Consider the following strategies:

Explainable AI and ML Models: Develop algorithms and machine learning models that are explainable and provide clear insights into the factors influencing decisions. This allows individuals to understand how decisions are made and detect any biases or unfair treatment.

Model Documentation: Maintain documentation that explains the logic, inputs, and outputs of algorithms used in decision-making processes. This documentation should be easily accessible to individuals and external auditors, promoting transparency and accountability.

Fairness Assessments: Conduct regular fairness assessments to identify potential biases or disparate impacts in algorithmic decision-making. Assess the impact of algorithms on different subgroups to ensure fairness and address any disparities that arise.

Data Governance and Auditing:

Robust data governance frameworks and regular audits promote accountability and transparency. Consider the following strategies:

Data Governance Policies: Establish clear data governance policies that outline roles, responsibilities, and accountability mechanisms for data management and decision-making processes.

Regular Data Audits: Conduct regular audits of data practices, processes, and decision-making to identify any gaps or areas for improvement. These audits help ensure compliance with ethical standards, regulations, and internal policies.

External Audits: Consider engaging external auditors or independent organizations to conduct audits of data practices. External audits provide an objective assessment of an organization's transparency and adherence to ethical data practices.

Stakeholder Engagement and Feedback:

Engaging with stakeholders and seeking feedback is crucial for transparency and accountability. Consider the following strategies:

Open Channels of Communication: Establish open channels for individuals, customers, employees, and external stakeholders to provide feedback, voice concerns, or seek clarification on data practices. Encourage active engagement and respond promptly to inquiries.

Data Advisory Boards: Create data advisory boards that include representatives from different stakeholder groups. These boards can provide input, oversight, and guidance on data practices, ensuring that decisions align with stakeholder expectations and ethical standards.

Public Reporting: Consider publishing reports or dashboards that provide insights into data practices, such as data usage statistics, data protection measures, or information on data breaches. Public reporting demonstrates a commitment to transparency and holds organizations accountable to the public.

Education and Training:

Educating employees and stakeholders about the importance of transparency and accountability is essential. Consider the following strategies:

Data Ethics Training: Provide regular training programs on data ethics, privacy, and responsible data practices. Raise awareness among employees about the importance of transparency, accountability, and the ethical implications of their work.

Embedding Transparency in Organizational Culture: Foster a culture that values transparency and accountability. Encourage employees to proactively share information, seek feedback, and embrace a data-driven decision-making process that aligns with ethical principles.

In conclusion, promoting transparency and accountability in data-driven decision-making is crucial for building trust, maintaining ethical standards, and ensuring responsible behavior. By adopting strategies such as clear communication of data practices, granting individuals access to their personal data, explainability of algorithms, robust data governance, stakeholder engagement, and education and training, organizations can foster a culture of transparency, accountability, and ethical data practices. Transparency and accountability not only benefit individuals but also contribute to the overall credibility and reputation of organizations in the digital age.

CHAPTER 13: DATA SCIENCE IN MARKETING AND SALES

Chapter 13 focuses on the application of data science in the field of marketing and sales. With the proliferation of digital technologies and the abundance of customer data, organizations have the opportunity to leverage data science techniques to gain insights, make data-driven decisions, and enhance marketing and sales strategies. This chapter explores the key concepts, techniques, and benefits of data science in marketing and sales.

Importance of Data Science in Marketing and Sales:

Data science has revolutionized the marketing and sales landscape by enabling organizations to derive valuable insights from large volumes of data. It empowers businesses to understand customer behavior, identify trends, optimize marketing campaigns, personalize customer experiences, and drive revenue growth. Data science provides a competitive advantage by helping organizations make informed decisions based on data-driven insights.

Customer Segmentation and Targeting:

Data science plays a crucial role in customer segmentation and targeting, allowing organizations to divide their customer base into distinct segments based on relevant characteristics. Consider the following:

Clustering Techniques: Apply clustering algorithms to group customers with similar traits, behaviors, or preferences. This enables targeted marketing campaigns tailored to the needs and interests of specific customer segments.

Predictive Modeling: Utilize predictive modeling techniques, such as regression or machine learning algorithms, to identify customer attributes that contribute to desired outcomes, such as purchase likelihood or customer lifetime value. This enables targeted marketing efforts to high-potential customers.

Personalization: Leverage data science techniques to personalize marketing messages and experiences for individual customers. By analyzing historical data and customer behavior, organizations can deliver relevant and customized content, recommendations, and offers.

Customer Churn Prediction and Retention:

Data science helps organizations identify customers who are likely to churn and implement strategies to retain them. Consider the following:

Churn Prediction Models: Build machine learning models that analyze customer data to predict the likelihood of churn. These models consider factors such as customer behavior, engagement patterns, purchase history, and demographic information to identify at-risk customers.

Retention Strategies: Develop targeted retention strategies based on churn predictions. This can include personalized offers, loyalty programs, proactive customer support, or engagement campaigns to re-engage and retain customers.

Customer Lifetime Value (CLV) Analysis: Calculate CLV to understand the long-term value of customers. This information helps prioritize marketing and sales efforts, focusing on high-value customers and optimizing resource allocation.

Marketing Campaign Optimization:

Data science enables organizations to optimize marketing campaigns by analyzing data and measuring campaign performance. Consider the following:

A/B Testing: Utilize controlled experiments, such as A/B testing, to compare the effectiveness of different marketing strategies, messages, or channels. Data science techniques help analyze the results and identify the most effective approach.

Attribution Modeling: Attribute the impact of marketing activities to conversions or sales using attribution modeling techniques. This provides insights into the effectiveness of each marketing channel or touchpoint in the customer journey, helping allocate resources efficiently.

Predictive Analytics: Leverage predictive analytics to forecast the outcomes of marketing campaigns, such as customer response rates, conversion rates, or revenue. This enables organizations to optimize campaign parameters, targeting, and messaging.

Pricing Optimization:

Data science techniques support pricing optimization strategies, allowing organizations to set optimal prices for products or services. Consider the following:

Demand Forecasting: Use data science models to forecast customer demand based on historical data, market conditions, and external factors. This information helps organizations set prices that maximize revenue while considering factors such as demand elasticity and market competition.

Dynamic Pricing: Implement dynamic pricing strategies that adjust prices based on real-time market dynamics, demand, or inventory levels. Data science techniques enable organizations to optimize pricing decisions dynamically.

Price Sensitivity Analysis: Analyze customer behavior and responses to price changes to understand price sensitivity. This information guides pricing strategies and helps determine optimal price points for different customer segments.

Sentiment Analysis and Customer Feedback:

Data science techniques can be applied to analyze customer sentiment and feedback, providing valuable insights for marketing and sales strategies. Consider the following:

Sentiment Analysis: Use natural language processing and machine learning techniques to analyze customer reviews, social media posts, or customer service interactions. Sentiment analysis provides insights into customer perceptions, preferences, and areas for improvement.

Social Listening: Monitor social media platforms and online forums to understand customer sentiments, trends, and discussions related to products or brands. This information can be used to adapt marketing messages, address customer concerns, or identify opportunities.

Voice of Customer Analysis: Analyze customer feedback and surveys to identify key themes, satisfaction levels, or areas where improvements can be made. Data science techniques enable organizations to derive actionable insights from unstructured customer feedback.

In conclusion, data science plays a vital role in marketing and sales, enabling organizations to leverage customer data, make data-driven decisions, and optimize marketing strategies. By applying data science techniques for customer segmentation, targeting, churn prediction, campaign optimization, pricing optimization, sentiment analysis, and customer feedback analysis, organizations can enhance customer experiences, increase customer retention, optimize marketing campaigns, and drive revenue growth. Embracing data science in marketing and sales empowers organizations to stay competitive in today's data-driven business landscape.

Personalizing Customer Experiences

Personalizing customer experiences is a strategic approach that focuses on tailoring interactions, products, and services to meet the specific needs, preferences, and expectations of individual customers. In today's digital age, organizations have access to vast amounts of customer data, allowing them to leverage data-driven techniques to deliver personalized experiences. This section explores the key strategies, benefits, and challenges of personalizing customer experiences.

Understanding Customer Needs and Preferences:

Personalization begins with gaining a deep understanding of customer needs, preferences, and behaviors. Consider the following strategies:

Customer Segmentation: Segment customers into distinct groups based on relevant characteristics such as demographics, behavior, preferences, or purchase history. This segmentation enables targeted and relevant personalization efforts for each group.

Customer Profiling: Develop comprehensive customer profiles by collecting and analyzing data from various touchpoints, including transactional data, browsing behavior, social media interactions, and customer feedback. These profiles help build a holistic view of each customer's preferences and behaviors.

Customer Journey Mapping: Map the customer’s journey to identify key touchpoints and interactions. Understand the customer's motivations, pain points, and expectations at each stage to deliver personalized experiences that address their specific needs.

Data-Driven Personalization:

Leveraging customer data is essential for effective personalization. Consider the following strategies:

Data Collection and Integration: Collect data from various sources, such as customer interactions, website analytics, CRM systems, social media, and third-party data providers. Integrate and centralize this data to create a unified customer view.

Predictive Analytics and Machine Learning: Utilize predictive analytics and machine learning techniques to analyze customer data and identify patterns, trends, and individual preferences. These techniques enable organizations to make data-driven predictions and recommendations for each customer.

Real-Time Data Analysis: Implement real-time data analysis capabilities to process customer data as it is generated. This enables immediate personalization of customer experiences, such as personalized product recommendations or tailored content.

Tailoring Products and Services:

Personalization extends beyond marketing messages and includes tailoring products and services to meet individual customer needs. Consider the following strategies:

Product Recommendations: Use collaborative filtering or recommendation algorithms to provide personalized product recommendations based on customer preferences, purchase history, and similarities with other customers. This enhances the customer's shopping experience and increases the likelihood of conversions.

Customized Offerings: Offer customization options that allow customers to personalize products or services based on their preferences. This can include customizable features, packaging, or pricing options that cater to individual needs.

Dynamic Pricing: Implement dynamic pricing strategies that adjust prices based on customer preferences, purchase history, or real-time market conditions. Dynamic pricing ensures that customers receive personalized pricing offers based on their unique characteristics and behaviors.

Personalized Marketing Communications:

Personalization in marketing communications involves delivering tailored messages to customers. Consider the following strategies:

Email Marketing: Utilize customer data to personalize email communications, such as using the customer's name, referencing past purchases, or recommending relevant products based on their preferences.

Behavioral Triggers: Set up behavioral triggers that automatically send targeted messages or offers based on specific customer actions or events. For example, sending a follow-up email after a customer abandons a cart or offering a discount on a customer's birthday.

Omni-Channel Personalization: Consistently personalize customer experiences across multiple channels, such as websites, mobile apps, social media, and physical stores. Ensure a seamless and consistent experience as customers interact with the brand across different touchpoints.

Privacy and Data Security:

Respecting customer privacy and maintaining data security are essential considerations in personalization efforts. Consider the following strategies:

Consent and Transparency: Obtain customer consent for data collection and ensure transparency by clearly communicating how customer data will be used. Provide options for customers to control the types of data collected and how it is used for personalization.

Data Security Measures: Implement robust data security measures to protect customer data from unauthorized access or breaches. This includes encryption, secure data storage, access controls, and regular security audits.

Compliance with Regulations: Adhere to data protection regulations, such as the General Data Protection Regulation (GDPR) or the California Consumer Privacy Act (CCPA). Ensure compliance with privacy laws and regulations governing data collection, usage, and storage.

Challenges and Considerations:

While personalization offers significant benefits, it also presents challenges that organizations need to address. Consider the following:

Data Quality and Integration: Ensure the accuracy, completeness, and reliability of customer data. Clean and integrate data from various sources to create a comprehensive and accurate customer profile.

Overpersonalization: Strive for a balance between personalization and avoiding overpersonalization. Respect customer boundaries and preferences to prevent personalization efforts from becoming intrusive or overwhelming.

Scalability: Develop systems and infrastructure that can handle the scalability requirements of personalization efforts. As the customer base grows, organizations need to ensure that personalization efforts can be effectively managed and scaled.

Ethical Considerations: Consider ethical implications in personalization efforts, such as the fair and unbiased treatment of customers, avoiding discriminatory practices, and respecting individuals' privacy rights.

In conclusion, personalizing customer experiences is a powerful strategy for organizations to enhance customer satisfaction, drive customer loyalty, and improve business outcomes. By understanding customer needs, leveraging customer data, tailoring products and services, delivering personalized marketing communications, and ensuring privacy and data security, organizations can create meaningful and engaging experiences that resonate with individual customers. Personalization establishes a competitive advantage, strengthens customer relationships, and positions organizations as customer-centric in today's highly competitive marketplace.

Optimizing Marketing Campaigns

Marketing campaigns play a vital role in driving business growth and reaching target audiences. Optimizing marketing campaigns involves continuously improving their effectiveness and efficiency to maximize return on investment (ROI) and achieve desired business outcomes. This section explores the key strategies, techniques, and benefits of optimizing marketing campaigns.

Define Clear Goals and Key Performance Indicators (KPIs):

To optimize marketing campaigns, it is crucial to establish clear goals and KPIs that align with overall business objectives. Consider the following:

SMART Goals: Set Specific, Measurable, Achievable, Relevant, and Time-bound (SMART) goals that define the desired outcomes of the campaign. For example, increasing website traffic by 20% or improving conversion rates by 15%.

Key Performance Indicators: Identify relevant KPIs to measure the success of the campaign. These may include metrics such as click-through rates (CTR), conversion rates, cost per acquisition (CPA), return on ad spend (ROAS), or customer lifetime value (CLV).

Audience Segmentation and Targeting:

Effective audience segmentation and targeting are crucial for optimizing marketing campaigns. Consider the following strategies:

Customer Segmentation: Divide the target audience into distinct segments based on relevant characteristics such as demographics, behavior, preferences, or purchase history. This enables personalized messaging and tailored marketing efforts for each segment.

Persona Development: Create detailed buyer personas that represent ideal customers within each segment. Develop an in-depth understanding of their needs, pain points, motivations, and preferences to craft targeted messages and offers.

Custom Audiences: Leverage custom audience targeting options on advertising platforms to reach specific segments or groups based on existing customer data, such as email lists or website visitors.

Data-Driven Decision Making:

Optimizing marketing campaigns requires data-driven decision making. Consider the following strategies:

Data Collection and Analysis: Collect and analyze relevant data from various sources, including website analytics, CRM systems, social media, and advertising platforms. Gain insights into customer behavior, campaign performance, and market trends.

A/B Testing: Conduct A/B tests to compare different elements of the campaign, such as ad variations, landing page designs, or call-to-action buttons. Analyze the results to identify the most effective elements and refine campaign strategies accordingly.

Attribution Modeling: Utilize attribution modeling techniques to assign credit to different marketing touchpoints along the customer journey. This helps understand the contribution of each channel or tactic in driving conversions and optimize resource allocation.

Continuous Monitoring and Optimization:

Optimizing marketing campaigns requires continuous monitoring and iterative improvements. Consider the following strategies:

Real-Time Analytics: Implement real-time analytics to monitor campaign performance and track key metrics. Identify opportunities for optimization and make data-driven adjustments on an ongoing basis.

Conversion Rate Optimization (CRO): Focus on improving conversion rates at each stage of the customer journey. Test and optimize landing pages, forms, checkout processes, and other elements to maximize conversions.

Campaign Iteration: Regularly review campaign performance, analyze data, and iterate based on insights. Test new ideas, refine targeting strategies, and adjust messaging to improve campaign effectiveness.

Personalization and Relevance:

Delivering personalized and relevant content is crucial for optimizing marketing campaigns. Consider the following strategies:

Dynamic Content: Utilize dynamic content capabilities to deliver personalized messages and offers based on customer segments, preferences, or behaviors. Tailor content to match the interests and needs of individual customers.

Marketing Automation: Implement marketing automation tools to deliver targeted messages at the right time and through the right channels. Automate personalized email sequences, trigger-based campaigns, and personalized recommendations.

Behavioral Targeting: Use behavioral targeting techniques to identify customer intent and preferences based on their online behavior. Serve relevant ads or content based on their browsing history, search queries, or previous interactions with the brand.

Campaign Performance Tracking and Reporting:

Effectively tracking and reporting campaign performance is essential for optimization. Consider the following strategies:

Marketing Analytics Dashboards: Develop dashboards that provide real-time insights into campaign performance and KPIs. Monitor metrics, track progress towards goals, and identify areas requiring improvement.

Customized Reports: Generate customized reports that highlight key performance metrics, trends, and actionable insights. Share these reports with stakeholders to facilitate data-driven decision making and align campaign efforts with business objectives.

Attribution Reporting: Use attribution models to generate reports that demonstrate the impact of different marketing channels and touchpoints on campaign performance. Attribute conversions and revenue to each marketing tactic accurately.

In conclusion, optimizing marketing campaigns is a continuous process that involves defining clear goals, segmenting and targeting the audience, leveraging data-driven decision making, continuous monitoring and optimization, personalization, and effective tracking and reporting. By implementing these strategies, organizations can improve the effectiveness and efficiency of their marketing campaigns, maximize ROI, drive customer engagement, and achieve desired business outcomes. Optimization allows organizations to refine their marketing strategies based on insights and deliver personalized, relevant, and impactful campaigns to their target audience.

Forecasting Demand and Sales

Accurate forecasting of demand and sales is essential for organizations to effectively plan production, manage inventory, optimize resources, and make informed business decisions. By using historical data, market trends, and advanced analytical techniques, organizations can predict future demand and sales patterns. This section explores the key strategies, techniques, and benefits of forecasting demand and sales.

Data Collection and Analysis:

The first step in forecasting demand and sales is collecting and analyzing relevant data. Consider the following strategies:

Historical Data: Gather historical sales data, including information on product sales, customer behavior, market trends, and external factors that may influence demand. Ensure the data is accurate, comprehensive, and representative of the business's operations.

Market Research: Conduct market research to identify trends, consumer preferences, competitive dynamics, and other factors that impact demand. Collect data on market size, customer demographics, purchasing behavior, and industry-specific indicators.

Data Integration: Integrate data from various sources, including sales records, customer databases, market research reports, social media, web analytics, and other relevant sources. Consolidating data provides a holistic view and improves the accuracy of demand forecasting models.

Time-Series Analysis:

Time-series analysis is a widely used technique for demand and sales forecasting. It involves analyzing historical data to identify patterns, trends, and seasonality. Consider the following techniques:

Moving Averages: Calculate moving averages to smooth out fluctuations and identify underlying trends. Simple moving averages or weighted moving averages can be used to forecast future sales based on historical averages.

Exponential Smoothing: Exponential smoothing techniques assign different weights to historical data points, giving more importance to recent observations. Models like simple exponential smoothing, Holt's linear exponential smoothing, or Holt-Winters' method can be applied for more accurate forecasts.

ARIMA Models: Autoregressive Integrated Moving Average (ARIMA) models capture the temporal dependence and seasonality in time series data. ARIMA models are useful for capturing complex patterns and predicting future demand.

Regression Analysis:

Regression analysis is another powerful technique for demand and sales forecasting. It identifies relationships between demand/sales and various explanatory variables. Consider the following techniques:

Simple Linear Regression: Use linear regression to analyze the relationship between demand/sales and a single explanatory variable, such as price, advertising expenditure, or promotional activities. The model can then be used to forecast sales based on these variables.

Multiple Regression: Extend the analysis to multiple explanatory variables, considering factors such as price, marketing spend, seasonality, economic indicators, or competitor activities. Multiple regression models provide a more comprehensive understanding of the drivers of demand and enable more accurate forecasting.

Machine Learning and Artificial Intelligence:

Machine learning and artificial intelligence (AI) techniques can be leveraged to forecast demand and sales. These methods can handle complex data patterns and adapt to changing market dynamics. Consider the following techniques:

Neural Networks: Neural networks can learn complex relationships between demand/sales and multiple variables. They can capture nonlinear patterns and seasonality in data, making them suitable for forecasting tasks.

Random Forests: Random forests use an ensemble of decision trees to analyze data and make predictions. They can handle high-dimensional datasets, identify important variables, and provide accurate forecasts.

Support Vector Regression (SVR): SVR is a supervised learning algorithm that can capture nonlinear relationships between demand/sales and explanatory variables. SVR models can handle large datasets and high-dimensional feature spaces.

Incorporating External Factors:

Forecasting demand and sales should consider external factors that can influence demand patterns. Consider the following strategies:

Economic Indicators: Include relevant economic indicators such as GDP growth, inflation rates, interest rates, or consumer confidence indices. These factors provide insights into the overall economic environment and consumer spending behavior.

Seasonality: Account for seasonal patterns, such as holidays, weather conditions, or cultural events that impact demand. Seasonal adjustments ensure accurate forecasts by considering historical patterns and anticipated fluctuations.

Marketing and Promotional Activities: Consider the impact of marketing campaigns, advertising expenditure, promotions, or pricing strategies on demand and sales. These factors directly influence consumer behavior and can significantly impact demand forecasts.

Continuous Monitoring and Evaluation:

Forecasting demand and sales is an ongoing process that requires continuous monitoring and evaluation. Consider the following strategies:

Monitor Actual Sales: Continuously track actual sales data to compare with forecasted values. Regularly update forecasting models based on new data to improve accuracy.

Forecast Accuracy Metrics: Use forecast accuracy metrics, such as mean absolute percentage error (MAPE), mean absolute error (MAE), or root mean squared error (RMSE), to evaluate the performance of forecasting models. Assessing accuracy helps identify areas for improvement and fine-tune forecasting techniques.

Incorporate Feedback Loops: Incorporate feedback from sales teams, customers, and other stakeholders to refine forecasting models. Feedback provides valuable insights into changing market conditions, customer preferences, and emerging trends.

In conclusion, forecasting demand and sales plays a critical role in effective business planning and decision making. By employing data-driven techniques, such as time-series analysis, regression analysis, machine learning, and considering external factors, organizations can accurately predict future demand patterns. Accurate demand forecasts help optimize production, inventory management, resource allocation, and marketing strategies, resulting in improved customer satisfaction, reduced costs, and increased profitability. Continuous monitoring and evaluation ensure that forecasting models remain accurate and relevant in dynamic market environments.

CHAPTER 14: DATA SCIENCE IN OPERATIONS AND SUPPLY CHAIN

Chapter 14 delves into the applications of data science in operations and supply chain management. Operations and supply chain play a crucial role in organizations' overall efficiency, cost-effectiveness, and customer satisfaction. By leveraging data science techniques, organizations can optimize their operations, improve supply chain processes, and drive operational excellence. This chapter explores the key concepts, strategies, and benefits of data science in operations and supply chain management.

Importance of Data Science in Operations and Supply Chain:

Data science offers valuable insights and predictive capabilities that can significantly enhance operations and supply chain management. By analyzing vast amounts of data, organizations can identify bottlenecks, streamline processes, reduce costs, improve forecasting accuracy, and enhance overall operational efficiency. Data science empowers organizations to make data-driven decisions, optimize resource allocation, and respond quickly to changing market dynamics.

Demand Forecasting and Planning:

Data science plays a critical role in demand forecasting and planning, enabling organizations to align their production and inventory levels with customer demand. Consider the following strategies:

Historical Data Analysis: Analyze historical sales data, market trends, customer behavior, and external factors to forecast future demand accurately. Data science techniques, such as time-series analysis, regression, or machine learning, can identify patterns, seasonality, and demand drivers.

Collaborative Forecasting: Involve key stakeholders, such as sales teams, marketing, and customers, in the demand forecasting process. Leverage collaborative tools and techniques to gather insights and improve the accuracy of forecasts.

Demand Sensing: Utilize real-time data, such as point-of-sale data, social media trends, or weather information, to sense and respond quickly to changes in demand. Data science enables organizations to adjust production and inventory levels in real-time.

Inventory Optimization:

Data science enables organizations to optimize inventory levels, reduce costs, and minimize stockouts. Consider the following strategies:

Inventory Forecasting: Use data science techniques to forecast inventory requirements based on demand forecasts, lead times, seasonality, and other relevant factors. Accurate inventory forecasting helps prevent stockouts or excess inventory.

Demand Segmentation: Segment customer demand based on factors such as product preferences, order patterns, or geography. By understanding different demand patterns, organizations can optimize inventory allocation and ensure availability of high-demand products.

Just-in-Time (JIT) Inventory: Apply data science models to implement just-in-time inventory practices. By synchronizing production with demand, organizations can minimize inventory holding costs while meeting customer requirements.

Supply Chain Optimization:

Data science techniques play a vital role in optimizing supply chain processes, ensuring efficient and reliable delivery of products or services. Consider the following strategies:

Supply Chain Analytics: Utilize data analytics to gain insights into supply chain performance, identify bottlenecks, and streamline processes. Analyze data related to suppliers, transportation, warehousing, and order fulfillment to improve efficiency and reduce costs.

Supplier Performance Analysis: Evaluate supplier performance using data-driven metrics, such as on-time delivery, quality, and responsiveness. This enables organizations to identify top-performing suppliers and establish strategic partnerships.

Supply Chain Risk Management: Apply data science techniques to assess and mitigate supply chain risks. Analyze historical data, market trends, and external factors to identify potential disruptions and develop contingency plans.

Predictive Maintenance:

Data science enables organizations to implement predictive maintenance practices, ensuring the reliability and uptime of critical assets. Consider the following strategies:

Sensor Data Analysis: Utilize sensor data from machinery and equipment to monitor performance, detect anomalies, and predict maintenance needs. Data science techniques, such as anomaly detection, machine learning, or predictive modeling, can identify signs of equipment failure before it occurs.

Condition Monitoring: Implement condition monitoring techniques to continuously track asset performance and health. By analyzing data related to temperature, vibration, noise, or other sensor measurements, organizations can proactively identify maintenance requirements.

Predictive Analytics: Leverage historical maintenance data and equipment performance data to develop predictive maintenance models. These models can optimize maintenance schedules, reduce unplanned downtime, and extend asset lifecycles.

Continuous Improvement and Optimization:

Data science enables organizations to drive continuous improvement and optimization in operations and supply chain management. Consider the following strategies:

Performance Metrics and Dashboards: Define key performance metrics and develop dashboards to monitor operational performance in real-time. Visualize data to identify areas of improvement, track progress, and facilitate data-driven decision making.

Process Optimization: Apply data science techniques, such as process mining, optimization algorithms, or simulation modeling, to identify process inefficiencies and optimize workflow. Improve process cycle times, resource allocation, or task sequencing based on data-driven insights.

Root Cause Analysis: Utilize data analysis and statistical techniques to conduct root cause analysis for operational issues or supply chain disruptions. Identify underlying factors contributing to problems and implement targeted improvements.

In conclusion, data science plays a crucial role in optimizing operations and supply chain management. By leveraging data-driven insights, organizations can enhance demand forecasting, optimize inventory levels, streamline supply chain processes, implement predictive maintenance, and drive continuous improvement. The application of data science techniques helps organizations improve operational efficiency, reduce costs, increase customer satisfaction, and maintain a competitive edge in the market. Embracing data science in operations and supply chain management empowers organizations to make informed decisions, optimize resource allocation, and adapt to evolving market conditions.

Improving Supply Chain Efficiency

Supply chain efficiency is crucial for organizations to deliver products or services in a timely, cost-effective, and customer-centric manner. In today's competitive business landscape, organizations are constantly seeking ways to optimize their supply chain processes and enhance overall efficiency. This section explores key strategies, techniques, and benefits of improving supply chain efficiency.

Supply Chain Visibility:

Achieving supply chain visibility is the foundation for improving efficiency. It involves gaining real-time insights into the movement of goods, inventory levels, and process performance. Consider the following strategies:

Data Integration: Integrate data from various sources, including suppliers, logistics partners, inventory systems, and production facilities. Create a centralized platform or system that consolidates data and provides a holistic view of the supply chain.

Track and Trace Technologies: Implement technologies such as RFID (Radio Frequency Identification), barcodes, or IoT (Internet of Things) sensors to track and trace products throughout the supply chain. Real-time tracking enables organizations to monitor inventory levels, identify bottlenecks, and proactively address issues.

Collaborative Platforms: Utilize collaborative platforms that allow stakeholders, including suppliers, logistics providers, and customers, to access and share relevant supply chain information. Collaboration fosters transparency, improves communication, and facilitates coordination among all parties.

Demand Planning and Forecasting:

Accurate demand planning and forecasting are crucial for optimizing inventory levels and meeting customer requirements. Consider the following strategies:

Data Analytics: Utilize historical sales data, market trends, customer behavior, and external factors to develop accurate demand forecasts. Data analytics techniques, such as time-series analysis, regression, or machine learning, help identify patterns, seasonality, and demand drivers.

Collaboration with Customers: Engage with customers to gather insights on demand patterns, preferences, and upcoming promotions or events. Collaborative forecasting allows organizations to align production and inventory levels with customer demand.

Demand Sensing: Leverage real-time data, such as point-of-sale data, social media trends, or market intelligence, to sense changes in demand quickly. Data science techniques enable organizations to respond proactively by adjusting production plans and inventory levels.

Lean and Agile Supply Chain Principles:

Adopting lean and agile principles helps organizations streamline supply chain processes and respond effectively to changing market dynamics. Consider the following strategies:

Lean Manufacturing: Implement lean principles, such as reducing waste, optimizing processes, and improving flow, to minimize lead times, eliminate non-value-added activities, and enhance overall efficiency.

Agile Supply Chain Network: Develop an agile supply chain network that can quickly adapt to market changes and customer demands. This includes flexible manufacturing capabilities, responsive logistics, and dynamic sourcing strategies.

Continuous Improvement: Foster a culture of continuous improvement by encouraging employee involvement, implementing Kaizen methodologies, and regularly reviewing and optimizing supply chain processes. Continuous improvement drives efficiency gains over time.

Inventory Optimization:

Efficient inventory management is critical for reducing costs and ensuring product availability. Consider the following strategies:

ABC Analysis: Classify inventory items based on their value and usage frequency using the ABC analysis technique. This helps organizations prioritize inventory management efforts and allocate resources effectively.

Safety Stock Optimization: Use statistical models, such as the service level method or demand variability analysis, to optimize safety stock levels. This ensures an appropriate buffer to handle demand variability while minimizing excess inventory.

Just-in-Time (JIT) Principles: Implement JIT principles to synchronize production with demand. By reducing lead times, minimizing work-in-progress inventory, and optimizing production schedules, organizations can achieve greater efficiency and cost savings.

Supplier Relationship Management:

Effective supplier relationship management enhances supply chain efficiency and resilience. Consider the following strategies:

Supplier Collaboration: Collaborate closely with key suppliers to share information, align production plans, and improve demand forecasting accuracy. This enables organizations to optimize inventory levels, reduce lead times, and enhance responsiveness.

Supplier Performance Monitoring: Establish performance metrics and regularly evaluate suppliers based on criteria such as quality, delivery reliability, and responsiveness. This helps identify top-performing suppliers and enables organizations to establish strategic partnerships.

Supplier Integration: Integrate suppliers into the supply chain processes by providing them with real-time access to demand forecasts, production plans, or inventory levels. This fosters collaboration, improves communication, and enhances supply chain visibility.

Technology Adoption:

Leveraging technology solutions can significantly improve supply chain efficiency. Consider the following strategies:

Supply Chain Management Systems: Implement integrated supply chain management systems that automate processes, provide real-time visibility, and facilitate data-driven decision making. These systems streamline operations and improve collaboration.

Warehouse Management Systems (WMS): Utilize WMS to optimize warehouse operations, including inventory management, order fulfillment, and labor allocation. WMS solutions enable efficient space utilization, accurate picking, and streamlined workflows.

Transportation Management Systems (TMS): Implement TMS to optimize transportation operations, route planning, and carrier selection. TMS solutions enhance shipment visibility, improve delivery times, and reduce transportation costs.

Advanced Analytics and Artificial Intelligence: Utilize advanced analytics and AI techniques to analyze large volumes of supply chain data, identify patterns, detect anomalies, and predict future demand or supply disruptions. These techniques help organizations make proactive decisions and optimize supply chain processes.

In conclusion, improving supply chain efficiency is essential for organizations to remain competitive and meet customer expectations. By adopting strategies such as enhancing supply chain visibility, improving demand planning, embracing lean and agile principles, optimizing inventory levels, managing supplier relationships, and leveraging technology solutions, organizations can streamline operations, reduce costs, and enhance customer satisfaction. Efficient supply chain management enables organizations to respond quickly to market changes, mitigate risks, and deliver products or services in a timely and cost-effective manner.

Optimizing Inventory Management

Effective inventory management is crucial for organizations to maintain the right balance between supply and demand, reduce costs, and ensure customer satisfaction. Optimizing inventory management involves strategic planning, efficient processes, and leveraging data-driven techniques to optimize inventory levels, improve accuracy, and enhance overall operational efficiency. This section explores key strategies, techniques, and benefits of optimizing inventory management.

Demand Forecasting and Planning:

Accurate demand forecasting is the foundation of inventory management optimization. Consider the following strategies:

Historical Data Analysis: Analyze historical sales data, market trends, customer behavior, and external factors to develop accurate demand forecasts. Utilize data science techniques, such as time-series analysis, regression, or machine learning, to identify patterns, seasonality, and demand drivers.

Collaboration with Customers: Engage with customers to gather insights on demand patterns, preferences, and upcoming promotions or events. Collaborative forecasting allows organizations to align production and inventory levels with customer demand.

Demand Sensing: Leverage real-time data, such as point-of-sale data, social media trends, or market intelligence, to sense changes in demand quickly. Data science techniques enable organizations to respond proactively by adjusting production plans and inventory levels.

ABC Analysis and Inventory Classification:

ABC analysis is a widely used technique to classify inventory items based on their value and usage frequency. Consider the following strategies:

ABC Classification: Categorize inventory items into three groups: A, B, and C, based on their value. A-items represent high-value items that contribute significantly to revenue, B-items are moderately important, and C-items have lower value and usage frequency.

Differentiated Management Approach: Apply different management approaches for each inventory category. A-items require closer monitoring and tighter control due to their higher value, while C-items can be managed with less attention.

Optimal Inventory Policies: Develop optimal inventory policies for each category based on factors such as lead time, demand variability, or service level targets. This ensures that resources are allocated efficiently, and inventory levels are optimized based on the criticality and demand characteristics of each item.

Safety Stock Optimization:

Safety stock is a buffer inventory held to mitigate the risk of stockouts. Optimizing safety stock levels helps organizations reduce costs while ensuring adequate availability. Consider the following strategies:

Statistical Analysis: Utilize statistical techniques, such as demand variability analysis, to understand the demand patterns and calculate appropriate safety stock levels. Analyzing historical demand variability helps strike a balance between customer service levels and inventory holding costs.

Service Level Optimization: Determine the desired service level, which represents the probability of meeting customer demand without stockouts. Calculate safety stock levels that align with the desired service level for each inventory item.

Demand Collaboration: Collaborate with customers, suppliers, and other stakeholders to gather insights and align safety stock levels with customer demand patterns, lead times, and supply chain risks. Sharing information helps reduce uncertainty and optimize safety stock levels.

Inventory Turnover and Lead Time Reduction:

Improving inventory turnover and reducing lead times are effective ways to optimize inventory management. Consider the following strategies:

Supplier Collaboration: Collaborate closely with key suppliers to streamline procurement processes, reduce lead times, and improve supplier performance. Engage in demand planning, implement vendor-managed inventory, or establish strategic partnerships to minimize lead times.

Lean Principles: Adopt lean principles to eliminate waste, reduce lead times, and improve overall operational efficiency. Streamline internal processes, eliminate non-value-added activities, and implement just-in-time (JIT) inventory practices to minimize inventory holding costs.

Continuous Improvement: Foster a culture of continuous improvement by encouraging employee involvement, implementing Kaizen methodologies, and regularly reviewing and optimizing inventory management processes. Continuous improvement drives efficiency gains over time.

Inventory Visibility and Tracking Technologies:

Enhancing inventory visibility and implementing tracking technologies improves accuracy and streamlines inventory management processes. Consider the following strategies:

Inventory Tracking Systems: Utilize barcode scanning, RFID (Radio Frequency Identification), or IoT (Internet of Things) sensors to track and monitor inventory movement. Real-time tracking enables organizations to identify discrepancies, reduce manual errors, and streamline inventory control processes.

Warehouse Management Systems (WMS): Implement WMS solutions to automate inventory management processes, including receiving, put-away, picking, and replenishment. WMS optimizes space utilization, improves accuracy, and provides real-time visibility into inventory levels.

Data Integration: Integrate inventory data with other systems, such as demand forecasting, order management, and production planning. Data integration enables accurate and up-to-date inventory information, facilitating proactive decision making and efficient resource allocation.

Performance Measurement and Continuous Monitoring:

Implementing performance metrics and continuous monitoring ensures ongoing improvement and optimization of inventory management. Consider the following strategies:

Key Performance Indicators (KPIs): Define and track KPIs that measure inventory performance, such as inventory turnover ratio, stockout rate, carrying cost, or fill rate. KPIs provide insights into inventory performance and highlight areas for improvement.

Exception Management: Implement exception-based management techniques to focus attention on items that deviate from predefined thresholds or require immediate action. Proactively identify and resolve issues, such as stockouts, excess inventory, or obsolete items.

Regular Inventory Audits: Conduct regular physical inventory audits to verify accuracy and identify discrepancies. Implement cycle counting techniques to continuously monitor inventory accuracy and identify potential issues.

In conclusion, optimizing inventory management is essential for organizations to balance supply and demand, reduce costs, and improve operational efficiency. By implementing strategies such as demand forecasting and planning, inventory classification, safety stock optimization, reducing lead times, enhancing visibility through technology, and implementing performance measurement and continuous monitoring, organizations can achieve efficient and effective inventory management.

Optimized inventory management leads to improved customer satisfaction, reduced carrying costs, streamlined processes, and increased profitability.

Predictive Maintenance and Quality Control

Predictive maintenance and quality control are critical components of effective asset management and product quality assurance. By leveraging data-driven techniques and advanced analytics, organizations can proactively identify maintenance needs and ensure product quality, thereby minimizing downtime, reducing costs, and enhancing customer satisfaction. This section explores the key strategies, techniques, and benefits of predictive maintenance and quality control.

Predictive Maintenance:

Predictive maintenance utilizes data and analytics to predict equipment failure, identify maintenance needs, and optimize maintenance schedules. By proactively addressing maintenance issues, organizations can minimize unplanned downtime, extend asset lifecycles, and reduce maintenance costs. Consider the following strategies:

Condition Monitoring: Utilize sensors and monitoring systems to collect real-time data on equipment performance, such as temperature, vibration, or pressure. Analyze this data using data science techniques, including anomaly detection, pattern recognition, or machine learning, to identify signs of impending failures.

Predictive Analytics: Leverage historical maintenance data and equipment performance data to develop predictive maintenance models. These models can predict future maintenance needs based on patterns and trends, enabling organizations to schedule maintenance activities proactively.

Maintenance Optimization: Optimize maintenance schedules based on predictive insights and prioritization of maintenance tasks. This allows organizations to allocate resources efficiently, reduce maintenance costs, and minimize equipment downtime.

Remote Monitoring: Implement remote monitoring capabilities to track equipment performance and receive real-time alerts on potential issues. Remote monitoring enables organizations to address maintenance needs promptly, even for geographically dispersed assets.

Quality Control:

Quality control focuses on ensuring that products or services meet or exceed customer expectations. By implementing data-driven techniques and quality control processes, organizations can improve product quality, reduce defects, and enhance customer satisfaction. Consider the following strategies:

Statistical Process Control (SPC): Utilize statistical techniques, such as control charts, to monitor and control manufacturing processes. SPC helps identify process variations and ensures products are within acceptable quality limits.

Six Sigma: Implement Six Sigma methodologies to reduce process variations and defects. By applying statistical analysis, organizations can identify root causes of quality issues and implement corrective actions to improve product quality.

Real-time Quality Monitoring: Implement real-time quality monitoring systems that capture data at various stages of the production process. Analyze this data to identify deviations, trends, or patterns that may impact product quality.

Automated Inspection: Utilize automated inspection technologies, such as machine vision systems, to detect defects, measure dimensions, and assess product quality. Automated inspections ensure consistent and accurate quality assessments.

Data Integration and Analytics:

Effective predictive maintenance and quality control require data integration and advanced analytics capabilities. Consider the following strategies:

Data Integration: Integrate data from various sources, including sensors, equipment, maintenance records, and quality control systems. Centralize the data to create a comprehensive view of asset performance and product quality.

Data Analytics: Apply data analytics techniques, such as machine learning, pattern recognition, or anomaly detection, to analyze large volumes of data and identify patterns or deviations that indicate maintenance needs or quality issues.

Predictive Models: Develop predictive models that leverage historical data and advanced algorithms to predict equipment failures or assess product quality. These models enable organizations to make data-driven decisions and take proactive measures.

Predictive Insights: Utilize predictive insights to drive decision making and action. For predictive maintenance, organizations can schedule maintenance tasks based on predicted failure probabilities. In quality control, insights can be used to identify process improvements or adjust production parameters.

Continuous Improvement and Feedback Loops:

To maximize the benefits of predictive maintenance and quality control, organizations should embrace continuous improvement and feedback loops. Consider the following strategies:

Root Cause Analysis: Conduct root cause analysis to identify underlying factors contributing to equipment failures or quality issues. This analysis helps implement corrective actions and prevent future occurrences.

Cross-Functional Collaboration: Foster collaboration among maintenance, operations, quality control, and data analytics teams. Cross-functional collaboration ensures a holistic approach to problem-solving and facilitates knowledge sharing.

Feedback from Field: Collect feedback from field technicians, operators, or customers to improve predictive maintenance models or quality control processes. Field feedback provides valuable insights into real-world conditions and helps refine predictive algorithms or quality control strategies.

Performance Evaluation: Continuously monitor and evaluate the performance of predictive maintenance models and quality control processes. Assess key performance indicators (KPIs) such as equipment uptime, maintenance costs, defect rates, or customer satisfaction to identify areas for improvement.

In conclusion, predictive maintenance and quality control are essential for optimizing asset management and ensuring product quality. By leveraging data integration, advanced analytics, and feedback loops, organizations can proactively identify maintenance needs, optimize maintenance schedules, reduce equipment downtime, and enhance product quality. These practices result in cost savings, increased asset lifespan, improved customer satisfaction, and a competitive advantage in the market. Embracing predictive maintenance and quality control enables organizations to make data-driven decisions, drive continuous improvement, and deliver high-quality products and services to their customers.

CHAPTER 15: DATA SCIENCE IN FINANCE AND RISK MANAGEMENT

Chapter 15 explores the applications of data science in the field of finance and risk management. The finance industry deals with vast amounts of data, making it an ideal domain for leveraging data science techniques to gain insights, make informed decisions, and manage risks effectively. This chapter provides an overview of how data science is transforming finance and revolutionizing risk management practices.

Importance of Data Science in Finance and Risk Management:

Data science plays a pivotal role in the finance industry, enabling organizations to harness the power of data to drive strategic decision-making, improve operational efficiency, and manage risks. With the increasing availability of big data and advancements in data analytics, organizations can gain deeper insights into financial markets, customer behavior, and risk factors.

Data-driven Financial Analysis and Modeling:

Data science techniques enable organizations to analyze financial data, extract meaningful insights, and develop predictive models for financial analysis. Consider the following applications:

Financial Forecasting: Utilize historical financial data, market trends, and economic indicators to develop accurate financial forecasts. Data science techniques, such as time-series analysis, regression, or machine learning, help identify patterns, seasonality, and factors influencing financial performance.

Portfolio Optimization: Employ data-driven approaches to optimize investment portfolios. Data analytics models can consider risk profiles, return expectations, and correlations between assets to recommend optimal portfolio allocations.

Fraud Detection: Apply data science techniques, including anomaly detection, pattern recognition, or machine learning algorithms, to detect fraudulent activities in financial transactions. Advanced analytics can identify suspicious patterns, deviations, or anomalies that may indicate fraudulent behavior.

Risk Management and Compliance:

Data science plays a vital role in managing risks, ensuring compliance with regulations, and enhancing risk assessment practices. Consider the following applications:

Credit Risk Assessment: Utilize data analytics to assess the creditworthiness of individuals or businesses. Predictive models can analyze credit history, financial ratios, and other relevant factors to estimate default probabilities and assign appropriate credit ratings.

Market Risk Analysis: Apply data science techniques to analyze financial market data, historical trends, and external factors to assess market risk exposures. Data-driven models can evaluate portfolio risk, measure value-at-risk (VaR), and identify potential risks arising from market volatility.

Regulatory Compliance: Leverage data analytics to ensure compliance with regulatory requirements. Data science techniques can help organizations monitor transactions, detect potential violations, and generate regulatory reports accurately and efficiently.

Algorithmic Trading and Quantitative Finance:

Data science has revolutionized algorithmic trading and quantitative finance, enabling organizations to make data-driven trading decisions and develop sophisticated trading strategies. Consider the following applications:

High-Frequency Trading: Utilize data science techniques, such as machine learning and natural language processing, to analyze large volumes of market data in real-time. Algorithms can identify patterns, execute trades, and capitalize on short-term market opportunities.

Quantitative Modeling: Develop quantitative models that leverage historical data, statistical analysis, and machine learning algorithms to identify market trends, price patterns, or arbitrage opportunities. These models enable organizations to make data-driven trading decisions.

Risk Arbitrage: Apply data analytics to identify potential risk arbitrage opportunities by analyzing pricing discrepancies, corporate actions, or market inefficiencies. Data-driven approaches can help organizations capture profit opportunities arising from mispricing or market anomalies.

Customer Analytics and Personalized Services:

Data science techniques enhance customer analytics, enabling organizations to offer personalized financial services and improve customer satisfaction. Consider the following applications:

Customer Segmentation: Utilize data analytics to segment customers based on their financial needs, preferences, or risk profiles. Segmentation enables organizations to offer tailored products, services, and targeted marketing strategies.

Customer Lifetime Value (CLV) Analysis: Apply data science models to predict the CLV of customers. By understanding the long-term value of customers, organizations can prioritize customer acquisition, retention, and relationship management strategies.

Recommender Systems: Utilize machine learning algorithms to develop recommender systems that provide personalized financial recommendations, such as investment options, insurance products, or credit offerings, based on customer profiles and preferences.

In conclusion, data science has revolutionized the finance industry, enabling organizations to make data-driven decisions, manage risks effectively, and offer personalized financial services. By leveraging data analytics, advanced modeling techniques, and algorithmic trading strategies, organizations can gain deeper insights into financial markets, enhance risk management practices, and provide customized solutions to customers. The integration of data science in finance and risk management empowers organizations to drive innovation, improve operational efficiency, and navigate the complexities of the financial landscape.

Fraud Detection and Prevention

Fraud is a pervasive issue that can cause significant financial losses, damage reputations, and erode customer trust. Organizations across various industries face the challenge of detecting and preventing fraud. However, with the advancements in data science techniques, organizations now have powerful tools to identify fraudulent activities, mitigate risks, and enhance fraud prevention efforts. This section explores the key strategies, techniques, and benefits of fraud detection and prevention using data science.

Importance of Fraud Detection and Prevention:

Fraud can occur in different forms, including financial fraud, identity theft, insurance fraud, and cybercrime. Detecting and preventing fraud is essential for organizations to protect their assets, ensure compliance with regulations, and maintain the trust of customers. Data science plays a crucial role in identifying patterns, anomalies, and suspicious activities, thereby strengthening fraud prevention measures.

Data Analytics for Fraud Detection:

Data analytics techniques are pivotal in detecting fraud by analyzing large volumes of data and identifying patterns or anomalies that may indicate fraudulent activities. Consider the following strategies:

Anomaly Detection: Employ statistical methods and machine learning algorithms to identify deviations from normal behavior or patterns that may indicate fraudulent activities. Anomalies may manifest as unusual transaction patterns, outliers, or unexpected changes in data.

Network Analysis: Utilize network analysis techniques to identify relationships or connections between individuals, entities, or accounts involved in fraudulent activities. Network analysis helps uncover complex fraud schemes, such as money laundering or organized fraud rings.

Text Mining and Natural Language Processing (NLP): Analyze textual data, such as emails, chat logs, or customer complaints, using NLP techniques to identify fraud-related keywords, suspicious patterns, or fraudulent claims.

Machine Learning Models: Train machine learning models using historical data to detect patterns indicative of fraud. Models such as logistic regression, decision trees, random forests, or neural networks can learn from past fraud cases and identify new instances of fraud.

Behavioral Analytics:

Behavioral analytics focuses on understanding and analyzing patterns of human behavior to identify anomalies or deviations that may signal fraudulent activities. Consider the following strategies:

User Behavior Analysis: Analyze user behavior, such as browsing patterns, transaction history, or login activities, to establish baseline behavior profiles. Deviations from these profiles can indicate fraudulent activities, such as account takeovers or identity theft.

Machine Learning Algorithms: Leverage machine learning algorithms, such as clustering or classification techniques, to identify groups of users or transactions that exhibit similar patterns of fraudulent behavior. These algorithms can adapt and improve over time as new data becomes available.

User Authentication and Verification: Implement multi-factor authentication, biometric identification, or identity verification techniques to ensure that users are who they claim to be. By confirming user identities, organizations can reduce the risk of fraudulent activities.

Real-Time Monitoring and Alert Systems:

Real-time monitoring and alert systems are crucial for identifying and responding to fraud in a timely manner. Consider the following strategies:

Rule-Based Systems: Implement rule-based systems that trigger alerts based on predefined rules or thresholds. These rules can be based on known fraud patterns or suspicious activities identified through data analysis.

Machine Learning-Based Systems: Train machine learning models to detect fraud in real-time by continuously analyzing incoming data and identifying patterns or anomalies that match fraud profiles. These models can adapt and improve over time as new data is collected.

Automated Alerts and Case Management: Establish automated alert systems that notify relevant stakeholders when potential fraud is detected. Implement robust case management processes to ensure timely investigation and resolution of flagged cases.

Collaboration and Data Sharing:

Fraud detection and prevention efforts can be strengthened through collaboration and data sharing among organizations, industry partners, and law enforcement agencies. Consider the following strategies:

Fraud Data Exchange: Participate in fraud data exchanges or consortiums where organizations can share anonymized data related to fraud incidents, patterns, or trends. Collaborative data sharing helps identify emerging fraud trends and improve overall detection capabilities.

Information Sharing Platforms: Engage in information-sharing platforms or industry forums to exchange knowledge, best practices, and fraud prevention strategies. Learning from the experiences of others can help organizations stay ahead of evolving fraud techniques.

Public-Private Partnerships: Foster partnerships with law enforcement agencies, regulatory bodies, and industry associations to share information, collaborate on investigations, and advocate for stronger fraud prevention measures.

Continuous Improvement and Adaptive Systems:

Fraudsters are constantly evolving their techniques, necessitating adaptive and continuously improving fraud detection and prevention systems.

Consider the following strategies:

Feedback Loops: Establish feedback loops to gather insights from fraud analysts, investigators, and data scientists. Continuous feedback enables organizations to refine models, update rules, and improve the effectiveness of fraud detection systems.

Learning from False Positives and False Negatives: Analyze cases of false positives (legitimate transactions flagged as fraud) and false negatives (fraudulent transactions not detected) to identify areas for improvement. These analyses help organizations fine-tune their fraud detection algorithms and reduce false alarms.

Regular Assessments: Conduct regular assessments of fraud prevention strategies, processes, and technologies to identify gaps and areas for improvement. Stay updated with emerging fraud techniques and new data science advancements to enhance fraud prevention capabilities.

In conclusion, data science techniques provide powerful tools for detecting and preventing fraud. By leveraging data analytics, behavioral analysis, real-time monitoring, collaboration, and continuous improvement, organizations can stay ahead of fraudsters and protect themselves from financial losses and reputational damage. Implementing robust fraud detection and prevention measures not only safeguards organizational assets but also instills confidence in customers and stakeholders.

Risk Modeling and Assessment

Risk modeling and assessment are essential components of effective risk management strategies. Organizations face various types of risks, including financial risks, operational risks, cybersecurity risks, and compliance risks. By leveraging data-driven techniques and advanced analytics, organizations can identify, quantify, and mitigate risks more effectively. This section explores the key strategies, techniques, and benefits of risk modeling and assessment.

Importance of Risk Modeling and Assessment:

Risk modeling and assessment provide organizations with a systematic approach to identify, understand, and manage risks. By quantifying risks and their potential impacts, organizations can make informed decisions, allocate resources effectively, and develop appropriate risk mitigation strategies. Risk modeling and assessment help organizations improve their resilience, protect their assets, and maintain a competitive advantage.

Risk Identification and Categorization:

The first step in risk modeling and assessment is to identify and categorize risks. Consider the following strategies:

Risk Registers: Develop risk registers that list potential risks specific to the organization's industry, operations, and objectives. Engage stakeholders from different departments to ensure comprehensive risk identification.

Risk Categorization: Categorize risks into different types, such as financial risks, operational risks, strategic risks, or compliance risks. This categorization helps in understanding the nature of risks and tailoring risk management strategies accordingly.

Risk Heat Maps: Use risk heat maps to visualize and prioritize risks based on their likelihood and potential impact. Heat maps provide a quick overview of the risk landscape and assist in focusing resources on high-risk areas.

Data Collection and Analysis:

Data plays a crucial role in risk modeling and assessment. Consider the following strategies:

Historical Data: Analyze historical data related to risk incidents, losses, or near misses. This data helps identify patterns, trends, and root causes of risks, enabling organizations to develop effective risk mitigation strategies.

External Data Sources: Utilize external data sources, such as industry reports, regulatory information, or market data, to gain insights into industry-specific risks and emerging trends. External data enhances the organization's understanding of the broader risk landscape.

Data Analytics Techniques: Apply data analytics techniques, such as statistical analysis, regression modeling, or machine learning, to identify relationships, correlations, or predictive patterns within the data. Data analytics helps in quantifying risks and assessing their potential impacts.

Quantitative and Qualitative Risk Assessment:

Risk assessment involves quantifying and qualitatively assessing risks to determine their significance and potential impacts. Consider the following strategies:

Quantitative Risk Assessment: Utilize quantitative techniques, such as Monte Carlo simulation, value-at-risk (VaR) analysis, or scenario analysis, to quantify risks in terms of probability and potential financial impacts. These techniques help organizations understand the potential range of outcomes and make risk-informed decisions.

Qualitative Risk Assessment: Conduct qualitative assessments to evaluate risks based on their potential non-financial impacts, such as reputational damage, operational disruptions, or regulatory penalties. Qualitative assessments consider factors such as severity, likelihood, and the organization's risk tolerance.

Risk Scoring and Rating: Develop risk scoring or rating systems to assess risks based on predefined criteria. These systems help prioritize risks, allocate resources, and establish risk tolerance thresholds.

Risk Modeling and Simulation:

Risk modeling and simulation techniques provide a deeper understanding of complex risk scenarios and potential outcomes. Consider the following strategies:

Scenario Analysis: Develop scenarios that represent different risk events or situations and assess their potential impacts on the organization. Scenario analysis helps organizations anticipate risks and evaluate alternative risk mitigation strategies.

Stress Testing: Conduct stress tests to evaluate the organization's resilience under adverse conditions or extreme risk scenarios. Stress testing helps identify vulnerabilities, assess the adequacy of risk controls, and enhance risk mitigation strategies.

Sensitivity Analysis: Perform sensitivity analysis to understand how changes in key variables or assumptions impact risk exposures. Sensitivity analysis helps identify critical risk drivers and assess the organization's sensitivity to changes in external factors.

Risk Mitigation Strategies:

Based on the results of risk modeling and assessment, organizations can develop risk mitigation strategies to manage and reduce risks. Consider the following strategies:

Risk Transfer: Transfer risks to external parties through insurance, hedging, or contractual arrangements. Risk transfer helps mitigate the financial impacts of risks and enhances the organization's ability to absorb losses.

Risk Avoidance: Avoid risks by refraining from engaging in activities or investments with high-risk exposures. Risk avoidance may involve diversifying operations, exiting high-risk markets, or discontinuing high-risk products or services.

Risk Reduction: Implement measures to reduce the likelihood or potential impacts of risks. This may include implementing controls, enhancing cybersecurity measures, improving safety protocols, or conducting employee training.

Risk Acceptance: Accept certain risks when the potential benefits outweigh the potential impacts or when risks cannot be effectively mitigated. Risk acceptance requires a clear understanding of risk tolerance and the ability to monitor and manage risks effectively.

Continuous Monitoring and Review:

Risk modeling and assessment are not one-time exercises. They require continuous monitoring and periodic review to adapt to changing circumstances and emerging risks. Consider the following strategies:

Key Risk Indicators (KRIs): Establish KRIs to track and monitor key risk metrics or indicators that provide early warning signs of potential risks. Regularly review and analyze KRIs to identify emerging risks and trigger appropriate risk mitigation actions.

Risk Culture and Awareness: Foster a risk-aware culture across the organization by promoting risk awareness, accountability, and proactive risk management. Encourage employees to report risks and provide mechanisms for anonymous reporting.

Regular Reviews and Updates: Conduct regular reviews of risk models, assumptions, and mitigation strategies to ensure their relevance and effectiveness. Update risk assessments based on new information, changes in the business environment, or lessons learned from risk incidents.

In conclusion, risk modeling and assessment provide organizations with a systematic approach to identify, analyze, and manage risks effectively. By leveraging data-driven techniques, conducting quantitative and qualitative assessments, and developing appropriate risk mitigation strategies, organizations can enhance their resilience, protect their assets, and make informed risk-informed decisions. Risk modeling and assessment contribute to the overall risk management framework, enabling organizations to navigate uncertainties, seize opportunities, and achieve their objectives while minimizing potential risks.

Portfolio Optimization and Trading Strategies

Portfolio optimization and trading strategies are critical components of investment management and financial decision-making. Efficiently allocating assets and implementing effective trading strategies can help investors maximize returns, manage risks, and achieve their investment objectives. This section explores the key strategies, techniques, and benefits of portfolio optimization and trading strategies.

Importance of Portfolio Optimization and Trading Strategies:

Portfolio optimization involves determining the ideal allocation of assets within a portfolio to achieve a desired risk-return tradeoff. Trading strategies, on the other hand, involve executing trades based on various factors such as market conditions, asset valuation, or technical indicators. Both portfolio optimization and trading strategies are vital in improving investment performance, managing risks, and adapting to changing market conditions.

Modern Portfolio Theory and Asset Allocation:

Modern Portfolio Theory (MPT) forms the foundation for portfolio optimization. MPT emphasizes diversification and the efficient allocation of assets to maximize returns for a given level of risk. Key aspects include:

Risk-Return Tradeoff: MPT recognizes that investors seek to maximize returns while minimizing risks. By optimizing the allocation of assets, investors can achieve the desired level of risk exposure and potential returns.

Asset Allocation: Asset allocation involves determining the optimal mix of asset classes, such as stocks, bonds, cash, or alternative investments, within a portfolio. Asset allocation decisions are guided by factors such as risk tolerance, investment objectives, and market conditions.

Efficient Frontier: The efficient frontier represents the set of portfolios that offer the highest expected return for a given level of risk. Portfolio optimization techniques aim to identify portfolios that lie on the efficient frontier.

Mean-Variance Optimization:

Mean-Variance Optimization (MVO) is a widely used technique for portfolio optimization. It considers the expected returns and risk (measured by variance or standard deviation) of different assets to determine the optimal asset allocation. Key aspects include:

Expected Returns: Develop expected return estimates for each asset based on historical data, fundamental analysis, or predictive models. These estimates help quantify the potential returns associated with different asset classes or individual securities.

Risk Assessment: Assess the risk of assets by calculating their variances or standard deviations. This risk measure is crucial in understanding the potential volatility or downside risk associated with each asset.

Efficient Frontier Construction: Use optimization algorithms to identify the asset allocation that offers the maximum return for a given level of risk or the minimum risk for a target level of return. The result is the efficient frontier, which represents the optimal tradeoff between risk and return.

Factor-Based and Risk-Based Strategies:

In addition to traditional mean-variance optimization, investors may consider factor-based or risk-based strategies for portfolio optimization. These strategies involve allocating assets based on specific factors or risk exposures. Key aspects include:

Factor Investing: Allocate assets based on specific factors such as value, growth, momentum, or low volatility. Factor-based strategies aim to capture excess returns associated with these factors and enhance portfolio diversification.

Risk Parity: Allocate assets based on their risk contributions rather than market value. Risk parity strategies focus on balancing risk across different asset classes, reducing concentration risk, and improving risk-adjusted returns.

Trading Strategies and Execution:

Once the optimal portfolio allocation is determined, implementing effective trading strategies becomes crucial. Trading strategies involve executing trades based on market conditions, technical analysis, or fundamental analysis. Key aspects include:

Market Timing: Attempt to profit by predicting short-term market movements. Market timing strategies involve monitoring market indicators, trends, or news events to identify buy or sell signals.

Trend Following: Identify and follow prevailing trends in the market. Trend-following strategies aim to capture profits by riding the momentum of price movements.

Fundamental Analysis: Analyze financial statements, company fundamentals, or economic factors to identify undervalued or overvalued securities. Fundamental analysis helps in making informed investment decisions based on the intrinsic value of assets.

Quantitative Trading: Utilize quantitative models and algorithms to execute trades based on predefined rules, statistical analysis, or machine learning. Quantitative trading strategies leverage technology and data analysis to execute trades swiftly and systematically.

Risk Management and Rebalancing:

Effective risk management and periodic portfolio rebalancing are integral to maintaining the desired risk-return characteristics of a portfolio. Key aspects include:

Stop Loss Orders: Implement stop loss orders to automatically sell a security when it reaches a predetermined price level. Stop loss orders help limit potential losses and manage downside risk.

Rebalancing: Periodically review and rebalance the portfolio to maintain the desired asset allocation. Rebalancing involves selling or buying assets to restore the target weights based on changes in asset values or market conditions.

Risk Monitoring: Continuously monitor portfolio risk using risk metrics such as value-at-risk (VaR), tracking error, or maximum drawdown. Regular risk monitoring helps identify deviations from the desired risk levels and triggers risk mitigation actions.

Performance Evaluation and Continuous Improvement:

Evaluate portfolio performance regularly to assess the effectiveness of portfolio optimization and trading strategies. Key aspects include:

Performance Metrics: Measure portfolio performance using metrics such as returns, risk-adjusted returns (e.g., Sharpe ratio), or benchmark comparisons. Performance metrics provide insights into the effectiveness of the chosen strategies.

Backtesting: Conduct historical simulations or backtests to assess the performance of trading strategies based on past market data. Backtesting helps validate the efficacy of trading strategies and identify areas for improvement.

Continuous Learning and Adaptation: Stay updated with market trends, investment research, and advances in data science techniques. Continuous learning enables investors to refine their strategies, incorporate new information, and adapt to changing market conditions.

In conclusion, portfolio optimization and trading strategies are vital components of investment management. By utilizing techniques such as mean-variance optimization, factor-based strategies, and risk-based approaches, investors can optimize asset allocation and manage risks effectively. Implementing trading strategies based on market analysis, technical indicators, or fundamental research helps in executing trades efficiently. Regular performance evaluation, risk management, and continuous improvement ensure the ongoing success of portfolio management and enhance investment outcomes.

CHAPTER 16: DATA SCIENCE IN HEALTHCARE AND LIFE SCIENCES

Chapter 16 explores the applications of data science in the fields of healthcare and life sciences. Data science has the potential to revolutionize healthcare delivery, medical research, drug discovery, and patient outcomes. This chapter provides an overview of how data science techniques and analytics are transforming the healthcare and life sciences industry.

Importance of Data Science in Healthcare and Life Sciences:

Data science plays a crucial role in improving healthcare outcomes, enhancing patient care, and driving medical advancements. With the vast amount of data generated in healthcare and life sciences, organizations can leverage data science techniques to gain insights, improve diagnosis, optimize treatments, and accelerate research and development.

Electronic Health Records (EHR) and Clinical Decision Support:

Electronic Health Records (EHR) systems store comprehensive patient health information and provide a valuable source of data for analysis and decision support. Key aspects include:

Data Integration: Integrate data from various sources, including EHRs, medical devices, wearables, and genetic data, to create a comprehensive patient profile. Integrated data enables a holistic view of patient health and facilitates data-driven decision-making.

Clinical Decision Support Systems: Develop decision support systems that leverage data analytics and machine learning algorithms to assist healthcare providers in diagnosing diseases, selecting treatments, and optimizing patient care. Decision support systems improve accuracy, reduce errors, and ensure evidence-based medical practices.

Predictive Analytics and Disease Prevention:

Predictive analytics enables healthcare providers to identify individuals at risk of developing diseases, predict disease progression, and implement preventive measures. Key aspects include:

Risk Stratification: Utilize predictive models to identify individuals at higher risk of developing specific diseases based on factors such as genetics, lifestyle, medical history, or demographic characteristics. Risk stratification helps target preventive interventions and allocate healthcare resources more efficiently.

Early Detection: Apply data analytics techniques to detect early signs of diseases or abnormalities, enabling early intervention and potentially improving patient outcomes. Early detection enhances the effectiveness of treatments and reduces healthcare costs.

Precision Medicine and Personalized Treatment:

Data science plays a critical role in advancing precision medicine and personalized treatment approaches. Key aspects include:

Genomic Data Analysis: Analyze genomic data to identify genetic variations, biomarkers, and potential therapeutic targets. Genomic analysis helps tailor treatments to individual patients based on their genetic profiles, maximizing treatment effectiveness.

Predictive Modeling for Treatment Response: Develop predictive models that leverage patient data, genetic information, and clinical factors to predict treatment response. These models enable healthcare providers to make informed decisions and select treatments that are more likely to be effective for specific patients.

Real-Time Monitoring and Feedback: Leverage real-time patient monitoring systems and wearable devices to collect data on patient health, treatment adherence, and response. Real-time monitoring enables healthcare providers to adjust treatments, provide timely interventions, and optimize patient care.

Drug Discovery and Development:

Data science techniques have the potential to revolutionize the drug discovery and development process, leading to more efficient and targeted therapies. Key aspects include:

High-Throughput Screening: Utilize data analytics and machine learning algorithms to analyze large datasets generated through high-throughput screening. This approach helps identify potential drug candidates, predict drug-target interactions, and prioritize molecules for further investigation.

Drug Repurposing: Apply data mining and analytics techniques to identify existing drugs that may have potential applications in new therapeutic areas. Drug repurposing allows for faster and cost-effective drug development by leveraging existing safety and efficacy data.

Clinical Trial Optimization: Use data analytics to optimize the design and conduct of clinical trials. Data-driven approaches can help identify patient populations, optimize recruitment strategies, and analyze trial data to accelerate the development and approval of new treatments.

Public Health and Population Analytics:

Data science plays a vital role in analyzing population health data, tracking disease outbreaks, and improving public health interventions. Key aspects include:

Disease Surveillance: Analyze epidemiological data, syndromic surveillance data, social media data, or environmental data to identify disease outbreaks, monitor disease patterns, and implement timely interventions.

Health Policy and Planning: Utilize data analytics to inform health policy decisions, resource allocation, and public health planning. Data-driven insights enable policymakers to identify priority areas, address health disparities, and optimize resource utilization.

Social Determinants of Health: Analyze social and demographic data to understand the impact of social determinants on health outcomes. This knowledge helps in designing interventions that address social factors and promote health equity.

In conclusion, data science and analytics are transforming healthcare and life sciences by improving patient care, enabling precision medicine, accelerating drug discovery, and enhancing public health interventions. The integration of data from various sources, advanced analytics techniques, and machine learning algorithms facilitate evidence-based decision-making, personalized treatments, and better healthcare outcomes. Embracing data science in healthcare and life sciences enables organizations to harness the power of data, drive medical advancements, and ultimately improve the well-being of individuals and populations.

Clinical Decision Support Systems (CDSS) are powerful tools that leverage data science and information technology to assist healthcare providers in making informed decisions regarding patient care. CDSS integrates patient-specific data, medical knowledge, and evidence-based guidelines to provide recommendations, alerts, and reminders at the point of care. This section explores the key features, benefits, and challenges of Clinical Decision Support Systems.

Features of Clinical Decision Support Systems:

CDSS incorporates several features to support clinical decision-making processes. These features include:

Patient Data Integration: CDSS integrates patient-specific data from electronic health records (EHRs), diagnostic test results, medical imaging, and other sources. This comprehensive patient profile allows for personalized decision support.

Knowledge Base: CDSS relies on a vast knowledge base that includes medical literature, clinical practice guidelines, best practices, and expert knowledge. This knowledge base is continuously updated to reflect the latest research and medical advancements.

Decision Support Rules: CDSS employs decision support rules that are based on medical guidelines and protocols. These rules are designed to trigger alerts, reminders, or recommendations based on specific patient conditions or medical events.

Clinical Algorithms: CDSS utilizes clinical algorithms to process patient data, perform risk assessments, and generate recommendations. Algorithms can range from simple rules-based logic to complex machine learning models that learn from data.

Real-Time Monitoring: CDSS enables real-time monitoring of patient data, enabling prompt identification of critical changes or deviations from normal values. This real-time monitoring facilitates early intervention and timely decision-making.

Benefits of Clinical Decision Support Systems:

CDSS offers numerous benefits to healthcare providers, patients, and the healthcare system as a whole. These benefits include:

Enhanced Patient Safety: CDSS helps reduce medical errors by providing alerts for potential drug interactions, allergies, contraindications, or incorrect dosages. It promotes adherence to evidence-based guidelines, thereby improving patient safety.

Improved Clinical Outcomes: CDSS supports evidence-based medicine by providing clinicians with relevant and up-to-date information. It helps clinicians select appropriate diagnostic tests, treatments, and interventions, leading to improved clinical outcomes.

Increased Efficiency: CDSS optimizes clinical workflows by providing clinicians with relevant information at the point of care. It reduces the need for manual searching and data retrieval, saving time and improving efficiency.

Standardized Care: CDSS promotes standardized and consistent care by ensuring that healthcare providers follow established guidelines and protocols. It reduces unwarranted variations in care delivery and improves care quality.

Cost Savings: CDSS can lead to cost savings by avoiding unnecessary tests, treatments, or hospitalizations. It helps identify cost-effective interventions and promotes efficient resource utilization.

Clinical Decision Support System Applications:

CDSS has diverse applications across various healthcare settings and domains. Some key applications include:

Medication Management: CDSS helps healthcare providers in prescribing appropriate medications, dosages, and schedules. It provides alerts for potential drug-drug interactions, drug allergies, or medication errors.

Diagnostic Support: CDSS aids clinicians in interpreting diagnostic tests, analyzing results, and generating differential diagnoses. It compares patient data against clinical guidelines, research findings, and reference databases to support accurate diagnoses.

Disease Management: CDSS assists in managing chronic diseases by providing guidelines and reminders for preventive care, monitoring disease progression, and guiding treatment decisions.

Risk Assessment and Prevention: CDSS facilitates risk assessment by integrating patient data and generating risk scores or predictive models. It identifies patients at higher risk for specific conditions and supports preventive interventions.

Clinical Pathways and Protocols: CDSS helps in adhering to clinical pathways and protocols by providing decision support at each step of the care process. It ensures that healthcare providers follow established care guidelines and protocols consistently.

Challenges and Considerations:

Implementing and effectively utilizing CDSS in healthcare settings presents certain challenges and considerations. These include:

Data Quality and Integration: CDSS relies on accurate, complete, and well-integrated patient data. Data quality issues, such as incorrect or incomplete data, can adversely affect the reliability and performance of CDSS.

Alert Fatigue: CDSS generates numerous alerts and reminders, which can lead to alert fatigue among clinicians. Overwhelming clinicians with excessive alerts may result in important alerts being ignored or overlooked.

User Interface and Usability: CDSS should have a user-friendly interface that integrates seamlessly into clinicians' workflows. A well-designed user interface and intuitive usability ensure easy adoption and effective utilization of CDSS.

Evidence-Based Guidelines: CDSS relies on evidence-based guidelines, which may not always reflect individual patient characteristics or preferences. It is important to continuously update and customize guidelines to ensure relevance and accuracy.

Legal and Ethical Considerations: CDSS raises legal and ethical considerations, such as liability, privacy, and informed consent. Ensuring patient privacy, informed consent, and transparency in CDSS algorithms and recommendations is crucial.

In conclusion, Clinical Decision Support Systems play a significant role in improving healthcare outcomes, enhancing patient safety, and promoting evidence-based medicine. By leveraging patient data, medical knowledge, and decision support algorithms, CDSS assists healthcare providers in making informed decisions at the point of care. Despite the challenges, the benefits of CDSS in terms of patient safety, clinical outcomes, and efficiency make it a valuable tool in modern healthcare.

Drug discovery and development is a complex and intricate process aimed at identifying, designing, testing, and bringing safe and effective medications to market. It involves a multidisciplinary approach that combines scientific research, data analysis, regulatory compliance, and clinical trials. This section provides an overview of the key stages, challenges, and advancements in the drug discovery and development process.

Drug Discovery Process:

The drug discovery process involves the identification of new therapeutic targets and the development of compounds that can modulate these targets. Key stages include:

Target Identification: Scientists identify specific molecules, proteins, receptors, or genetic targets associated with a disease or condition. This can be achieved through various methods, including genomics, proteomics, and computational modeling.

Target Validation: The identified targets undergo rigorous validation to ensure their relevance and potential as drug targets. This involves preclinical studies, such as in vitro experiments and animal models, to demonstrate the target's involvement in disease pathology.

Hit Discovery: Researchers explore vast libraries of compounds, natural products, or design novel molecules to find initial hits that interact with the target of interest. High-throughput screening and computational modeling techniques assist in identifying potential hit compounds.

Lead Optimization: Promising hits undergo a series of modifications and optimizations to enhance their drug-like properties, such as potency, selectivity, bioavailability, and safety. Medicinal chemists iteratively synthesize and test analogs to improve lead compounds.

Preclinical Development:

Once lead compounds are optimized, preclinical studies are conducted to assess their safety and efficacy before moving to human trials. Key aspects include:

In vitro Studies: Lead compounds are tested in vitro to evaluate their pharmacological activity, mechanism of action, toxicity, and metabolic properties. These studies help identify the most promising candidates for further evaluation.

Animal Studies: Lead compounds undergo in vivo studies using animal models to assess their efficacy, safety, and pharmacokinetics. These studies provide crucial data on dosing, drug distribution, toxicity, and potential side effects.

Formulation Development: Formulation scientists develop suitable drug formulations to optimize drug delivery, stability, and bioavailability. The goal is to ensure that the drug can be effectively administered to patients in the desired dosage form.

Clinical Development:

Clinical development involves testing the safety, efficacy, and dosage of the drug in human subjects. It consists of three main phases:

Phase 1: In this phase, a small group of healthy volunteers receives the drug to evaluate its safety, dosage, and pharmacokinetics. The focus is on assessing the drug's tolerability, absorption, distribution, metabolism, and excretion.

Phase 2: A larger group of patients with the target disease or condition receives the drug to assess its effectiveness and further evaluate safety. This phase aims to determine the optimal dosage, dosing regimen, and potential side effects.

Phase 3: The drug is tested on a larger population of patients to confirm its efficacy, safety, and effectiveness in comparison to existing treatments or placebos. This phase provides critical data for regulatory approval and labeling.

Regulatory Approval and Post-Marketing Surveillance:

Upon successful completion of clinical trials, the drug manufacturer submits an application to regulatory authorities for approval. Key aspects include:

Regulatory Submission: The drug manufacturer compiles all the necessary data, including preclinical and clinical trial results, manufacturing processes, and labeling information, to submit to regulatory authorities for approval.

Regulatory Review: Regulatory agencies, such as the Food and Drug Administration (FDA) in the United States, review the submitted data to assess the drug's safety, efficacy, and benefits in relation to the target population. They also evaluate the drug's manufacturing quality and labeling.

Post-Marketing Surveillance: After regulatory approval and market launch, post-marketing surveillance ensures continued monitoring of the drug's safety and effectiveness. Adverse events and patient outcomes are tracked to identify any unexpected side effects or long-term risks.

Advances in Drug Discovery and Development:

Advancements in technology and data science have revolutionized the drug discovery and development process. Some key advancements include:

High-Throughput Screening: Automated robotic systems enable the screening of large compound libraries, accelerating the hit discovery process.

Computational Modeling and Artificial Intelligence: Computer-aided drug design techniques, molecular simulations, and machine learning algorithms assist in predicting drug-target interactions, designing novel compounds, and optimizing lead candidates.

Biomarkers and Precision Medicine: The identification of biomarkers helps in patient stratification, predicting treatment response, and selecting the most appropriate patients for clinical trials. Precision medicine approaches enable targeted therapies based on individual genetic profiles.

Virtual Clinical Trials: The use of digital technologies, remote monitoring, and virtual patient data facilitate the conduct of decentralized clinical trials, reducing costs, and improving patient participation.

Challenges in Drug Discovery and Development:

The drug discovery and development process faces several challenges, including:

High Failure Rates: The majority of drug candidates fail to progress beyond preclinical or clinical stages due to lack of efficacy, safety concerns, or inadequate data.

Time and Cost: Developing a new drug can take more than a decade and cost billions of dollars. The high cost of research and development poses challenges for smaller companies and limits innovation.

Regulatory and Safety Requirements: Meeting stringent regulatory requirements and ensuring patient safety are essential but can be resource-intensive and time-consuming.

Data Integration and Analysis: Handling and analyzing large amounts of data generated from various sources require robust data management and analytics infrastructure.

Ethical Considerations: Balancing the need for rapid drug development with ethical considerations, such as patient rights, informed consent, and data privacy, is a continuous challenge.

In conclusion, drug discovery and development involve a complex and multi-stage process that requires scientific expertise, collaboration, and significant resources. Advances in technology, data science, and personalized medicine have opened new avenues for more targeted and effective treatments. Overcoming challenges in the drug discovery process is crucial to bring safe and innovative therapies to patients, ultimately improving healthcare outcomes and advancing medical science.

Precision medicine, also known as personalized medicine, is an approach to healthcare that aims to tailor medical treatments and interventions to individual patients based on their unique characteristics, such as genetics, lifestyle, environment, and medical history. By considering these factors, precision medicine seeks to improve patient outcomes, enhance treatment efficacy, and minimize adverse effects. This section explores the key concepts, benefits, and challenges of precision medicine in relation to patient outcomes.

Key Concepts of Precision Medicine:

Precision medicine incorporates several key concepts to guide treatment decisions and optimize patient outcomes. These concepts include:

Genomic Medicine: Genomic information plays a significant role in precision medicine. Genetic testing and analysis help identify genetic variants, biomarkers, and genetic predispositions that influence disease susceptibility, treatment response, and prognosis.

Personalized Risk Assessment: Precision medicine assesses an individual's risk of developing specific diseases based on their genetic, environmental, and lifestyle factors. This allows for targeted preventive measures and early interventions to reduce disease occurrence or progression.

Targeted Therapies: Precision medicine involves the use of targeted therapies that specifically address the molecular or genetic characteristics of a patient's disease. These therapies are designed to maximize treatment effectiveness while minimizing side effects.

Biomarkers and Companion Diagnostics: Biomarkers, such as genetic markers or molecular signatures, are used to identify patients who are more likely to benefit from specific treatments. Companion diagnostics help match patients with the most appropriate therapies based on biomarker profiles.

Benefits of Precision Medicine on Patient Outcomes:

Precision medicine has the potential to significantly impact patient outcomes by improving treatment efficacy, reducing adverse effects, and optimizing healthcare delivery. Some key benefits include:

More Accurate Diagnosis: Precision medicine enables the identification of specific genetic mutations or biomarkers associated with diseases. This improves diagnostic accuracy, leading to earlier detection and intervention.

Targeted Treatments: By tailoring treatments to individual patients, precision medicine increases the likelihood of treatment success and minimizes ineffective treatments. This leads to improved patient response rates and treatment outcomes.

Personalized Risk Assessment and Prevention: Precision medicine allows for the identification of individuals at higher risk for certain diseases. This enables targeted preventive measures, early screening, and interventions to reduce disease occurrence or severity.

Reduced Adverse Effects: By considering an individual's genetic profile and specific characteristics, precision medicine helps avoid treatments that may have adverse effects or limited efficacy. This reduces the risk of unnecessary side effects and improves patient safety.

Optimized Treatment Selection: Precision medicine assists in selecting the most appropriate treatment options based on a patient's unique genetic profile, disease characteristics, and treatment response predictors. This leads to more informed decision-making and improved treatment outcomes.

Challenges in Precision Medicine:

Despite its immense potential, precision medicine faces several challenges that impact its widespread adoption and implementation. Some key challenges include:

Data Integration and Privacy: Precision medicine relies on the integration of large and diverse datasets, including genomic data, clinical records, and lifestyle information. Integrating and securely managing these data sources while protecting patient privacy is a complex task.

Limited Access to Genetic Testing: Widespread implementation of precision medicine requires broad access to genetic testing and analysis. However, access barriers, such as cost, infrastructure, and awareness, limit the availability of genetic testing for all patients.

Interpreting Genetic Variants: Understanding the clinical significance of genetic variants and interpreting their impact on disease risk, treatment response, or prognosis can be challenging. Standardized guidelines and databases are necessary to aid accurate interpretation.

Ethical and Social Implications: Precision medicine raises ethical considerations related to genetic privacy, informed consent, and potential discrimination. Addressing these ethical and social implications is crucial for the responsible and equitable implementation of precision medicine.

Health Equity: Ensuring equitable access to precision medicine technologies and interventions is essential. Disparities in access to genetic testing, therapies, and specialized healthcare resources can exacerbate existing health inequities.

Integration of Precision Medicine into Healthcare Systems:

Integrating precision medicine into healthcare systems requires collaboration among healthcare providers, researchers, policymakers, and technology developers. Key aspects include:

Infrastructure and Data Management: Developing robust infrastructure for data storage, integration, and analysis is essential. Healthcare systems need to invest in secure and scalable platforms that facilitate data sharing and analysis.

Education and Training: Healthcare professionals need education and training to understand the principles of precision medicine, genetic testing, and the interpretation of genetic data. This ensures their ability to effectively incorporate precision medicine into clinical practice.

Regulatory Framework: Establishing regulatory frameworks that ensure patient privacy, data protection, and adherence to ethical guidelines is crucial. Regulatory bodies play a vital role in overseeing the responsible implementation of precision medicine.

Collaborative Research: Collaborations between researchers, clinicians, and industry partners are necessary to advance precision medicine research, validate biomarkers, and develop targeted therapies.

Patient Empowerment and Education: Engaging patients in the precision medicine process, providing genetic counseling, and promoting patient understanding of the benefits and limitations of precision medicine are key factors for successful implementation.

In conclusion, precision medicine holds tremendous potential to transform healthcare by individualizing patient care, improving treatment efficacy, and enhancing patient outcomes. By leveraging genetic information, biomarkers, and personalized risk assessment, precision medicine enables tailored treatments and preventive interventions. However, addressing challenges related to data integration, access, interpretation, ethics, and equity is crucial for the widespread adoption and success of precision medicine.

CHAPTER 17: DATA SCIENCE IN HUMAN RESOURCES

Chapter 17 explores the application of data science techniques and analytics in the field of Human Resources (HR). Data science has revolutionized HR practices by enabling organizations to make data-driven decisions, improve workforce management, and enhance employee experiences. This chapter provides an overview of the key concepts, benefits, and challenges of using data science in HR.

Importance of Data Science in HR:

Data science has transformed HR from a traditional administrative function to a strategic business partner. By leveraging data and analytics, HR professionals can gain insights into employee behavior, workforce trends, talent management, and organizational performance. Data science in HR helps organizations make informed decisions and improve overall business outcomes.

HR Analytics and Predictive Modeling:

HR analytics involves collecting and analyzing HR-related data to derive insights and inform decision-making. Predictive modeling utilizes statistical techniques and machine learning algorithms to forecast future HR outcomes. Key aspects include:

Workforce Planning: HR analytics helps organizations plan for future workforce needs by forecasting talent demand and identifying skill gaps. Predictive modeling enables HR professionals to anticipate attrition rates, retirements, and workforce trends.

Talent Acquisition and Recruitment: Data science in HR enables organizations to optimize the recruitment process, identify the best sourcing channels, and predict candidate success. Analytics can help identify key candidate characteristics and improve hiring decisions.

Employee Engagement and Retention: By analyzing employee feedback, performance data, and other relevant factors, HR professionals can identify drivers of engagement and predict employee retention. This helps organizations proactively address employee concerns and improve retention strategies.

People Analytics and Employee Experience:

People analytics focuses on understanding and optimizing the employee experience within an organization. Key aspects include:

Employee Surveys and Sentiment Analysis: Data science techniques, such as natural language processing, can analyze employee surveys, feedback, and sentiment to understand employee experiences, satisfaction, and engagement levels.

Employee Journey Mapping: Data science enables HR professionals to map the employee journey, identifying critical touchpoints and moments that impact employee experiences. This helps organizations design interventions and improve the overall employee experience.

Diversity and Inclusion: Data science can help organizations measure and track diversity and inclusion metrics, identify biases in hiring and promotion processes, and develop strategies to foster a more inclusive work environment.

Performance Management and Talent Development:

Data science in HR enhances performance management and talent development processes. Key aspects include:

Performance Metrics and KPIs: By leveraging data analytics, organizations can define and track performance metrics and key performance indicators (KPIs) for individual employees, teams, and departments. This enables effective performance management and goal setting.

Learning and Development: Data science can analyze training data, performance data, and employee feedback to identify skill gaps, recommend personalized learning paths, and optimize talent development programs.

Succession Planning: By analyzing employee performance, potential, and career aspirations, HR professionals can identify high-potential employees for future leadership roles and implement succession planning strategies.

Challenges in Data Science in HR:

Implementing data science in HR faces certain challenges that need to be addressed for successful adoption. Some key challenges include:

Data Quality and Integration: Ensuring the accuracy, completeness, and integration of HR data from various sources is crucial for effective data analysis. Poor data quality can lead to erroneous insights and decision-making.

Data Privacy and Ethics: Respecting employee privacy rights and ensuring ethical use of employee data is essential. Organizations must adhere to data protection regulations and establish transparent and ethical data practices.

Skill Gaps and Talent: Developing data science skills within HR teams and recruiting data science professionals with HR domain knowledge can be a challenge. Building a multidisciplinary team is crucial for successful data science implementation.

Change Management: Introducing data-driven decision-making and analytics in HR requires organizational change management. HR professionals need to embrace analytics, understand its value, and develop the necessary skills to effectively use data.

In conclusion, data science has transformed HR practices by enabling data-driven decision-making, improving workforce management, and enhancing employee experiences. By leveraging HR analytics, predictive modeling, and people analytics, organizations can optimize talent acquisition, employee engagement, performance management, and talent development. Overcoming challenges related to data quality, privacy, skills, and change management is key to successfully implementing data science in HR and reaping its benefits for the organization and its employees.

Talent acquisition and retention are critical aspects of Human Resources (HR) that significantly impact an organization's success. In today's competitive job market, attracting top talent and keeping them engaged and committed is essential for business growth. This section explores the key strategies, challenges, and benefits of talent acquisition and retention.

Talent Acquisition Strategies:

Talent acquisition focuses on identifying, attracting, and recruiting individuals with the skills, knowledge, and attributes required for a specific role or the overall success of the organization. Effective talent acquisition strategies include:

Employer Branding: Building a strong employer brand helps attract top talent. Organizations need to showcase their unique value proposition, company culture, employee benefits, and career growth opportunities to stand out in the competitive job market.

Recruitment Marketing: Utilizing various marketing techniques, such as job advertisements, social media campaigns, and targeted messaging, helps reach potential candidates and create awareness about career opportunities within the organization.

Candidate Experience: Providing a positive candidate experience throughout the recruitment process is crucial. Clear communication, efficient processes, timely feedback, and a smooth application experience contribute to a positive impression of the organization.

Proactive Sourcing: Adopting proactive sourcing methods, such as talent pipelines, networking, and employee referrals, helps identify and engage potential candidates before they actively start job searching.

Data-Driven Approaches: Leveraging data and analytics in talent acquisition enables organizations to identify effective sourcing channels, track recruitment metrics, and make data-driven decisions to optimize the recruitment process.

Employee Retention Strategies:

Employee retention focuses on creating an environment that fosters employee satisfaction, engagement, and loyalty. Organizations need effective strategies to retain top talent and reduce turnover. Key retention strategies include:

Competitive Compensation and Benefits: Offering competitive compensation packages, including salaries, bonuses, and benefits, is essential to attract and retain talented employees. Regular market analysis helps ensure that compensation remains competitive.

Career Development and Growth Opportunities: Providing clear career paths, mentoring programs, training, and development opportunities demonstrate a commitment to employee growth. Employees are more likely to stay with an organization that supports their career aspirations.

Work-Life Balance and Flexibility: Promoting work-life balance and offering flexible work arrangements, such as remote work options and flexible schedules, contribute to employee satisfaction and retention.

Recognition and Rewards: Implementing employee recognition programs and rewards for exceptional performance or milestones helps foster a positive work environment and reinforces employee engagement.

Employee Engagement Initiatives: Actively engaging employees through regular feedback, employee surveys, and initiatives that promote a sense of belonging, teamwork, and collaboration enhances employee satisfaction and retention.

Benefits and Impact of Effective Talent Acquisition and Retention:

Effective talent acquisition and retention strategies have several benefits and impact on organizational success:

Access to Top Talent: Successful talent acquisition enables organizations to attract and hire highly skilled and talented individuals, giving them a competitive edge in the marketplace.

Reduced Recruitment Costs: Effective retention strategies help reduce turnover, resulting in cost savings associated with recruitment, onboarding, and training new employees.

Increased Productivity and Performance: Engaged and satisfied employees are more likely to be productive, innovative, and committed to achieving organizational goals. They contribute to higher performance and overall business success.

Enhanced Employer Brand: Positive talent acquisition and retention practices enhance an organization's employer brand. This, in turn, attracts more top talent and makes the organization an employer of choice.

Improved Employee Morale and Satisfaction: Effective retention strategies lead to higher employee morale and job satisfaction, creating a positive work culture and reducing turnover.

Continuity and Knowledge Retention: Retaining experienced employees ensures continuity in operations, preserves institutional knowledge, and facilitates the transfer of knowledge to new employees.

Challenges in Talent Acquisition and Retention:

While talent acquisition and retention are crucial, organizations face certain challenges in these areas:

Competition for Talent: Organizations often compete with each other to attract and retain top talent. This competition increases the challenge of finding qualified candidates and keeping them engaged.

Skills Gap: Rapidly evolving industries and technologies create skill gaps, making it challenging to find individuals with the required expertise. Organizations may need to invest in training and development programs to bridge these gaps.

Employee Turnover: Employee turnover can disrupt operations, impact morale, and result in additional recruitment and training costs. Retaining key talent becomes essential to minimize turnover.

Changing Workforce Preferences: The modern workforce values flexibility, work-life balance, and meaningful work. Organizations must adapt to changing preferences to attract and retain talent.

Diversity and Inclusion: Building a diverse and inclusive workforce is crucial for organizations. However, achieving diversity and inclusion goals may require additional efforts and strategies to attract underrepresented talent.

In conclusion, talent acquisition and retention are key priorities for organizations seeking to build high-performing teams and achieve business success. By implementing effective talent acquisition strategies, organizations can attract top talent, while robust retention strategies foster employee satisfaction, engagement, and loyalty. Overcoming challenges related to competition, skills gaps, and changing workforce preferences requires proactive and data-driven approaches. Ultimately, investing in talent acquisition and retention efforts pays off in improved employee performance, reduced turnover, and a strong employer brand.

Performance evaluation and workforce planning are essential components of Human Resources (HR) management that contribute to the success of an organization. Performance evaluation assesses individual and team performance, while workforce planning ensures that the organization has the right talent in place to meet current and future business needs. This section explores the key concepts, strategies, and benefits of performance evaluation and workforce planning.

Performance Evaluation:

Performance evaluation involves assessing the performance, skills, and contributions of individual employees, teams, and departments. It provides feedback, identifies areas for improvement, and recognizes achievements. Key aspects of performance evaluation include:

Goal Setting: Setting clear, measurable, and achievable goals is crucial for effective performance evaluation. Goals should align with the organization's objectives and provide a framework for evaluating performance.

Performance Metrics and KPIs: Defining performance metrics and key performance indicators (KPIs) helps measure progress, track results, and evaluate performance objectively. Metrics can include quantitative measures, such as sales targets or customer satisfaction scores, as well as qualitative assessments, such as teamwork or communication skills.

Performance Reviews: Regular performance reviews provide an opportunity for managers and employees to discuss performance, provide feedback, and set development goals. Performance reviews can be conducted annually, semi-annually, or on a more frequent basis depending on organizational needs.

Feedback and Coaching: Ongoing feedback and coaching are essential for employee development and continuous improvement. Managers should provide constructive feedback, offer guidance, and support employees in their professional growth.

Performance Improvement Plans: When performance falls below expectations, a performance improvement plan may be implemented to address specific areas of improvement. This plan outlines goals, timelines, and support mechanisms to help employees enhance their performance.

Workforce Planning:

Workforce planning involves assessing current and future talent needs and developing strategies to ensure that the organization has the right workforce in place to achieve its objectives. Key aspects of workforce planning include:

Talent Demand Forecasting: Analyzing business goals, growth projections, and market trends helps determine the future talent requirements of the organization. This analysis considers factors such as retirements, attrition rates, and anticipated skill gaps.

Succession Planning: Succession planning identifies high-potential employees and develops a pool of talent ready to assume key roles within the organization. It ensures continuity in leadership and critical positions, mitigating the risk of talent gaps.

Skill Gap Analysis: Assessing the skills and competencies required for future roles helps identify skill gaps within the workforce. This analysis informs recruitment strategies, training programs, and talent development initiatives to address those gaps.

Recruitment and Hiring Strategies: Workforce planning informs recruitment strategies, including identifying sourcing channels, defining candidate profiles, and optimizing selection processes. It ensures that the organization attracts and hires individuals with the required skills and expertise.

Talent Retention: Workforce planning considers employee retention strategies to retain key talent and reduce turnover. This includes creating a positive work culture, providing career development opportunities, and offering competitive compensation and benefits.

Benefits of Performance Evaluation and Workforce Planning:

Effective performance evaluation and workforce planning practices offer numerous benefits to organizations, employees, and stakeholders:

Improved Performance and Productivity: Performance evaluation provides feedback, identifies strengths and areas for improvement, and helps employees align their efforts with organizational goals. Workforce planning ensures that the organization has the right talent to meet current and future demands, enhancing overall performance and productivity.

Talent Development and Engagement: Performance evaluation fosters employee development by providing opportunities for learning, growth, and skill enhancement. Workforce planning identifies career paths, provides development opportunities, and engages employees by aligning their skills and aspirations with organizational needs.

Effective Succession and Talent Management: Workforce planning, coupled with performance evaluation, facilitates succession planning and talent management initiatives. Organizations can identify high-potential employees, develop their skills, and prepare them for future leadership roles.

Alignment with Organizational Goals: Performance evaluation and workforce planning ensure that individual and team goals align with organizational objectives. This alignment improves coordination, enhances collaboration, and drives overall organizational success.

Cost and Resource Optimization: Effective workforce planning helps organizations optimize costs and resources by ensuring the right talent is available at the right time. This reduces recruitment costs, minimizes talent gaps, and enhances operational efficiency.

Agility and Adaptability: Workforce planning enables organizations to anticipate and respond to changes in the business environment. By identifying emerging skill requirements and proactively addressing talent needs, organizations can adapt quickly to market demands.

Challenges in Performance Evaluation and Workforce Planning:

Organizations may encounter challenges when implementing performance evaluation and workforce planning practices. Some common challenges include:

Subjectivity and Bias: Performance evaluation can be subjective, influenced by personal biases and perceptions. Organizations need to establish clear evaluation criteria and provide training to reduce bias and ensure fairness.

Data Accuracy and Accessibility: Performance evaluation and workforce planning rely on accurate and accessible data. Organizations must have reliable systems in place to collect, analyze, and store employee data securely.

Resistance to Change: Introducing performance evaluation and workforce planning practices may face resistance from employees who are accustomed to traditional evaluation methods. Change management strategies, communication, and training can help overcome resistance and gain employee buy-in.

Changing Skill Requirements: Rapidly evolving industries and technologies pose challenges in workforce planning as skill requirements continuously evolve. Organizations need to anticipate and address these skill gaps to stay competitive.

Integration with HR Systems: Integrating performance evaluation and workforce planning with HR systems and processes can be complex. Organizations need to ensure seamless integration and data flow between various HR systems.

In conclusion, performance evaluation and workforce planning are critical HR practices that contribute to organizational success. Effective performance evaluation provides feedback, improves employee development, and enhances individual and team performance. Workforce planning ensures that the organization has the right talent to meet current and future demands. Overcoming challenges, such as bias, data accuracy, and skill gaps, requires strategic approaches, clear criteria, and continuous improvement. By implementing robust performance evaluation and workforce planning strategies, organizations can optimize talent management, drive performance, and achieve their strategic objectives.

Diversity and inclusion analytics is a data-driven approach that helps organizations measure, analyze, and improve diversity and inclusion within their workforce. It involves collecting and analyzing data related to employee demographics, representation, hiring practices, promotion rates, employee experiences, and other factors. By leveraging diversity and inclusion analytics, organizations can gain insights into their current state, identify areas for improvement, and develop strategies to foster a more diverse and inclusive workplace. This section explores the key concepts, benefits, challenges, and best practices of diversity and inclusion analytics.

Key Concepts of Diversity and Inclusion Analytics:

Diversity and inclusion analytics involve the following key concepts:

Demographic Data: Collecting data on employee demographics, such as gender, race, ethnicity, age, disability status, and sexual orientation, provides a baseline understanding of the composition of the workforce.

Representation Analysis: Analyzing the representation of different demographic groups within the organization helps identify any underrepresented or overrepresented groups at various levels and departments.

Hiring and Promotion Practices: Evaluating hiring and promotion practices, including applicant demographics, interview processes, and selection outcomes, helps assess whether there are any biases or barriers affecting the representation of diverse talent.

Employee Experience and Engagement: Assessing employee experiences, satisfaction, engagement, and perceptions of inclusion through surveys or feedback mechanisms provides insights into the organizational culture and potential areas for improvement.

Intersectionality: Considering the intersection of multiple dimensions of diversity, such as race and gender, or age and disability, allows for a more nuanced understanding of the experiences and challenges faced by employees with intersecting identities.

Benefits of Diversity and Inclusion Analytics:

Implementing diversity and inclusion analytics provides several benefits to organizations:

Data-Driven Decision-Making: Diversity and inclusion analytics enable data-driven decision-making, moving beyond assumptions and biases. Organizations can make evidence-based decisions to foster a more inclusive workplace and drive positive change.

Enhanced Recruitment and Retention: By analyzing diversity and inclusion data, organizations can identify areas of improvement in their recruitment and retention practices. This helps attract and retain diverse talent, leading to a more diverse and inclusive workforce.

Improved Organizational Performance: Research shows that diverse and inclusive organizations tend to outperform their peers. Diversity and inclusion analytics help organizations leverage the diverse perspectives, experiences, and skills of their employees, leading to increased innovation, productivity, and business outcomes.

Compliance with Legal and Ethical Standards: Diversity and inclusion analytics assist organizations in monitoring and ensuring compliance with legal requirements and ethical standards related to diversity, non-discrimination, and equal opportunity.

Enhanced Employer Brand and Reputation: Demonstrating a commitment to diversity and inclusion through data-driven initiatives enhances an organization's employer brand and reputation. It attracts top talent, improves customer perception, and fosters positive relationships with stakeholders.

Challenges of Diversity and Inclusion Analytics:

Implementing diversity and inclusion analytics may face certain challenges:

Data Collection and Accuracy: Collecting accurate and comprehensive diversity data can be challenging, especially in organizations with decentralized systems or privacy concerns. Ensuring data accuracy and maintaining employee confidentiality are crucial.

Data Interpretation and Contextualization: Analyzing diversity and inclusion data requires an understanding of the broader organizational context, historical trends, and industry benchmarks. Interpreting data without considering these factors may lead to misinterpretations.

Intersectionality and Multiple Dimensions of Diversity: Analyzing multiple dimensions of diversity and considering intersectionality adds complexity to diversity and inclusion analytics. Organizations need to develop frameworks and methodologies that capture and address the unique experiences of individuals with intersecting identities.

Addressing Unconscious Bias: Unconscious bias can influence the collection and interpretation of diversity data. Organizations should provide training and awareness programs to mitigate bias in data collection, analysis, and decision-making processes.

Engaging Stakeholders: Engaging stakeholders, including employees, leaders, and external partners, is essential for successful implementation of diversity and inclusion analytics. Ensuring buy-in, communicating the purpose and benefits of analytics, and involving stakeholders in the process are critical for success.

Best Practices in Diversity and Inclusion Analytics:

To effectively leverage diversity and inclusion analytics, organizations should consider the following best practices:

Establish Clear Objectives: Clearly define the goals and objectives of diversity and inclusion analytics, aligning them with the organization's overall diversity and inclusion strategy and business objectives.

Collect Comprehensive and Relevant Data: Collect data that captures a broad range of diversity dimensions while respecting employee privacy and legal requirements. Ensure that the data collected is relevant to the organization's diversity and inclusion goals.

Analyze Data Intersectionally: Analyze diversity data intersectionally to understand the unique experiences of individuals with intersecting identities. This helps identify specific challenges and opportunities for creating an inclusive environment.

Involve Stakeholders: Engage employees, leaders, and external partners in the diversity and inclusion analytics process. Seek their input, address concerns, and involve them in the interpretation of data and development of action plans.

Communicate Findings and Take Action: Communicate the findings of diversity and inclusion analytics to employees, leaders, and other stakeholders. Use the insights gained to develop targeted initiatives, policies, and practices that foster a more inclusive workplace.

Monitor Progress and Evaluate Impact: Continuously monitor the progress of diversity and inclusion initiatives and evaluate their impact. Regularly assess the effectiveness of strategies, adjust approaches as needed, and celebrate successes.

In conclusion, diversity and inclusion analytics play a crucial role in creating a more inclusive and equitable workplace. By collecting and analyzing diversity data, organizations can gain insights, identify areas for improvement, and develop evidence-based strategies to foster diversity and inclusion. Overcoming challenges related to data collection, interpretation, and bias is key to successful implementation. Leveraging diversity and inclusion analytics benefits organizations by driving better decision-making, attracting and retaining top talent, and enhancing overall organizational performance.

CHAPTER 18: DATA SCIENCE IN INTERNET OF THINGS (IOT)

Chapter 18 explores the intersection of data science and the Internet of Things (IoT). The IoT refers to the network of interconnected devices and sensors that collect and exchange data. This chapter delves into the key concepts, challenges, and applications of data science in the IoT ecosystem.

Key Concepts of Data Science in IoT:

Data science in the IoT involves leveraging data analytics techniques to extract insights, patterns, and actionable information from the vast amounts of data generated by IoT devices. Key concepts include:

Data Collection: IoT devices generate massive volumes of data through sensors, actuators, and connected systems. Data scientists focus on collecting, storing, and organizing this data for further analysis.

Data Integration: IoT data often comes from diverse sources and formats. Data scientists work on integrating data from different devices and systems, ensuring consistency and compatibility for analysis.

Data Preprocessing: IoT data may contain noise, missing values, and anomalies. Data scientists employ preprocessing techniques to clean, transform, and prepare the data for analysis, ensuring its quality and reliability.

Data Analytics: Data scientists use various statistical, machine learning, and deep learning algorithms to extract insights from IoT data. These techniques help discover patterns, anomalies, correlations, and predictions to drive decision-making.

Challenges in Data Science in IoT:

Implementing data science in the IoT ecosystem faces several challenges:

Data Volume and Velocity: The sheer volume and high velocity of data generated by IoT devices require scalable and efficient data processing and analysis techniques.

Data Variety and Heterogeneity: IoT data comes in various formats, protocols, and structures, making it challenging to integrate and analyze. Data scientists need to handle different data types and develop methods to extract meaningful insights.

Data Security and Privacy: IoT devices collect sensitive data, raising concerns about data security and privacy. Data scientists must ensure proper encryption, access controls, and anonymization techniques to protect the data and comply with regulations.

Edge Computing: IoT devices often have limited computing power and storage capacity. Data scientists need to develop algorithms and techniques that can be deployed on edge devices for real-time analysis and decision-making.

Interoperability and Standards: The IoT landscape encompasses a wide range of devices, platforms, and protocols. Data scientists face the challenge of interoperability and the need to develop standards that facilitate seamless data integration and analysis.

Applications of Data Science in IoT:

Data science has numerous applications in the IoT ecosystem:

Predictive Maintenance: Data science enables predictive maintenance by analyzing sensor data to identify potential equipment failures and schedule maintenance activities proactively.

Anomaly Detection: Data scientists leverage anomaly detection algorithms to identify unusual patterns or behavior in IoT data. This helps detect and mitigate security breaches, system malfunctions, or environmental deviations.

Smart Cities: Data science in the IoT helps analyze data from various sources, such as sensors, traffic cameras, and weather stations, to optimize city operations, improve transportation systems, and enhance overall urban living.

Industrial IoT: Data science plays a crucial role in optimizing industrial processes by analyzing sensor data to identify bottlenecks, improve efficiency, and reduce downtime.

Environmental Monitoring: Data science enables the analysis of environmental sensor data to monitor air quality, water quality, and other environmental parameters. This information helps in managing and mitigating environmental risks.

Healthcare IoT: Data science contributes to healthcare IoT applications by analyzing sensor data from wearable devices, remote patient monitoring, and medical equipment. This analysis helps in early detection of health issues, personalized medicine, and remote patient care.

Benefits of Data Science in IoT:

The integration of data science in the IoT ecosystem offers several benefits:

Real-time Decision-Making: Data science techniques applied to IoT data enable real-time analysis and decision-making, allowing organizations to respond quickly to emerging situations and optimize operations.

Predictive and Prescriptive Analytics: By leveraging historical and real-time IoT data, data science helps organizations predict future trends, identify patterns, and make data-driven decisions. This allows for proactive actions and improved outcomes.

Enhanced Efficiency and Cost Savings: Data science in the IoT enables organizations to optimize processes, reduce waste, and improve efficiency. This leads to cost savings and improved resource utilization.

Improved Safety and Security: Data science helps in detecting and mitigating security threats, identifying potential hazards, and enhancing overall safety in various IoT applications, such as smart homes and industrial systems.

Innovation and New Business Opportunities: Data science in the IoT ecosystem drives innovation and opens up new business opportunities. By uncovering insights from IoT data, organizations can develop new products, services, and revenue streams.

In conclusion, data science plays a vital role in unlocking the value of data generated by IoT devices. By applying data analytics techniques, organizations can gain insights, optimize operations, enhance decision-making, and create innovative solutions. Overcoming challenges related to data volume, variety, security, and interoperability is crucial for successful implementation. The application areas of data science in IoT are diverse, ranging from predictive maintenance to smart cities and healthcare. Embracing data science in the IoT ecosystem offers numerous benefits, empowering organizations to harness the power of data and drive meaningful outcomes.

Analyzing sensor data for predictive maintenance is a critical application of data science in the Internet of Things (IoT) ecosystem. Predictive maintenance aims to identify potential equipment failures or malfunctions before they occur, allowing organizations to schedule maintenance activities proactively. By analyzing sensor data collected from IoT devices, data scientists can extract valuable insights and patterns that help optimize maintenance processes, reduce downtime, and improve operational efficiency. This section explores the key concepts, challenges, benefits, and best practices of analyzing sensor data for predictive maintenance.

Key Concepts of Analyzing Sensor Data for Predictive Maintenance:

Analyzing sensor data for predictive maintenance involves the following key concepts:

Sensor Data Collection: IoT devices equipped with sensors continuously collect data related to equipment performance, temperature, vibration, pressure, humidity, and other relevant parameters.

Data Preprocessing: Before analysis, sensor data undergoes preprocessing steps to clean, normalize, and transform the data. This ensures data quality and consistency, enabling accurate analysis.

Feature Extraction: Data scientists extract meaningful features from the sensor data that capture important patterns or indicators of equipment health. These features serve as inputs for predictive models.

Predictive Modeling: Data scientists apply various machine learning and statistical techniques to develop predictive models. These models learn from historical sensor data to identify patterns and anomalies associated with equipment failures.

Thresholds and Alarms: By setting thresholds and alarms based on predictive models, organizations can receive alerts when sensor data indicates potential equipment issues, enabling timely maintenance intervention.

Challenges in Analyzing Sensor Data for Predictive Maintenance:

Implementing sensor data analysis for predictive maintenance may encounter several challenges:

Data Volume and Velocity: IoT devices generate vast amounts of sensor data in real-time. Processing and analyzing this data in a timely manner requires scalable and efficient data storage and processing infrastructure.

Data Quality and Reliability: Sensor data may contain noise, outliers, or missing values. Ensuring data quality and reliability is crucial to avoid inaccurate predictions and false alarms.

Feature Selection and Engineering: Identifying the most relevant features from the sensor data is essential for accurate predictive modeling. Choosing appropriate features and engineering them effectively require domain knowledge and expertise.

Data Interpretability: Predictive models applied to sensor data may produce complex results that are difficult to interpret. Interpreting the models and explaining their findings to maintenance personnel and stakeholders can be a challenge.

Real-Time Analysis: Predictive maintenance requires real-time analysis of sensor data to enable timely intervention. Implementing real-time analytics capabilities and processing the data in near real-time is necessary for effective predictive maintenance.

Benefits of Analyzing Sensor Data for Predictive Maintenance:

Analyzing sensor data for predictive maintenance offers several benefits:

Reduced Downtime: By identifying potential equipment failures in advance, organizations can schedule maintenance activities proactively, reducing unplanned downtime and production disruptions.

Cost Savings: Predictive maintenance helps organizations optimize maintenance schedules, reducing the need for unnecessary preventive maintenance and minimizing equipment repair or replacement costs.

Increased Equipment Lifespan: Early detection and intervention based on predictive models help prolong the lifespan of equipment. Regular maintenance can prevent further deterioration and extend equipment reliability.

Enhanced Operational Efficiency: Analyzing sensor data allows organizations to optimize equipment utilization and improve operational efficiency by identifying inefficiencies, patterns, or conditions that affect performance.

Improved Safety: Predictive maintenance helps identify potential safety hazards, allowing organizations to address them before accidents or incidents occur, ensuring a safer working environment.

Efficient Resource Allocation: By identifying equipment issues in advance, organizations can allocate resources more efficiently, including manpower, spare parts, and maintenance schedules.

Best Practices in Analyzing Sensor Data for Predictive Maintenance:

To effectively analyze sensor data for predictive maintenance, organizations should consider the following best practices:

Data Quality Assurance: Ensure data quality by implementing data validation, cleaning, and normalization techniques. Monitor sensor data collection processes to minimize noise, outliers, and missing values.

Feature Engineering: Invest in domain expertise to identify relevant features from sensor data that have strong correlations with equipment failures. Use domain knowledge to engineer additional features that capture important patterns.

Model Selection and Validation: Select appropriate machine learning algorithms or statistical techniques that fit the predictive maintenance use case. Validate the models using historical sensor data and evaluate their performance metrics.

Real-Time Processing: Implement real-time data processing capabilities to enable timely analysis and intervention. Leverage technologies such as stream processing or edge computing to process sensor data in near real-time.

Collaboration between Data Scientists and Maintenance Teams: Foster collaboration between data scientists and maintenance personnel to understand domain-specific requirements, validate models, and interpret results effectively.

Continuous Improvement: Regularly monitor and evaluate the performance of predictive models. Incorporate feedback from maintenance teams and stakeholders to refine and improve the models over time.

In conclusion, analyzing sensor data for predictive maintenance is a powerful application of data science in the IoT ecosystem. By leveraging sensor data and applying predictive modeling techniques, organizations can optimize maintenance processes, reduce downtime, and improve operational efficiency. Overcoming challenges related to data volume, quality, interpretability, and real-time analysis is crucial for successful implementation. The benefits of analyzing sensor data for predictive maintenance include reduced downtime, cost savings, increased equipment lifespan, and enhanced operational efficiency. Adhering to best practices, such as data quality assurance, feature engineering, model selection, and collaboration, enables organizations to derive actionable insights and maximize the benefits of predictive maintenance.

Optimizing energy consumption and resource allocation is a crucial aspect of data science in various domains, including manufacturing, buildings, transportation, and renewable energy. This practice involves leveraging data analytics techniques to analyze energy consumption patterns, identify inefficiencies, and develop strategies for optimizing energy usage and resource allocation. By optimizing energy consumption and resource allocation, organizations can reduce costs, improve sustainability, and enhance overall operational efficiency. This section explores the key concepts, challenges, benefits, and best practices of optimizing energy consumption and resource allocation through data science.

Key Concepts of Optimizing Energy Consumption and Resource Allocation:

Optimizing energy consumption and resource allocation entails the following key concepts:

Energy Data Collection: Collecting energy consumption data from various sources, such as smart meters, sensors, or monitoring systems, provides a foundation for analysis and optimization.

Data Preprocessing: Preprocessing energy data involves cleaning, aggregating, and normalizing the data to ensure its quality and consistency. This step may involve handling missing values, outliers, or data inconsistencies.

Energy Efficiency Metrics: Defining energy efficiency metrics, such as energy intensity, energy consumption per unit of output, or energy performance indicators, helps assess the efficiency of energy usage.

Predictive Modeling: Developing predictive models using machine learning techniques helps forecast energy consumption and identify patterns or anomalies that can be used for optimization.

Resource Allocation Strategies: Optimizing resource allocation involves developing strategies to allocate energy, equipment, personnel, or other resources effectively based on data-driven insights and optimization algorithms.

Challenges in Optimizing Energy Consumption and Resource Allocation:

Implementing optimization strategies for energy consumption and resource allocation may encounter several challenges:

Data Availability and Quality: Accessing reliable and comprehensive energy consumption data can be challenging. Inaccurate or incomplete data may hinder the accuracy and effectiveness of optimization efforts.

Complex Energy Systems: Energy consumption in large-scale systems, such as manufacturing plants or smart grids, involves multiple interconnected processes and variables, making optimization complex.

Regulatory and Operational Constraints: Compliance with regulatory requirements and operational constraints can limit the flexibility of resource allocation and optimization strategies.

Integration of Multiple Data Sources: Integrating data from various sources, such as energy meters, production systems, or weather data, requires data integration techniques to provide a comprehensive view of energy consumption and resource utilization.

Behavioral and Human Factors: Optimizing energy consumption requires considering human behavior and organizational practices, as they significantly influence energy usage patterns and resource allocation decisions.

Benefits of Optimizing Energy Consumption and Resource Allocation:

Optimizing energy consumption and resource allocation through data science offers several benefits:

Cost Reduction: By identifying and eliminating energy inefficiencies, organizations can reduce energy costs significantly. Optimized resource allocation also minimizes waste and increases operational efficiency, leading to cost savings.

Sustainability and Environmental Impact: Energy optimization contributes to sustainability goals by reducing greenhouse gas emissions, promoting energy conservation, and supporting environmentally friendly practices.

Enhanced Operational Efficiency: Optimization strategies improve operational efficiency by identifying bottlenecks, streamlining processes, and reallocating resources to areas with high energy demand or inefficiencies.

Predictive Maintenance: Analyzing energy consumption patterns can help identify potential equipment failures or performance issues, enabling proactive maintenance interventions to avoid downtime and optimize resource allocation.

Demand Response and Load Management: Optimization techniques allow organizations to participate in demand response programs and effectively manage peak loads, reducing energy costs during periods of high demand.

Decision-Making Support: Data-driven insights enable better decision-making regarding resource allocation, equipment upgrades, energy-saving initiatives, and investment in energy-efficient technologies.

Best Practices in Optimizing Energy Consumption and Resource Allocation:

To effectively optimize energy consumption and resource allocation, organizations should consider the following best practices:

Data Collection and Monitoring: Implement automated data collection systems, such as smart meters or IoT sensors, to gather accurate and timely energy consumption data. Continuously monitor energy usage and resource allocation to identify inefficiencies.

Data Integration and Analysis: Integrate energy consumption data with other relevant data sources, such as production data or weather data, to gain a holistic view of resource allocation and energy performance. Apply data analytics techniques to identify patterns, anomalies, and optimization opportunities.

Predictive Modeling and Forecasting: Develop predictive models to forecast energy consumption, demand, and performance indicators. These models enable proactive planning and resource allocation based on predicted energy needs.

Optimization Algorithms and Tools: Utilize optimization algorithms and tools, such as mathematical programming, machine learning, or simulation-based optimization, to identify optimal resource allocation strategies considering operational constraints and objectives.

Stakeholder Engagement: Involve stakeholders, including energy managers, operators, and employees, in the optimization process. Raise awareness, provide training, and encourage behavior change to support energy-saving initiatives and resource allocation optimization.

Continuous Monitoring and Improvement: Establish a feedback loop to continuously monitor and evaluate the effectiveness of optimization strategies. Regularly review and update energy efficiency metrics, benchmarks, and targets to drive continuous improvement.

In conclusion, optimizing energy consumption and resource allocation through data science is a powerful approach to reduce costs, enhance sustainability, and improve operational efficiency. Overcoming challenges related to data availability, complexity, and behavioral factors is crucial for successful implementation. The benefits of optimizing energy consumption and resource allocation include cost reduction, sustainability improvements, and better operational decision-making. Adhering to best practices, such as data collection, integration, predictive modeling, optimization algorithms, stakeholder engagement, and continuous improvement, enables organizations to make data-driven decisions and achieve optimal energy usage and resource allocation.

Improving product design and user experience is a key focus area for organizations seeking to create innovative and user-centric products. Data science plays a crucial role in this process by leveraging user data, feedback, and analytics to inform and enhance product design decisions. By analyzing user behavior, preferences, and needs, organizations can optimize product features, user interfaces, and overall user experience. This section explores the key concepts, challenges, benefits, and best practices of using data science to improve product design and user experience.

Key Concepts of Improving Product Design and User Experience:

Improving product design and user experience involves the following key concepts:

User Research and Feedback: Collecting user data, feedback, and conducting user research helps understand user needs, preferences, and pain points. This data serves as a foundation for product design improvements.

User Behavior Analysis: Analyzing user behavior data, such as clickstream data, interaction patterns, or navigation flows, provides insights into how users engage with the product and identifies areas for improvement.

User Journey Mapping: Mapping the user journey from initial contact to product usage and beyond helps identify touchpoints, pain points, and opportunities to enhance user experience at each stage.

A/B Testing and Experimentation: Conducting controlled experiments, A/B tests, or multivariate tests helps evaluate the impact of design changes on user behavior and experience, guiding iterative improvements.

Personalization and Recommendation: Leveraging user data and machine learning algorithms, organizations can personalize product experiences and provide relevant recommendations based on user preferences and behavior.

Challenges in Improving Product Design and User Experience:

Implementing data-driven improvements in product design and user experience may encounter several challenges:

Data Quality and Availability: Ensuring the availability of high-quality and relevant user data can be challenging. Data collection mechanisms, privacy considerations, and data governance need to be carefully addressed.

User Privacy and Ethics: Organizations must handle user data ethically and responsibly, adhering to privacy regulations and obtaining appropriate user consent. Balancing data utilization with user privacy concerns is crucial.

Interpreting User Feedback: Analyzing and interpreting user feedback, which can be subjective or ambiguous, requires careful consideration. Organizations need to employ techniques such as sentiment analysis and text mining to derive meaningful insights.

Design-Data Integration: Integrating data science practices into the product design process can be challenging. Collaboration between designers, data scientists, and product teams is essential for effective integration.

Scalability and Real-Time Analysis: Scaling data analysis processes to handle large user datasets and conducting real-time analysis for immediate insights pose technical challenges. Organizations need robust infrastructure and tools to address these challenges.

Benefits of Improving Product Design and User Experience:

Improving product design and user experience through data science offers several benefits:

Enhanced User Satisfaction: By identifying user needs, pain points, and preferences, organizations can make targeted design improvements that enhance user satisfaction and loyalty.

Increased User Engagement and Adoption: Improving user experience leads to increased user engagement, longer usage sessions, and higher adoption rates, ultimately driving business growth.

Competitive Advantage: Organizations that prioritize user-centric design and continually improve user experience gain a competitive edge in the market. Customers are more likely to choose products that provide a seamless and delightful experience.

Improved Conversion and Retention: Optimizing product design and user experience increases conversion rates, encourages repeat usage, and improves customer retention.

Data-Driven Decision-Making: Data science empowers organizations to make data-driven design decisions, reducing reliance on subjective opinions and assumptions.

Innovation and Differentiation: Leveraging user data and analytics enables organizations to identify innovation opportunities and differentiate their products by delivering unique and tailored experiences.

Best Practices in Improving Product Design and User Experience:

To effectively improve product design and user experience using data science, organizations should consider the following best practices:

User-Centric Design: Place users at the center of the design process. Conduct user research, user testing, and usability studies to understand their needs, expectations, and pain points.

Data Collection and Integration: Collect user data from multiple sources, such as web analytics, customer feedback channels, or user surveys. Integrate this data with product design and development processes to inform design decisions.

User Segmentation and Personalization: Segment users based on their preferences, behavior, or demographics. Use this segmentation to personalize product experiences and tailor recommendations to individual users.

Iterative Design and Testing: Adopt an iterative design approach, incorporating A/B testing, user feedback, and continuous improvement cycles to refine the product design and user experience over time.

Collaboration between Designers and Data Scientists: Foster collaboration and effective communication between designers and data scientists. Encourage cross-functional teams that combine design expertise and data science capabilities.

Continuous User Feedback: Implement mechanisms to collect user feedback, such as surveys, feedback forms, or user ratings. Regularly analyze this feedback to identify trends, pain points, and areas for improvement.

User Experience Monitoring and Analytics: Implement user experience monitoring tools and analytics platforms to track user behavior, interactions, and engagement metrics. Leverage these insights to optimize the user experience.

In conclusion, data science plays a vital role in improving product design and user experience. By leveraging user data, feedback, and analytics, organizations can gain valuable insights, optimize product features, and create seamless and delightful experiences for users. Overcoming challenges related to data quality, privacy, and design-data integration is crucial for successful implementation. The benefits of improving product design and user experience include enhanced user satisfaction, increased engagement, and competitive advantage. Adhering to best practices, such as user-centric design, data integration, iterative testing, and collaboration, enables organizations to leverage data science to create innovative and user-centric products.

CHAPTER 19: EVALUATING DATA SCIENCE PROJECTS

Chapter 19 focuses on the critical process of evaluating data science projects. Evaluating the effectiveness and impact of data science initiatives is essential for organizations to measure their return on investment, make informed decisions, and drive continuous improvement. This chapter explores the key concepts, methodologies, challenges, and best practices involved in evaluating data science projects.

Key Concepts in Evaluating Data Science Projects:

Evaluating data science projects involves considering the following key concepts:

Project Objectives: Clearly define the objectives and expected outcomes of the data science project. Align these objectives with the organization's overall goals and priorities.

Key Performance Indicators (KPIs): Identify relevant KPIs that measure the project's success. These may include metrics such as accuracy, precision, recall, revenue impact, customer satisfaction, or cost savings.

Evaluation Framework: Develop an evaluation framework that defines the methodologies, metrics, and data sources to assess the project's performance. This framework provides a structured approach to evaluate different aspects of the project.

Data Quality and Availability: Ensure that data used for evaluation is of high quality, relevant, and representative of the project's objectives. Address any data quality issues or limitations that may impact the evaluation.

Stakeholder Engagement: Involve key stakeholders, including business leaders, project sponsors, and end-users, in the evaluation process. Seek their input, address concerns, and incorporate their feedback in the evaluation criteria.

Methodologies for Evaluating Data Science Projects:

There are various methodologies and techniques for evaluating data science projects:

Accuracy Metrics: Measure the accuracy of the predictive models or algorithms used in the project. Common metrics include precision, recall, F1 score, and area under the curve (AUC) for classification tasks, as well as mean squared error (MSE) or R-squared for regression tasks.

Business Impact Analysis: Assess the project's impact on key business metrics, such as revenue, cost savings, customer acquisition, or retention rates. Conduct before-and-after analysis or A/B testing to measure the project's influence on business outcomes.

User Feedback and Satisfaction: Gather user feedback and conduct surveys or interviews to assess user satisfaction and acceptance of the project's outputs or recommendations.

Return on Investment (ROI): Calculate the financial return on investment by comparing the project's costs (e.g., resources, infrastructure, data acquisition) to the benefits generated (e.g., revenue increase, cost savings).

Decision-Making Improvement: Evaluate the project's contribution to improved decision-making processes, such as more informed strategic choices, optimized resource allocation, or reduced risks.

Challenges in Evaluating Data Science Projects:

Evaluating data science projects comes with its own set of challenges:

Data Quality and Availability: Access to high-quality data that represents the project's objectives and business context is crucial for accurate evaluation. Addressing data quality issues and ensuring data availability can be challenging.

Causality vs. Correlation: Distinguishing between correlation and causation is important when evaluating the impact of a data science project. It can be challenging to attribute changes solely to the project's outputs and rule out confounding factors.

Alignment with Business Objectives: Ensuring alignment between the evaluation metrics and the organization's business objectives is essential. Defining meaningful KPIs that capture the project's impact on business outcomes can be a challenge.

Time and Resource Constraints: Evaluating data science projects requires time, resources, and expertise. Balancing evaluation efforts with ongoing project needs and limited resources can pose challenges.

Best Practices in Evaluating Data Science Projects:

To effectively evaluate data science projects, organizations should consider the following best practices:

Clearly Define Objectives and KPIs: Clearly articulate project objectives and establish measurable KPIs that align with business goals. These objectives and KPIs serve as the foundation for evaluation.

Plan Evaluation in Advance: Incorporate evaluation planning from the project's outset. Define evaluation milestones, data requirements, and evaluation methodologies to ensure a systematic and well-structured evaluation process.

Establish Baselines: Establish baseline metrics or benchmarks to provide a point of comparison for evaluation. Compare project performance against these baselines to assess the project's impact.

Involve Stakeholders: Engage key stakeholders throughout the evaluation process. Seek their input, address concerns, and incorporate their perspectives in the evaluation criteria and methodologies.

Continuously Monitor and Iterate: Evaluate data science projects iteratively and continuously. Monitor performance over time, gather feedback, and use the evaluation results to drive ongoing improvement.

Communicate Results and Insights: Effectively communicate the evaluation findings, insights, and recommendations to relevant stakeholders. Provide actionable insights that inform decision-making and guide future project iterations.

In conclusion, evaluating data science projects is essential for assessing their impact, ensuring alignment with business objectives, and driving continuous improvement. By establishing clear objectives, defining relevant KPIs, and using appropriate evaluation methodologies, organizations can measure the success of their data science initiatives. Overcoming challenges related to data quality, causality, and resource constraints is crucial for effective evaluation. Adhering to best practices, such as planning evaluation in advance, involving stakeholders, establishing baselines, and communicating results, enables organizations to make informed decisions and optimize the value derived from data science projects.

Measuring the success of data initiatives is essential for organizations to assess the impact, effectiveness, and value derived from their data-driven projects. By establishing appropriate metrics and evaluation methodologies, organizations can track progress, identify areas for improvement, and make data-informed decisions. This section explores the key concepts, challenges, benefits, and best practices of measuring the success of data initiatives.

Key Concepts in Measuring the Success of Data Initiatives:

Measuring the success of data initiatives involves considering the following key concepts:

Goals and Objectives: Clearly define the goals and objectives of the data initiative. These should be aligned with the organization's overall strategy and address specific business challenges or opportunities.

Key Performance Indicators (KPIs): Identify relevant KPIs that measure the success of the data initiative. These metrics may include quantitative measures such as revenue impact, cost savings, customer satisfaction, or operational efficiency.

Data Quality and Accuracy: Ensure that the data used for evaluation is of high quality, accurate, and representative of the initiative's objectives. Address any data quality issues or limitations that may impact the evaluation.

Impact on Decision-Making: Assess the extent to which the data initiative has influenced decision-making processes within the organization. Measure the adoption and utilization of data-driven insights in decision-making.

Stakeholder Engagement: Involve key stakeholders, including business leaders, project sponsors, and end-users, in the evaluation process. Seek their input, address concerns, and incorporate their feedback in the evaluation criteria.

Challenges in Measuring the Success of Data Initiatives:

Measuring the success of data initiatives can encounter several challenges:

Defining Relevant Metrics: Identifying and defining metrics that accurately capture the impact and value of the data initiative can be challenging. It requires a clear understanding of business objectives and alignment with organizational priorities.

Data Quality and Availability: Access to high-quality data that represents the initiative's objectives and business context is crucial for accurate evaluation. Data availability and data integration across systems can pose challenges.

Causality vs. Correlation: Distinguishing between correlation and causation is important when assessing the impact of a data initiative. It can be challenging to attribute changes solely to the data initiative and rule out confounding factors.

Organizational Change and Adoption: Evaluating the success of data initiatives involves assessing the extent to which the organization has embraced data-driven decision-making. Overcoming resistance to change and fostering a data-driven culture can be challenging.

Benefits of Measuring the Success of Data Initiatives:

Measuring the success of data initiatives offers several benefits:

Performance Assessment: Evaluate the performance and impact of data initiatives, enabling organizations to identify areas of success and areas that need improvement.

Decision-Making Improvement: Measure the extent to which the data initiative has improved decision-making processes, leading to more informed and effective strategic choices.

Return on Investment (ROI): Calculate the ROI by comparing the costs of implementing and maintaining the data initiative to the benefits generated. This helps assess the financial value and efficiency of the initiative.

Alignment with Business Objectives: Evaluate the degree to which the data initiative aligns with the organization's business objectives and contributes to overall goals and priorities.

Continuous Improvement: Use evaluation results to drive continuous improvement. Identify lessons learned, insights, and recommendations that can inform future data initiatives and enhance their effectiveness.

Best Practices in Measuring the Success of Data Initiatives:

To effectively measure the success of data initiatives, organizations should consider the following best practices:

Clearly Define Goals and Objectives: Clearly articulate the goals and objectives of the data initiative. Align these goals with the organization's overall strategy and ensure they address specific business challenges or opportunities.

Establish Relevant KPIs: Identify and define KPIs that align with the initiative's objectives and provide meaningful insights into its impact. Choose KPIs that are measurable, relevant, and aligned with business goals.

Define Evaluation Methodologies: Develop evaluation methodologies that outline the data collection process, data analysis techniques, and evaluation frameworks. These methodologies provide a structured approach to assess the success of the data initiative.

Regular Monitoring and Reporting: Implement a regular monitoring and reporting process to track progress and evaluate the initiative's performance against defined KPIs. Provide stakeholders with timely and actionable insights.

Stakeholder Engagement: Involve key stakeholders throughout the evaluation process. Seek their input, address concerns, and incorporate their perspectives in the evaluation criteria and methodologies.

Continuous Improvement and Iteration: Use evaluation results to drive continuous improvement. Learn from successes and failures, iterate on data initiatives, and apply insights gained to enhance future projects.

In conclusion, measuring the success of data initiatives is crucial for organizations to assess the impact, effectiveness, and value derived from their data-driven projects. By establishing clear objectives, defining relevant KPIs, and using appropriate evaluation methodologies, organizations can track progress, make data-informed decisions, and drive continuous improvement. Overcoming challenges related to defining metrics, data quality, causality, and organizational change is essential for effective measurement. Adhering to best practices, such as clearly defining goals, establishing relevant KPIs, engaging stakeholders, and fostering a culture of continuous improvement, enables organizations to assess the success of their data initiatives and optimize their data-driven strategies.

Identifying areas for improvement is a critical step in the data science and analytics process. It enables organizations to optimize their strategies, address weaknesses, and drive continuous improvement. By evaluating current practices, analyzing results, and seeking feedback, organizations can identify areas where they can enhance efficiency, effectiveness, and overall performance. This section explores the key concepts, challenges, benefits, and best practices of identifying areas for improvement in data science and analytics.

Key Concepts in Identifying Areas for Improvement:

Identifying areas for improvement involves considering the following key concepts:

Evaluation and Assessment: Evaluate existing data science and analytics practices, processes, and outcomes against predefined goals and objectives. Assess the effectiveness and efficiency of current strategies and identify areas that require improvement.

Performance Metrics: Define key performance metrics that align with organizational goals. These metrics may include accuracy, efficiency, customer satisfaction, cost-effectiveness, or timeliness.

Feedback and Collaboration: Gather feedback from stakeholders, including users, clients, and internal teams, to gain insights into their experiences and perspectives. Collaboration and communication foster a culture of continuous improvement.

Benchmarking: Compare performance against industry standards or best practices to identify gaps and areas where improvement is needed. Benchmarking provides a reference point for evaluating performance.

Root Cause Analysis: Conduct root cause analysis to identify the underlying factors contributing to suboptimal performance. This analysis helps pinpoint the specific areas that require improvement.

Challenges in Identifying Areas for Improvement:

Identifying areas for improvement can encounter several challenges:

Data Quality and Availability: Access to high-quality, relevant data is crucial for accurate evaluation. Addressing data quality issues and ensuring data availability can be challenging.

Subjectivity and Bias: Evaluating performance and identifying areas for improvement may involve subjective judgment and interpretation. Avoiding bias and ensuring objectivity in the evaluation process is important.

Complexity and Interdependencies: Data science and analytics involve complex systems and interdependencies. Isolating specific areas for improvement within this complex ecosystem can be challenging.

Resistance to Change: Overcoming resistance to change and fostering a culture of continuous improvement can be challenging. Resistance may arise from organizational dynamics, lack of awareness, or fear of disruption.

Benefits of Identifying Areas for Improvement:

Identifying areas for improvement offers several benefits:

Enhanced Performance: Identifying areas for improvement enables organizations to enhance their performance, efficiency, and effectiveness in data science and analytics initiatives.

Increased Efficiency: By addressing inefficiencies and streamlining processes, organizations can optimize resource allocation, reduce costs, and improve overall efficiency.

Data-Informed Decision-Making: Identifying areas for improvement allows organizations to make data-informed decisions and prioritize investments in areas that yield the greatest impact.

Competitive Advantage: Continuously improving data science and analytics capabilities provides a competitive edge by staying ahead of industry trends, technological advancements, and customer expectations.

Innovation and Adaptability: Identifying areas for improvement fosters a culture of innovation and adaptability. Organizations can continuously learn, experiment, and adapt to changing business and technological landscapes.

Best Practices in Identifying Areas for Improvement:

To effectively identify areas for improvement in data science and analytics, organizations should consider the following best practices:

Define Clear Objectives and Metrics: Clearly articulate the objectives of data science and analytics initiatives and establish relevant metrics for evaluation. These metrics should align with organizational goals and priorities.

Continuously Monitor Performance: Implement a regular monitoring and evaluation process to track performance against predefined metrics. This includes reviewing key performance indicators, analyzing results, and identifying trends or patterns.

Gather Feedback from Stakeholders: Engage stakeholders, including users, clients, and internal teams, to gather feedback on their experiences, challenges, and suggestions. This feedback provides valuable insights into areas that require improvement.

Conduct Root Cause Analysis: Conduct a thorough analysis to identify the underlying causes of suboptimal performance. This involves examining processes, systems, data quality, and organizational dynamics to pinpoint specific areas for improvement.

Foster a Culture of Continuous Improvement: Encourage a culture of continuous improvement by fostering collaboration, knowledge sharing, and learning. Embrace feedback, experimentation, and innovation as drivers of growth and progress.

Prioritize and Plan Improvement Efforts: Prioritize areas for improvement based on their potential impact, feasibility, and alignment with organizational goals. Develop a roadmap and action plan to address identified areas, assigning responsibilities and setting timelines.

In conclusion, identifying areas for improvement in data science and analytics is crucial for organizations to optimize their strategies, enhance performance, and drive continuous improvement. By evaluating current practices, analyzing results, seeking feedback, and conducting root cause analysis, organizations can identify specific areas that require attention. Overcoming challenges related to data quality, subjectivity, complexity, and resistance to change is essential for effective identification of improvement areas. Adhering to best practices, such as defining clear objectives and metrics, monitoring performance, gathering feedback, conducting root cause analysis, and fostering a culture of continuous improvement, enables organizations to stay competitive, adapt to evolving needs, and excel in data science and analytics endeavors.

Creating a culture of experimentation and learning is essential for organizations that want to embrace innovation, adapt to change, and drive continuous improvement. This culture encourages individuals and teams to explore new ideas, take calculated risks, and learn from both successes and failures. By fostering an environment that values experimentation, organizations can unlock new insights, identify better solutions, and drive growth. This section explores the key concepts, challenges, benefits, and best practices of creating a culture of experimentation and learning.

Key Concepts in Creating a Culture of Experimentation and Learning:

Creating a culture of experimentation and learning involves considering the following key concepts:

Psychological Safety: Foster a psychologically safe environment where individuals feel comfortable taking risks, sharing ideas, and challenging the status quo without fear of negative consequences.

Innovation Mindset: Encourage an innovation mindset that values creativity, curiosity, and exploration. Emphasize the importance of experimentation and learning as drivers of growth and improvement.

Risk-Taking and Failure Acceptance: Encourage calculated risk-taking and accept that failure is an opportunity for learning and growth. Emphasize the importance of learning from failures and using them as steppingstones to success.

Continuous Improvement: Promote a culture of continuous improvement by encouraging individuals and teams to regularly assess their work, identify areas for enhancement, and iterate on their ideas and processes.

Knowledge Sharing and Collaboration: Foster a collaborative environment where knowledge and insights are shared openly across teams and departments. Encourage cross-functional collaboration to promote diverse perspectives and ideation.

Challenges in Creating a Culture of Experimentation and Learning:

Creating a culture of experimentation and learning can encounter several challenges:

Risk-Averse Culture: Overcoming a risk-averse culture where failure is stigmatized, and innovative ideas are not encouraged requires a significant shift in mindset and organizational norms.

Lack of Resources and Time: Experimentation and learning require dedicated resources and time, which can be challenging to allocate in fast-paced business environments focused on immediate results.

Fear of Failure and Repercussions: Fear of failure and potential negative consequences can hinder individuals' willingness to take risks and explore new ideas. Overcoming this fear requires building trust and psychological safety within the organization.

Resistance to Change: Resistance to change is common when introducing new practices or challenging existing processes. Overcoming resistance requires effective change management strategies and clear communication.

Benefits of Creating a Culture of Experimentation and Learning:

Creating a culture of experimentation and learning offers several benefits:

Innovation and Creativity: Encouraging experimentation and learning unlocks innovation and creativity within the organization. It fosters a mindset of exploration, leading to the development of new ideas, products, and solutions.

Adaptability and Agility: A culture of experimentation and learning enables organizations to adapt quickly to changing market conditions, technological advancements, and customer needs.

Continuous Improvement: Embracing experimentation and learning allows organizations to continually improve processes, products, and services based on insights gained from real-world experiments.

Employee Engagement and Empowerment: Encouraging individuals to experiment and learn empowers them to take ownership of their work, fostering higher levels of engagement and job satisfaction.

Risk Management: A culture of experimentation helps manage risks effectively by allowing organizations to test hypotheses, validate assumptions, and make informed decisions based on data and insights.

Best Practices in Creating a Culture of Experimentation and Learning:

To effectively create a culture of experimentation and learning, organizations should consider the following best practices:

Leadership Support and Role Modeling: Leadership plays a crucial role in promoting experimentation and learning. Leaders should actively support and engage in experimentation initiatives, role-modeling behaviors that encourage innovation and risk-taking.

Establish Psychological Safety: Create a psychologically safe environment where individuals feel comfortable sharing ideas, taking risks, and learning from failures. Foster an open and inclusive culture that values diverse perspectives.

Allocate Resources and Time: Allocate dedicated resources, including time and budget, to support experimentation and learning activities. This demonstrates the organization's commitment to fostering a culture of exploration.

Encourage Collaboration and Knowledge Sharing: Promote collaboration and knowledge sharing across teams and departments. Encourage cross-functional collaboration, provide platforms for idea exchange, and recognize and reward knowledge-sharing behaviors.

Celebrate and Learn from Failures: Encourage the celebration of failures as learning opportunities. Foster a growth mindset that views failures as steppingstones to success and encourages individuals to reflect on failures and extract valuable insights.

Provide Training and Development Opportunities: Offer training programs, workshops, and learning opportunities that help individuals develop skills in experimentation, data analysis, and innovation. This enhances their ability to contribute to the culture of experimentation and learning.

In conclusion, creating a culture of experimentation and learning is crucial for organizations to foster innovation, adaptability, and continuous improvement. By embracing risk-taking, promoting psychological safety, and encouraging collaboration and knowledge sharing, organizations can unlock new ideas, drive creativity, and stay ahead in a rapidly changing business landscape. Overcoming challenges related to risk aversion, resource constraints, and resistance to change is essential for creating a culture that values experimentation and learning. Adhering to best practices, such as leadership support, psychological safety, resource allocation, collaboration, and celebrating failures as learning opportunities, enables organizations to establish a culture of exploration, innovation, and continuous growth.

CHAPTER 20: FUTURE TRENDS IN DATA SCIENCE AND ANALYTICS

Chapter 20 explores the exciting and evolving landscape of data science and analytics, highlighting the future trends that are expected to shape the field. As technology advances and new opportunities emerge, organizations need to stay ahead of the curve to leverage data-driven insights for strategic decision-making. This chapter provides an overview of key trends and innovations that are likely to impact data science and analytics in the future.

Artificial Intelligence and Machine Learning Advancements:

Artificial Intelligence (AI) and Machine Learning (ML) continue to evolve and drive significant advancements in data science and analytics. The future will witness the development of more sophisticated algorithms, improved model interpretability, and increased automation. AI and ML will enable organizations to extract deeper insights, make more accurate predictions, and automate decision-making processes.

Deep Learning and Neural Networks:

Deep Learning techniques, powered by neural networks, have gained immense popularity in recent years. The future will see further advancements in deep learning models, enabling them to handle more complex data, solve intricate problems, and drive breakthroughs in various domains such as image recognition, natural language processing, and autonomous systems.

Natural Language Processing and Conversational AI:

Natural Language Processing (NLP) and Conversational AI are revolutionizing how humans interact with computers. The future will witness advancements in NLP models that can comprehend and generate human-like language, enabling more sophisticated chatbots, virtual assistants, and language translation systems.

Edge Computing and IoT Integration:

The proliferation of Internet of Things (IoT) devices generates vast amounts of data. In the future, edge computing will become more prevalent, enabling data processing and analytics at the edge of the network. This integration of edge computing and IoT will unlock real-time insights, improve response times, and optimize resource allocation.

Ethical and Responsible Data Science:

As the impact of data science and analytics continues to grow, ethical considerations become increasingly important. The future will see a greater focus on responsible data science practices, including addressing algorithmic bias, ensuring data privacy, and promoting transparency and accountability in AI-driven decision-making processes.

Explainable AI and Trustworthy Models:

With the increasing adoption of AI, there is a growing need for models that can explain their decisions. Explainable AI techniques will gain prominence in the future, allowing organizations to understand how models arrive at their predictions and build trust among users, regulators, and stakeholders.

Automated Machine Learning (AutoML):

Automated Machine Learning (AutoML) will simplify the process of building and deploying ML models. The future will witness the development of more sophisticated AutoML tools and platforms that automate tasks such as feature engineering, model selection, hyperparameter tuning, and model deployment, making data science more accessible to a wider range of users.

Quantum Computing and Advanced Analytics:

Quantum Computing holds immense promise for solving complex problems that are beyond the capabilities of classical computing. In the future, quantum computing will enable advanced analytics techniques, such as optimization, simulation, and cryptography, which can significantly accelerate data processing and analysis.

Data Governance and Privacy Regulations:

As data privacy concerns increase, governments and regulatory bodies are introducing more stringent data governance and privacy regulations. Organizations will need to adapt to evolving regulations and ensure compliance while effectively utilizing data for analytics purposes.

Augmented Analytics and Natural Language Interfaces:

Augmented Analytics combines human intelligence with machine intelligence, enabling users to gain insights and make data-driven decisions more intuitively. In the future, augmented analytics will incorporate natural language interfaces, enabling users to interact with data using voice commands and conversational queries.

Data Science Democratization:

Data Science democratization aims to make data science tools and techniques accessible to a broader audience, including non-technical users. The future will witness the development of user-friendly interfaces, low-code platforms, and automated workflows that empower individuals across the organization to perform data analysis and gain insights.

Continuous Learning and Upskilling:

The field of data science and analytics is rapidly evolving, and professionals need to continuously update their skills and knowledge. In the future, lifelong learning and upskilling will become integral to staying relevant and harnessing the full potential of emerging technologies and techniques.

In conclusion, the future of data science and analytics holds immense potential for innovation and transformative impact. Advancements in AI, ML, NLP, edge computing, and ethical practices will shape the landscape of data-driven decision-making. Organizations that embrace these future trends and adapt to evolving technologies, regulations, and user expectations will gain a competitive edge and drive success in the data-driven era. Continuous learning, experimentation, and a commitment to responsible and ethical practices will be crucial for navigating the future of data science and analytics.

Emerging technologies and techniques play a crucial role in shaping the field of data science and analytics. As technology continues to advance at a rapid pace, new tools, methodologies, and approaches are being developed to extract deeper insights, improve data processing capabilities, and drive innovation. This section explores some of the key emerging technologies and techniques that are transforming the landscape of data science and analytics.

Internet of Things (IoT):

The Internet of Things (IoT) has gained significant traction in recent years. IoT devices generate massive amounts of data that can be utilized for analytics purposes. By collecting data from various sensors and devices, organizations can gain insights into patterns, trends, and anomalies, enabling better decision-making and optimization of processes.

Blockchain Technology:

Blockchain technology, initially associated with cryptocurrencies, has found applications beyond the financial sector. Its decentralized and transparent nature makes it suitable for secure and auditable data storage and sharing. Blockchain can enhance data security, integrity, and traceability, particularly in industries where data provenance and trust are critical.

Edge Computing:

Edge computing refers to processing and analyzing data near the source, at the edge of the network, rather than relying on centralized cloud infrastructure. This approach enables real-time data processing, reduces latency, and conserves network bandwidth. Edge computing is particularly valuable in scenarios where immediate data analysis and response are essential, such as in IoT applications and real-time analytics.

Automated Machine Learning (AutoML):

Automated Machine Learning (AutoML) is an emerging technology that simplifies the process of building and deploying machine learning models. AutoML platforms and tools automate tasks such as feature engineering, model selection, hyperparameter tuning, and model deployment. By reducing the complexity and time required for model development, AutoML democratizes data science and makes it accessible to a broader range of users.

Explainable AI (XAI):

Explainable AI (XAI) aims to enhance the interpretability and transparency of machine learning models. As AI becomes more pervasive, there is a growing need to understand and explain the decisions made by AI algorithms. XAI techniques provide insights into how models arrive at their predictions, increasing trust and enabling humans to make more informed decisions based on AI outputs.

Natural Language Processing (NLP) Advancements:

Advancements in Natural Language Processing (NLP) techniques enable computers to understand and process human language more effectively. With improved language models, sentiment analysis, text summarization, and language translation, organizations can derive insights from unstructured text data, analyze customer feedback, and enhance chatbot and virtual assistant capabilities.

Robotic Process Automation (RPA):

Robotic Process Automation (RPA) involves automating repetitive and rule-based tasks using software robots or bots. RPA enables organizations to streamline workflows, reduce errors, and increase operational efficiency. By integrating RPA with data science and analytics processes, organizations can automate data collection, cleansing, and transformation, allowing data scientists to focus on higher-value tasks.

Deep Learning Techniques:

Deep learning techniques, powered by neural networks, have revolutionized areas such as computer vision, natural language processing, and speech recognition. Deep learning models, with their ability to automatically learn hierarchical representations from data, have led to significant advancements in image recognition, object detection, language generation, and recommendation systems.

Augmented Analytics:

Augmented Analytics combines human intelligence with machine intelligence to enhance data analysis and decision-making. By leveraging automated machine learning, natural language interfaces, and data visualization, augmented analytics enables business users to gain insights from complex data sets and make data-driven decisions more intuitively.

Quantum Computing:

Quantum computing holds immense promise for solving complex problems that are beyond the capabilities of classical computing. Quantum computers leverage the principles of quantum mechanics to perform calculations at an exponential scale, enabling faster and more efficient data processing and optimization. While still in the early stages, quantum computing has the potential to revolutionize areas such as cryptography, optimization, and drug discovery.

DataOps and MLOps:

DataOps and MLOps (Machine Learning Operations) are emerging practices aimed at improving the efficiency, collaboration, and scalability of data science and machine learning projects. DataOps focuses on streamlining data pipelines, data governance, and data quality, while MLOps focuses on managing the lifecycle of machine learning models, including model deployment, monitoring, and retraining.

Federated Learning:

Federated Learning is a distributed machine learning approach that enables training models on decentralized data sources while preserving data privacy.

Instead of centralizing data in a single location, federated learning allows training to occur on local devices or servers, ensuring data privacy and reducing data transfer requirements. This approach is particularly relevant in industries with sensitive data, such as healthcare and finance.

In conclusion, emerging technologies and techniques are driving significant advancements in the field of data science and analytics. IoT, blockchain, edge computing, AutoML, XAI, NLP advancements, RPA, deep learning, augmented analytics, quantum computing, DataOps, MLOps, and federated learning are reshaping how organizations extract insights, automate processes, and make data-driven decisions. By staying informed about these emerging trends and embracing the right technologies and methodologies, organizations can gain a competitive edge, unlock new opportunities, and achieve transformative outcomes in their data science and analytics initiatives.

The impact of artificial intelligence (AI) on various aspects of society and industry cannot be overstated. AI has the potential to revolutionize how we live, work, and interact. This section explores the profound impact of AI in different domains and its implications for the future.

Automation and Efficiency:

One of the most significant impacts of AI is automation. AI-powered systems and robots can perform tasks that traditionally required human intervention, leading to increased efficiency and productivity. Automated processes, such as robotic process automation (RPA) and AI-driven algorithms, can handle repetitive, mundane, and time-consuming tasks, freeing up human workers to focus on more creative and strategic endeavors.

Enhanced Decision-Making:

AI enables data-driven decision-making by analyzing vast amounts of data, identifying patterns, and generating insights. Machine learning algorithms can make predictions, classify data, and recommend optimal actions based on historical data. This empowers organizations to make more informed decisions, optimize operations, and achieve better outcomes across various industries, such as finance, healthcare, and marketing.

Personalized Experiences:

AI has transformed the way businesses engage with customers. Through AI-powered recommendation systems and personalization algorithms, organizations can deliver highly tailored experiences to individual users. E-commerce platforms, streaming services, and social media platforms use AI to understand user preferences and behavior, resulting in personalized product recommendations, content suggestions, and targeted advertisements.

Advanced Healthcare:

AI has the potential to revolutionize healthcare by improving diagnostics, treatment plans, and patient outcomes. Machine learning algorithms can analyze medical data, identify patterns, and assist in disease diagnosis. AI-powered robots and devices can perform complex surgeries with precision and accuracy. Additionally, AI-enabled wearable devices can monitor vital signs and alert healthcare professionals in real-time, leading to early detection and intervention.

Smart Cities and Infrastructure:

AI is transforming the concept of smart cities by optimizing infrastructure and resource allocation. AI algorithms can analyze data from sensors, cameras, and connected devices to manage traffic flow, optimize energy consumption, and enhance public safety. Smart grids, intelligent transportation systems, and predictive maintenance are some examples of AI-driven solutions that improve urban living.

Enhanced Customer Service:

AI-powered chatbots and virtual assistants have revolutionized customer service. These intelligent systems can understand natural language, provide instant responses to customer inquiries, and handle routine customer support tasks. AI algorithms can analyze customer sentiments and feedback to improve customer experience and identify areas for service enhancements.

Augmented Creativity:

AI is being used to augment human creativity in fields such as art, music, and design. AI algorithms can generate artwork, compose music, and assist in the design process by analyzing patterns and creating unique outputs. This collaboration between humans and AI sparks new possibilities and pushes the boundaries of creative expression.

Ethical Considerations:

The impact of AI also raises ethical considerations. Issues such as bias in algorithms, privacy concerns, and job displacement require careful consideration and regulation. It is essential to ensure that AI systems are designed and deployed ethically, transparently, and in alignment with societal values.

Employment and Workforce Changes:

AI's automation capabilities may disrupt certain job sectors, leading to changes in employment patterns. While AI may replace some tasks, it also creates new opportunities and demands for skillsets in managing and leveraging AI technologies. Organizations and governments must focus on re-skilling and upskilling the workforce to adapt to the changing job landscape.

Collaborative AI:

Collaborative AI refers to the integration of AI technologies with human collaboration. Humans and AI systems work together to leverage each other's strengths. This approach allows AI to augment human capabilities, improve decision-making, and drive innovation.

Continuous Advancements:

AI is a rapidly evolving field, and advancements are being made at an unprecedented pace. Ongoing research and development are pushing the boundaries of AI, leading to breakthroughs in areas such as deep learning, natural language processing, and computer vision. Continued progress in AI will further amplify its impact across various domains.

In conclusion, the impact of AI is transformative and far-reaching. It drives automation, enhances decision-making, personalizes experiences, revolutionizes healthcare, improves infrastructure, augments creativity, and raises ethical considerations. The future holds immense potential for AI to shape society, economy, and the way we live and work. Organizations and policymakers must navigate these advancements responsibly, with a focus on ethical deployment, job reskilling, and leveraging AI to benefit humanity as a whole.

The ethical and societal implications of data science are increasingly becoming significant as organizations and individuals harness the power of data to drive decision-making and innovation. While data science offers numerous benefits, it also raises complex ethical considerations that need to be carefully addressed. This section explores the ethical and societal implications of data science and the key considerations that organizations and data scientists must keep in mind.

Privacy and Data Protection:

The collection and analysis of vast amounts of personal data raise concerns about privacy and data protection. Organizations must ensure that data is collected and used in a transparent and responsible manner, with proper consent from individuals. Data security measures should be implemented to safeguard sensitive information and protect against data breaches.

Bias and Fairness:

Data science algorithms can inadvertently reflect biases present in the data used for training. This can result in unfair outcomes or discrimination against certain groups. Data scientists must be aware of these biases and take steps to mitigate them, such as careful dataset selection, feature engineering, and ongoing monitoring of algorithm performance.

Transparency and Explainability:

The lack of transparency in data science models can lead to a lack of trust and understanding among users. It is important to develop models and algorithms that are explainable and provide insights into how they arrive at their predictions or decisions. This promotes accountability and allows users to assess the reliability and fairness of the results.

Informed Consent and User Empowerment:

Organizations must ensure that individuals are well-informed about the collection and use of their data and have the ability to exercise control over their personal information. Transparency in data practices and providing options for users to opt-in or opt-out of data sharing and analysis are critical for respecting individual autonomy.

Ethical Use of Data:

Data scientists have a responsibility to ensure that the data they use is obtained legally and ethically. This includes respecting data licensing agreements, complying with relevant regulations and guidelines, and being mindful of the potential societal impact of their work. The use of data should align with ethical principles and respect the rights and dignity of individuals.

Social and Economic Impact:

Data science has the potential to exacerbate existing social and economic inequalities. It is important to consider the broader impact of data science initiatives on vulnerable populations and marginalized communities. Efforts should be made to address biases, bridge the digital divide, and ensure that the benefits of data science are accessible to all.

Accountability and Governance:

Accountability and governance mechanisms are crucial in ensuring that data science initiatives are conducted ethically. Organizations should establish clear policies and guidelines for data usage, conduct regular audits, and designate responsible individuals or teams to oversee ethical practices.

Collaboration with regulatory bodies and adherence to relevant laws and regulations are essential.

Ethical Decision-Making in AI:

The increasing use of AI and machine learning algorithms raises ethical dilemmas regarding the role of humans in decision-making. Ethical considerations should be integrated into the design and development of AI systems, ensuring that humans retain control and accountability for the decisions made by AI algorithms.

Long-Term Implications:

Data science initiatives should consider the long-term implications of their work on society and the environment. This includes assessing potential unintended consequences, addressing issues of sustainability, and considering the broader societal implications of data-driven decisions.

Data Sharing and Open Science:

Balancing the need for data sharing and open science with privacy concerns is a delicate challenge. Data scientists should promote responsible data sharing practices, adhere to data usage agreements, and consider the potential risks and benefits associated with sharing sensitive data.

In conclusion, data science has immense potential to drive innovation and positive societal impact. However, organizations and data scientists must navigate the ethical considerations associated with data collection, analysis, and decision-making. By prioritizing privacy, fairness, transparency, informed consent, and social responsibility, data science can be used to promote the well-being of individuals and society as a whole. Ethical decision-making in data science is not only a legal and regulatory requirement but also a moral imperative to ensure that the benefits of data-driven technologies are harnessed responsibly and ethically.

CHAPTER 21: APPENDIX OF RESOURCES AND TOOLS FOR DATA SCIENCE AND ANALYTICS

Chapter 21 serves as a valuable resource for data science and analytics professionals, providing an overview of various tools, platforms, frameworks, and resources that can enhance their work. This appendix aims to equip readers with a comprehensive list of resources to support their data science and analytics endeavors. It covers a wide range of categories, including data processing, machine learning, data visualization, programming languages, and online communities.

Data Processing and Manipulation:

This section includes popular tools for data processing and manipulation, such as Apache Hadoop, Apache Spark, and SQL-based platforms like MySQL and PostgreSQL. These tools enable users to handle large datasets efficiently, perform data cleaning and transformation, and carry out complex data manipulations.

Machine Learning Libraries and Frameworks:

Machine learning is a fundamental aspect of data science and analytics. This section highlights popular machine learning libraries and frameworks such as Scikit-learn, TensorFlow, and PyTorch. These resources provide a wide range of algorithms and tools for tasks such as regression, classification, clustering, and neural network modeling.

Data Visualization Tools:

Data visualization is crucial for effectively communicating insights and findings. This section introduces visualization tools like Tableau, Power BI, and Matplotlib. These tools enable users to create interactive and visually appealing charts, graphs, and dashboards to present data-driven insights in a compelling manner.

Programming Languages:

Programming languages are essential for data science and analytics tasks. This section covers widely used programming languages, including Python and R, known for their extensive libraries and packages specifically designed for data analysis and modeling. Additionally, it provides resources for learning and improving coding skills in these languages.

Big Data and Cloud Platforms:

As data volumes continue to grow, the need for scalable and distributed computing platforms becomes critical. This section highlights tools and platforms such as Apache Kafka, Amazon Web Services (AWS), and Google Cloud Platform (GCP). These platforms offer capabilities for big data storage, processing, and analysis in a distributed and cloud-based environment.

Data Science Online Communities and Forums:

Data science professionals thrive in communities where they can learn, collaborate, and seek guidance from peers. This section lists popular online communities and forums such as Kaggle, Stack Overflow, and GitHub. These platforms offer opportunities for networking, sharing insights, participating in competitions, and accessing code repositories.

Data Science Courses and Learning Platforms:

Continued learning is vital in the ever-evolving field of data science. This section provides an overview of online learning platforms such as Coursera, edX, and DataCamp. These platforms offer a wide range of data science courses and certifications, allowing professionals to enhance their skills and stay up to date with the latest advancements.

Books and Publications:

Books remain an invaluable resource for in-depth learning and reference in data science. This section recommends influential books such as "The Elements of Statistical Learning" by Trevor Hastie, Robert Tibshirani, and Jerome Friedman, and "Python for Data Analysis" by Wes McKinney.

These books cover foundational concepts, algorithms, and practical applications in data science.

Data Science Blogs and Podcasts:

Staying informed about the latest trends and advancements in data science is essential. This section highlights prominent data science blogs and podcasts such as Towards Data Science, DataCamp Community, and the Data Skeptic podcast. These resources offer insightful articles, tutorials, interviews, and discussions on various data science topics.

Data Science Competitions and Challenges:

Participating in data science competitions and challenges can sharpen skills and provide opportunities to work on real-world problems. This section highlights platforms like Kaggle and DrivenData that host data science competitions. These platforms offer datasets, problem statements, and opportunities to collaborate and showcase expertise.

By providing this comprehensive list of resources and tools, the appendix empowers data science and analytics professionals to explore and utilize a wide range of tools, platforms, and learning opportunities. This ensures that they have access to the necessary resources to enhance their knowledge, skills, and efficiency in the field of data science and analytics.

Recommended Books, Articles, and Online Courses for Data Science and Analytics

Books, articles, and online courses play a vital role in enhancing knowledge, skills, and understanding in the field of data science and analytics. This section provides a curated list of recommended resources that cover a wide range of topics, from foundational concepts to advanced techniques. Whether you are a beginner or an experienced professional, these resources will help you deepen your understanding and stay up to date with the latest developments in the field.

Recommended Books:

"The Elements of Statistical Learning" by Trevor Hastie, Robert Tibshirani, and Jerome Friedman:

This book is a comprehensive introduction to statistical learning methods, covering topics such as linear regression, classification, resampling methods, tree-based methods, support vector machines, and more. It provides a solid foundation in statistical learning theory and practical implementation.

"Python for Data Analysis" by Wes McKinney:

This book offers a practical guide to data analysis using Python. It covers data manipulation, cleaning, and preparation using pandas, data visualization with Matplotlib and Seaborn, and introduces the basics of machine learning with scikit-learn. It is a valuable resource for those working with data in Python.

"Hands-On Machine Learning with Scikit-Learn, Keras, and TensorFlow" by Aurélien Géron:

This book provides a hands-on approach to machine learning, focusing on practical implementation with popular libraries such as scikit-learn, Keras, and TensorFlow. It covers key topics like classification, regression, clustering, and neural networks, and provides practical examples and exercises.

"Data Science for Business" by Foster Provost and Tom Fawcett:

This book explores the intersection of data science and business, explaining how data-driven decision-making can create value and drive success. It covers fundamental concepts, machine learning techniques, and ethical considerations in data science, making it a valuable resource for both technical and non-technical professionals.

Recommended Articles:

"The Unreasonable Effectiveness of Data" by Peter Norvig:

This influential article discusses the power of large datasets in driving improvements in data science and machine learning. It highlights the importance of data availability and quality in enabling the development of effective models and algorithms.

"A Few Useful Things to Know About Machine Learning" by Pedro Domingos:

This article provides practical insights and tips for those working with machine learning. It covers key concepts, common pitfalls, and practical considerations for model development and evaluation.

"The Data Science Process" by John Rollins and Roger D. Peng:

This article outlines the essential steps and considerations in the data science process. It provides a framework for approaching data analysis projects, from formulating questions to communicating results effectively.

"The Ethics of Artificial Intelligence" by Nick Bostrom and Eliezer Yudkowsky:

This thought-provoking article explores the ethical implications of artificial intelligence. It discusses key considerations such as value alignment, control, and the potential risks associated with AI development.

Recommended Online Courses:

"Machine Learning" by Andrew Ng (Coursera):

This highly acclaimed course provides a comprehensive introduction to machine learning. It covers topics such as linear regression, logistic regression, neural networks, and support vector machines. The course includes practical assignments to reinforce learning.

"Applied Data Science with Python" by University of Michigan (Coursera):

This specialization covers various aspects of data science, including data visualization, data analysis, and applied machine learning. It provides hands-on experience using Python libraries such as pandas, NumPy, and scikit-learn.

"Deep Learning Specialization" by deeplearning.ai (Coursera):

This specialization offers a deep dive into deep learning techniques and applications. It covers topics such as neural networks, convolutional neural networks, recurrent neural networks, and generative models. The specialization includes practical coding assignments and a final project.

"Data Science and Machine Learning Bootcamp with R" by Udemy:

This comprehensive course provides a practical introduction to data science and machine learning using the R programming language. It covers topics such as data exploration, data visualization, statistical analysis, and machine learning algorithms.

These recommended resources provide a solid foundation for data science and analytics professionals. They cover a wide range of topics, from foundational concepts to advanced techniques, and offer practical insights and hands-on experience. By engaging with these books, articles, and online courses, professionals can enhance their skills, stay updated with the latest trends, and excel in the field of data science and analytics.

Data science platforms and tools are essential for performing data analysis, building machine learning models, and extracting insights from data. These platforms provide a comprehensive set of tools and functionalities that enable data scientists and analysts to effectively work with data, collaborate, and deploy models. This section highlights some popular data science platforms and tools that are widely used in the industry.

Python and R:

Python and R are two of the most popular programming languages for data science. They offer extensive libraries and packages specifically designed for data analysis, machine learning, and statistical modeling. Python libraries such as NumPy, pandas, scikit-learn, and TensorFlow, along with R packages like dplyr, ggplot2, and caret, provide powerful capabilities for data manipulation, visualization, and modeling.

Jupyter Notebooks:

Jupyter Notebooks is an open-source web application that allows users to create and share documents containing live code, equations, visualizations, and narrative text. It supports multiple programming languages, including Python, R, and Julia. Jupyter Notebooks provide an interactive and collaborative environment for data exploration, prototyping, and sharing analysis workflows.

Apache Hadoop and Apache Spark:

Apache Hadoop is a popular open-source framework for distributed storage and processing of big data. It provides a scalable and fault-tolerant platform for handling large datasets across clusters of commodity hardware. Apache Spark, built on top of Hadoop, is a fast and general-purpose data processing engine that supports in-memory computing and enables real-time data analysis, machine learning, and graph processing.

SQL and Relational Databases:

SQL (Structured Query Language) is a standard language for managing relational databases. Relational databases such as MySQL, PostgreSQL, and Oracle are widely used for storing and managing structured data. SQL allows users to query and manipulate data using declarative statements, making it a powerful tool for data exploration and analysis.

Tableau:

Tableau is a popular data visualization tool that allows users to create interactive and visually appealing dashboards, charts, and reports. It supports a wide range of data sources and provides intuitive drag-and-drop functionality for creating visualizations. Tableau enables users to explore data, uncover patterns, and communicate insights effectively.

Apache Kafka:

Apache Kafka is a distributed event streaming platform that provides real-time data integration, streaming, and messaging capabilities. It allows for high-throughput, fault-tolerance, and scalable data processing, making it suitable for handling large volumes of streaming data in real-time applications, such as IoT analytics and real-time monitoring.

TensorFlow and PyTorch:

TensorFlow and PyTorch are popular open-source libraries for deep learning and neural network modeling. They provide comprehensive tools and frameworks for building and training complex deep learning models. These libraries offer a range of pre-built neural network architectures, optimization algorithms, and tools for model deployment.

RapidMiner:

RapidMiner is a data science platform that provides a visual and intuitive interface for data preparation, modeling, and deployment. It offers a wide range of data mining and machine learning algorithms, automated modeling capabilities, and integration with popular programming languages like Python and R.

KNIME:

KNIME (Konstanz Information Miner) is an open-source data analytics platform that allows users to visually design data workflows. It provides a wide range of data manipulation, transformation, and analysis capabilities, along with machine learning and text mining functionalities. KNIME supports integration with various data sources and offers a user-friendly interface for building and deploying data science workflows.

DataRobot:

DataRobot is an automated machine learning platform that simplifies the process of building and deploying machine learning models. It offers a wide range of automated tasks, including feature engineering, model selection, hyperparameter tuning, and model deployment. DataRobot enables users to build accurate models efficiently and deploy them in production environments.

Alteryx:

Alteryx is a self-service analytics platform that combines data preparation, data blending, and advanced analytics capabilities. It provides a visual interface for building data workflows, enabling users to perform complex data transformations, spatial analysis, and predictive modeling. Alteryx offers an intuitive drag-and-drop interface and supports integration with various data sources.

Dataiku:

Dataiku is an end-to-end data science and analytics platform that enables organizations to build and deploy machine learning models at scale. It provides a collaborative environment for data scientists, data analysts, and business users to work together on data projects. Dataiku supports data preparation, feature engineering, model building, and model deployment.

These are just a few examples of the many data science platforms and tools available in the market. The choice of platform and tools depends on specific requirements, data volumes, computational needs, and the expertise of the data science team. Ultimately, selecting the right combination of platforms and tools is crucial for maximizing productivity, efficiency, and the quality of data science and analytics initiatives.

Useful Libraries and Frameworks for Data Science and Analytics

Libraries and frameworks play a crucial role in data science and analytics, providing pre-built functionalities, algorithms, and tools that accelerate development, enhance productivity, and enable complex data analysis. This section highlights some of the widely used libraries and frameworks in the field, covering various aspects of data manipulation, analysis, modeling, and visualization.

NumPy:

NumPy (Numerical Python) is a fundamental library for numerical computing in Python. It provides efficient array operations, mathematical functions, and tools for working with multi-dimensional arrays. NumPy forms the foundation for many other libraries in the Python data science ecosystem and enables efficient data manipulation and computation.

pandas:

pandas is a powerful data manipulation library built on top of NumPy. It provides data structures like DataFrames and Series, which allow for easy handling and analysis of structured data. pandas offers functions for data cleaning, preprocessing, merging, grouping, and more, making it a versatile library for data manipulation and analysis.

scikit-learn:

scikit-learn is a widely used machine learning library in Python. It provides a comprehensive set of algorithms for classification, regression, clustering, dimensionality reduction, and model selection. scikit-learn also offers tools for data preprocessing, model evaluation, and model deployment, making it a go-to library for many data science projects.

TensorFlow:

TensorFlow is an open-source machine learning library developed by Google. It specializes in deep learning and allows users to build and train complex neural network models. TensorFlow provides a flexible architecture for creating computational graphs and supports distributed computing, enabling efficient training on large datasets. It has extensive support for deep learning frameworks such as Keras.

Keras:

Keras is a high-level neural network library that runs on top of TensorFlow, Theano, or Microsoft Cognitive Toolkit (CNTK). It offers an intuitive and user-friendly interface for building and training deep learning models. Keras provides pre-built layers, activation functions, and optimization algorithms, making it accessible to both beginners and experienced deep learning practitioners.

PyTorch:

PyTorch is another popular open-source deep learning framework that provides dynamic computational graphs and efficient GPU acceleration. It offers a flexible and intuitive API for building and training deep learning models. PyTorch allows for dynamic computation, making it easier to debug and experiment with models. It has gained popularity due to its ease of use and strong community support.

Matplotlib:

Matplotlib is a widely used data visualization library in Python. It provides a comprehensive set of functions for creating static, animated, and interactive visualizations. Matplotlib allows users to create a wide range of plots, including line plots, scatter plots, bar plots, histograms, and more. It offers extensive customization options to create visually appealing and informative visualizations.

Seaborn:

Seaborn is a data visualization library built on top of Matplotlib. It provides a higher-level interface for creating attractive and informative statistical visualizations. Seaborn offers functions for statistical plotting, categorical plotting, distribution visualization, and multi-plot grids. It simplifies the creation of complex visualizations and provides aesthetically pleasing default styles.

XGBoost:

XGBoost is an optimized gradient boosting library that provides state-of-the-art performance for machine learning tasks. It is particularly effective for handling structured data and has gained popularity in Kaggle competitions and other data science challenges. XGBoost offers a wide range of hyperparameters for fine-tuning models and supports parallel processing for efficient training.

Spark:

Apache Spark is a distributed computing framework that provides efficient data processing and analysis capabilities. Spark offers APIs for working with large-scale datasets, enabling distributed data manipulation, machine learning, and graph processing. It provides a unified interface for data analysis across multiple programming languages, including Python, R, Scala, and Java.

Dask:

Dask is a parallel computing library that enables scalable and distributed data processing in Python. It provides a familiar interface for working with arrays, DataFrames, and parallel computations, similar to NumPy and pandas. Dask seamlessly integrates with other libraries like NumPy, pandas, and scikit-learn, allowing users to scale their data operations across multiple cores and clusters.

H2O.ai:

H2O.ai is an open-source machine learning platform that offers a range of tools and algorithms for data science and analytics. It provides a distributed computing environment, allowing users to train machine learning models on large datasets efficiently. H2O.ai supports various algorithms, including gradient boosting, generalized linear models, and deep learning.

These libraries and frameworks provide powerful tools and functionalities that enable data scientists and analysts to tackle complex data challenges, build accurate models, and extract valuable insights from data. Depending on the specific requirements and project goals, data professionals can leverage these libraries and frameworks to streamline their workflows, improve productivity, and deliver impactful results in data science and analytics projects.

Chapter 22: Book Conclusion

Congratulations on completing this comprehensive guide to implementing data science and analytics! Throughout this journey, you have explored the foundational principles, best practices, and strategies for success in the dynamic field of data science. You have gained insights into the importance of data-driven decision-making, building data science teams, defining objectives and metrics, data collection and management, data exploration and visualization, statistical analysis, machine learning, predictive analytics, and so much more.

Data science and analytics have transformed the way organizations operate, enabling them to uncover valuable insights, make informed decisions, and drive innovation. The advancements in technology, the availability of massive amounts of data, and the development of sophisticated algorithms have unlocked unprecedented opportunities for organizations across industries.

As you reflect on this journey, it is essential to recognize the immense potential and responsibility that data science and analytics hold. The ability to extract actionable insights from data comes with a duty to uphold ethical practices, protect privacy, and ensure fairness. The considerations of bias, transparency, accountability, and data governance are critical to maintain trust and maximize the positive impact of data-driven initiatives.

The future of data science and analytics is promising, with emerging technologies and techniques continuously pushing the boundaries of what is possible. Artificial intelligence, machine learning, big data, and the Internet of Things are reshaping industries, challenging traditional practices, and opening new avenues for innovation. It is crucial for data professionals to stay updated with the latest trends, embrace continuous learning, and adapt to evolving technologies to stay at the forefront of this rapidly changing landscape.

Moreover, collaboration and interdisciplinary efforts are becoming increasingly important in data science. Effective data science teams bring together individuals with diverse skills, including data scientists, analysts, domain experts, and business leaders. By fostering a culture of collaboration, organizations can leverage the collective expertise to tackle complex problems and drive meaningful outcomes.

As you move forward in your data science journey, remember the importance of constantly improving and refining your skills. Stay curious, seek out new challenges, and embrace a mindset of lifelong learning. Engage with the data science community, attend conferences, participate in hackathons, and contribute to open-source projects. By actively engaging with the community, you can not only enhance your knowledge but also share your expertise and inspire others.

Finally, always remember the impact that data science and analytics can have on society. Use your skills responsibly, ethically, and with a commitment to making a positive difference. Strive to address societal challenges, contribute to sustainable development, and promote inclusivity in the data-driven world.

As you close this chapter of your learning, consider it the beginning of an exciting journey. The world of data science and analytics is ever-evolving, and your contributions can shape the future. Embrace the challenges, seize the opportunities, and continue to make a meaningful impact in this data-driven era.

Best of luck on your future endeavors, and may your data science and analytics journey be filled with continuous growth, innovation, and success!

Chapter 23: Disclaimer and Copyright

 First Printing, 2023

www.ingramcontent.com/pod-product-compliance
Lightning Source LLC
LaVergne TN
LVHW080021210926
848481LV00011B/3075
* 9 7 9 8 2 2 3 1 2 9 3 5 6 *